Euripides, Michael Wodhull

Hecuba and Other Plays

Euripides, Michael Wodhull

Hecuba and Other Plays

ISBN/EAN: 9783337378073

Printed in Europe, USA, Canada, Australia, Japan

Cover: Foto ©Thomas Meinert / pixelio.de

More available books at **www.hansebooks.com**

HECUBA

AND OTHER PLAYS

BY

EURIPIDES

TRANSLATED INTO ENGLISH VERSE BY
MICHAEL WODHULL

WITH AN INTRODUCTION BY HENRY MORLEY
LL.D., PROFESSOR OF ENGLISH LITERATURE AT
UNIVERSITY COLLEGE, LONDON

LONDON
GEORGE ROUTLEDGE AND SONS
BROADWAY, LUDGATE HILL
GLASGOW AND NEW YORK
1888

MORLEY'S UNIVERSAL LIBRARY.

1. *Sheridan's Plays.*
2. *Plays from Molière.* By English Dramatists.
3. *Marlowe's Faustus* and *Goethe's Faust.*
4. *Chronicle of the Cid.*
5. *Rabelais' Gargantua* and the Heroic Deeds of Pantagruel.
6. *Machiavelli's Prince.*
7. *Bacon's Essays.*
8. *Defoe's Journal of the Plague Year.*
9. *Locke on Civil Government* and *Filmer's "Patriarcha."*
10. *Butler's Analogy of Religion.*
11. *Dryden's Virgil.*
12. *Scott's Demonology and Witchcraft.*
13. *Herrick's Hesperides.*
14. *Coleridge's Table-Talk.*
15. *Boccaccio's Decameron.*
16. *Sterne's Tristram Shandy.*
17. *Chapman's Homer's Iliad.*
18. *Mediæval Tales.*
19. *Voltaire's Candide,* and *Johnson's Rasselas.*
20. *Jonson's Plays and Poems.*
21. *Hobbes's Leviathan.*
22. *Samuel Butler's Hudibras.*
23. *Ideal Commonwealths.*
24. *Cavendish's Life of Wolsey.*
25 & 26. *Don Quixote.*
27. *Burlesque Plays and Poems.*
28. *Dante's Divine Comedy.* LONGFELLOW's Translation.
29. *Goldsmith's Vicar of Wakefield, Plays, and Poems.*
30. *Fables and Proverbs from the Sanskrit.* (*Hitopadesa.*)
31. *Lamb's Essays of Elia.*
32. *The History of Thomas Ellwood.*
33. *Emerson's Essays, &c.*
34. *Southey's Life of Nelson.*
35. *De Quincey's Confessions of an Opium-Eater, &c.*
36. *Stories of Ireland.* By Miss EDGEWORTH.
37. *Frere's Aristophanes: Acharnians, Knights, Birds.*
38. *Burke's Speeches and Letters.*
39. *Thomas à Kempis.*
40. *Popular Songs of Ireland.*
41. *Potter's Æschylus.*
42. *Goethe's Faust:* Part *II.* ANSTER's Translation.
43. *Famous Pamphlets.*
44. *Francklin's Sophocles.*
45. *M. G. Lewis's Tales of Terror and Wonder.*
46. *Vestiges of the Natural History of Creation.*
47. *Drayton's Barons' Wars, Nymphidia, &c.*
48. *Cobbett's Advice to Young Men.*
49. *The Banquet of Dante.*
50. *Walker's Original.*
51. *Schiller's Poems and Ballads.*
52. *Peele's Plays and Poems.*
53. *Harrington's Oceana.*
54. *Euripides: Alcestis and other Plays.*
55. *Praed's Essays.*
56. *Traditional Tales.* ALLAN CUNNINGHAM.
57. *Hooker's Ecclesiastical Polity.* Books *I.-IV.*
58. *Euripides: The Bacchanals and other Plays.*
59. *Izaak Walton's Lives.*
60. *Aristotle's Politics.*
61. *Euripides: Hecuba and other Plays.*

"Marvels of clear type and general neatness."—*Daily Telegraph.*

INTRODUCTION.

WE left the history of the House of Tantalus with a reference to Helen, as we find her in the translated play which is among those which here complete the collection of the extant works of Euripides.

Menelaus sent ambassadors to Troy to demand back Helen, his wife, whom Paris had carried off. The counsels of Antenor were set aside at Troy, by the persuasions of Paris that gave occasion to the Siege of Troy. Agamemnon, on the throne of the deposed Thyestes, had extended his dominion. Homer gave him command over a hundred ships in the expedition against Troy. Some were from Mycene, which although but six or seven miles from Argos had been capital of a separate kingdom until it was reunited to Argos after the defeat and death of Eurystheus; and when Agamemnon succeeded his father Atreus, he enlarged and beautified Mycene. Twenty-eight unsuccessful suitors of Helen were summoned by Menelaus to contribute aid, and under command of the strongest of the confederates, Agamemnon—who was the brother of Menelaus, and who then had by his wife Clytemnestra three daughters, Iphigenia, Chrysothemis, and Electra, also one son, Orestes, then an infant—the expedition sailed for Troy.

But first, when the confederate fleets met as agreed, in the haven of Aulis they were stayed by a dead calm. Guidance was sought from the Oracle, and the soothsayer Calchas reminded Agamemnon of a vow made in the year of Iphigenia's birth that he would sacrifice to Diana the most beautiful production of the year. That was his daughter, Iphigenia, whom now Diana claimed. The fleet would remain bound in Aulis until the sacrifice of Iphigenia. The story of the sacrifice, of the anger of the maiden's mother Clytemnestra, and her lover Achilles, is told by Euripides in his "Iphigenia in Aulis." The Goddess in the act of sacrifice miraculously substituted a hind for the daughter, whom she wafted in a cloud to her temple among the Scythians at Tauris, where she became a Priestess, and where it was the custom of the barbarous people to sacrifice every Greek who landed on their shores.

In the siege of Troy, Paris was slain by the arrows of Philoctetes. Helen then married his brother Deiphobus, whom she betrayed to the Greeks. When she came again into the hands of Menelaus, he was soon reconciled to her. In returning from the ten years' siege of Troy, many of the companions of Agamemnon were lost by wreck on the coast of Euboea, where the father of Palamedes, to avenge the unjust killing of his son in the camp of the Greeks, had set up false lights. Agamemnon came safely to Argos with the captive prophetess Cassandra, whom he intended for himself. This was a new affront to Clytemnestra; who remembered the murder of her first husband Tantalus and her first infant, who remembered also the sacrifice of Iphigenia, and who had found a paramour in Ægisthus, son of Thyestes. Clytemnestra murdered Agamemnon with an axe as he was coming out of the bath, and then married Ægisthus, who took Agamemnon's throne.

The young Orestes was saved from his stepfather by a faithful servant, who carried him to Phocis, and there put him under the protection of Strophius. Electra remained at Argos and was married to a peasant, lest a husband powerful in the State should help to restore to their birthrights the children of Agamemnon.

When Orestes had passed out of childhood, he went for guidance to the Oracle of Apollo at Delphi, and was directed to avenge the murder of his father. He went then, with his inseparable friend Pylades, in disguise to Argos, and was received in a cottage on the boundary of Argos, by Electra and her peasant husband. He learnt that the peasant, strongly attached to the family of Agamemnon, had cancelled the wrong intended by Ægisthus, and had never claimed rights of a husband. Electra was still a maiden princess. Brother and sister then devised and carried out a plan for the killing of their mother Clytemnestra and Ægisthus.

But when the hands of Orestes were stained with his mother's blood, the Furies rose from Hell, and drove him to distraction. Six days after the murder of Clytemnestra, the citizens of Argos met to pass sentence on Orestes and Electra. Menelaus after a voyage from Troy of seven years' long delays, then landed at Nauplia near Argos, and would have helped his nephew Orestes; but he gave up Orestes and Electra to the people of Argos upon being told by Tyndarus that if he interfered he should never return to Sparta. The Council of Argos gave leave to Orestes and Electra to carry out upon themselves its sentence of death. After consulting with Pylades they resolved to kill Helen and seize their uncle's one daughter, Hermione, as hostage. Helen had vanished; Menelaus breathed revenge; Apollo descended to save Orestes from his uncle, and from the people, by declaring that Orestes had done what the gods required. But Apollo bade him cleanse away pollution of his mother's blood by a year's banishment, after which he was to submit himself to the judgment of the Areopagus at Athens.

Before the Areopagus one of the Furies was his accuser, Apollo witnessed in his favour. The votes of the Court were equal, and Athené gave the casting vote for his acquittal. But still the Furies were implacable, and Orestes, again appealing to Apollo's Oracle, was ordered to bring the statue of Diana from Tauris to Athens. Orestes sailed upon this mission with Pylades, whom he had affianced to his sister Electra. When the friends landed on the coast of Tauris, the barbarous people seized them and they were carried to Iphigenia to be sacrificed according to the custom of the land. When on the point of being sacrificed, discovery was made, and, with help of Minerva, not only the image of the goddess Diana, but also Iphigenia her priestess, was conveyed to Athens, in whose territories, at Brauronia, Iphigenia remained priestess until her death.

Meanwhile Menelaus had married his only daughter, Hermione, to Neoptolemus, the son of Achilles. Neoptolemus, who had offended Apollo by making the god answerable for the death of Achilles, went to Delphi to appease his wrath. Orestes, who sought Hermione for wife, went also to Delphi and persuaded the people there that Neoptolemus sought plunder of the temple. Neoptolemus was, therefore, murdered by the people of Delphi, as he was going unarmed to the temple to propitiate the god. Then Orestes carried off Hermione, and married her, at the same time when his sister Electra was married to Pylades. The plays of Euripides here leave Orestes; ruler on the throne of Agamemnon, reconciled to Menelaus, and married to Hermione, through whom, by right of her mother Helen and her father Menelaus, he may hope to bring also under his rule the dominions of Sparta.

Here ends an abstract of an abstract of the History of the House of Tantalus, as given by Michael Wodhull, Esq., to show the relations to each other of the stories upon which Euripides based many of his plays.

This volume completes our set of English versions of all extant plays of Euripides.

H. M.

April 1888

TO THE READERS OF THE UNIVERSAL LIBRARY.

THE next volume of this Library, published in May 1888, will complete our household edition of Rabelais with the Sequel to Pantagruel. This will be followed in June by "A Miscellany" of short works of special interest taken from different periods of English life. The sixty-three volumes of the Universal Library, re-arranged in historical order, will then form a completed series, and the supply of standard literature in shilling monthly volumes will be left to other editors whose good work in this direction has been called into existence by the success of the Universal Library, which on its first appearance broke new ground.'

The work done in these volumes will be continued, without change of aim, in a new series that has been planned to permit issue of large books without the crowding of type which, in this series, has been now and then found necessary. In the New Series, there will be a complete change of form. Substantial and handsome volumes of the best literature will be published in alternate months at a price that will add not more than three shillings to the present annual cost of "The Universal Library." The name of the new Library will change from the Universal to the Particular. Its books may be named from their *habitat*, and they will usually be edited where the eye raised from the paper and ink rests upon Carisbrooke Castle.

THE FIRST VOLUME OF
Morley's Carisbrooke Library
Will be published on the First of October, 1888.

H. M.

EURIPIDES.

HECUBA.

PERSONS OF THE DRAMA.

POLYDORE'S GHOST.
HECUBA.
CHORUS OF CAPTIVE TROJAN DAMES.
POLYXENA.

ULYSSES.
FEMALE ATTENDANT OF HECUBA.
AGAMEMNON.
POLYMESTOR.
TALTHYBIUS.

SCENE.—THE THRACIAN CHERSONESUS.

THE GHOST OF POLYDORE.

LEAVING the cavern of the dead, and gates
Of darkness, where from all the gods apart
Dwells Pluto, come I Polydore, the son
Of Hecuba from royal Cisseus sprung,
And Priam, who, when danger threatened Troy,
Fearing his city by the Grecian arms
Would be laid low in dust, from Phrygia's realm
In privacy conveyed me to the house
Of Polymestor, of his Thracian friend,
Who tills the Chersonesus' fruitful soil,
Ruling a nation famed for generous steeds;
But secretly, with me, abundant gold
My father sent, that his surviving children
Might lack no sustenance, if Ilion's walls
Should by the foe be levelled with the ground.
I was the youngest of all Priam's sons,
By stealth he therefore sent me from the realm;
Nor could my feeble arm sustain the shield,
Or launch the javelin; but while yet entire
Each ancient landmark on our frontiers stood,
The turrets of the Phrygian state remained
Unshaken, and my brother Hector's spear

Prospered in battle; nurtured by the man
Of Thrace, my father's friend, I, wretched youth,
Grew like a vigorous scion. But when Troy,
When Hector failed, when my paternal dome
Was from its basis rent, and Priam's self,
My aged father, at the altar bled
Which to the gods his pious hands had reared,
Butchered by curst Achilles' ruthless son;
Me, his unhappy guest, my father's friend
Slew for the sake of gold, and having slain,
Plunged me into the sea, that he might keep
Those treasures in his house. My breathless corse,
In various eddies by the rising waves
Of ocean tost, lies on the craggy shore,
Unwept, unburied. But by filial love
For Hecuba now prompted, I ascend
A disembodied ghost, and thrice have seen
The morning dawn, to Chersonesus land,
Since my unhappy mother came from Troy.
But all the Grecian army, in their ships,
Here anchoring on this coast of Thrace remain
Inactive; for appearing on his tomb
Achilles, Peleus' son, restrained the troops,
Who homeward else had steered their barks, and claims
Polyxena my sister, as a victim
Most precious at his sepulchre to bleed;
And her will he obtain, nor will his friends
Withhold the gift; for fate this day decrees
That she shall die: my mother must behold
Two of her slaughtered children's corses, mine,
And this unhappy maid's—that in a tomb
I may be lodged, where the firm beach resists
The waves, I to her servant will appear,
Since from the powers of hell I have obtained
The privilege of honourable interment,
And that a mother's hand these rites perform:
I shall accomplish what my soul desired.
But on the aged Hecuba's approach,
Far hence must I retreat; for from the tent
Of Agamemnon she comes forth, alarmed
By my pale spectre. O my wretched mother,
How art thou torn from princely roofs to view
This hour of servitude! what sad reverse
Of fortune! some malignant god hath balanced
Thy present misery 'gainst thy former bliss. [*Exit.*

HECUBA, *attended by* TROJAN DAMSELS.

HEC. Forth from these doors, ye gentle virgins, lead me,
A weak old woman: O ye nymphs of Troy,

Support your fellow-servant, once your queen
Bear me along, uphold my tottering frame,
And take me by this aged hand ; your arm
Shall be my staff to lean on, while I strive
My tardy pace to quicken. O ye lightnings
Of Jove, O Night in tenfold darkness wrapt,
By such terrific phantoms from my couch
Why am I scared? Thou venerable earth,
Parent of dreams that flit on raven wing ;
The vision I abhor, which I in sleep
This night have seen, relating to my son,
Who here is fostered in the Thracian realm,
And to Polyxena my dearest daughter ;
For I too clearly saw and understood
The meaning of that dreadful apparition ;
Ye tutelary gods of this domain,
Preserve the only anchor of our house,
My son, who dwells in Thracian fields, o'erspread
With snow, protected by his father's friend.
Some fresh event awaits us, and ere long
By accents most unwelcome shall the ear
Of wretchedness be wounded : till this hour,
By such incessant horrors, such alarms,
My soul was never seized. Where shall I view
The soul of Helenus, on whom the god
Bestowed prophetic gifts, ye Phrygian maids?
Where my Cassandra to unfold the dream?
With bloody fangs I saw a wolf, who slew
A dappled hind, which forcibly he tore
From these reluctant arms, and what increased
My fears, was this—Achilles' spectre stalked
Upon the summit of his tomb, and claimed
A gift, some miserable Trojan captive.
You therefore I implore, ye gods, avert
Such doom from my loved daughter,

CHORUS, HECUBA.

CHOR.   I to thee,
To thee, O Hecuba, with breathless speed,
Fly from the tents of our imperious lords,
Where I by lot have been assigned, and doomed
To be a slave, driven by the pointed spear
From Troy; by their victorious arms the Greeks
Have made me captive : nothing can I bring,
Thy sorrows to alleviate ; but to thee
Laden with heaviest tidings am I come
The herald of affliction. For 'tis said,
Greece in full council hath resolved thy daughter
A victim to Achilles shall be given.

The warrior mounting on his tomb, thou know'st,
Appeared in golden armour, and restrained
The fleet just ready to unfurl its sails,
Exclaiming, " Whither would ye steer your course,
Ye Greeks, and leave no offering on my grave?"
A storm of violent contention rose,
And two opinions in the martial synod
Of Greece went forth; the victim, some maintained,
Ought on the sepulchre to bleed, and some
Such offering disapproved. But Agamemnon,
Who shares the bed of the Prophetic Dame,
Espoused thy interest; while the sons of Theseus,
Branches from the Athenian root, discussed
The question largely in each point of view,
But in the same opinion both concurred,
And said that never should Cassandra's love
To great Achilles' valour be preferred:
Equally balanced the debate still hung,
When he, that crafty orator, endued
With sweetest voice, the favourite of the crowd,
Laertes' son, persuaded all the host,
Not to reject the first of Grecian chiefs,
And yield the preference to a victim slave:
Lest some vindictive ghost, before the throne
Of Proserpine arising, might relate
How Greece, unmindful of her generous sons,
Who nobly perished for their native land,
From Ilion's fields departed. In a moment
Ulysses will come hither, from thy breast,
And aged arms to drag the tender maid.
But to the temples, to the altars, go,
In suppliant posture clasp Atrides' knees,
Invoke the gods of heaven and hell beneath,
For either thou wilt by thy prayers avert
Thy daughter's fate, else must thou at the tomb
Behold the virgin fall distained with gore,
And gushing from her neck a crimson stream.

HEC. Wretch that I am! ah me! what clamorous sounds,
What words, what plaints, what dirges shall I find,
Expressive of the anguish which I feel?
Opprest by miserable old age, bowed down
Under a load of servitude too heavy
To be endured: what sanctuary remains,
What valiant race, what city will protect me?
The hoary Priam is no more, my sons
Are now no more. Or to this path, or that,
Shall I direct my steps? or whither go?
Where shall I find some tutelary god?
Ye Phrygian captives, messengers of ill,

O ye who with unwelcome tidings fraught,
Come hither, ye have ruined me. The orb
Of day shall never rise to fill this breast
With any comfort more. Ye luckless feet,
Bear an infirm old woman to the tent
Of our captivity. Come forth, my daughter,
Come forth and listen to thy mother's voice,
That thou may'st know the rumour I have heard,
In which thy life is interested.

POLYXENA, HECUBA, CHORUS.

POLYX.   O mother,
What mean you by those shrieks? what fresh event
Proclaiming, from my chamber, like a bird,
Have you constrained me, urged by fear, to speed
My flight?
    HEC.   Ah, daughter!
    POLYX.   With foreboding voice,
Why do you call me? these are evil omens.
    HEC. Alas! thy life, Polyxena.
    POLYX.   Speak out,
Nor aggravate the horrors yet untold
By long suspense. I fear, O mother, much
I fear. What mean those oft repeated groans?
    HEC. Thou child of a most miserable mother!
    POLYX. Why speak you thus?
    HEC.   The Greeks, with one consent,
Resolve that on the tomb of Peleus' son
Thou shalt be sacrificed.
    POLYX.   What boundless woes
Are these which to your daughter you announce!
Yet, O my mother, with the tale proceed.
    HEC. Of a most horrible report I speak,
Which says, that, by the suffrage of the Greeks,
It is resolved to take away thy life.
    POLYX. O, my unhappy mother, doomed to suffer
Wrongs the most dreadful, doomed to lead a life
Of utter wretchedness: what grievous curse,
Such as no language can express, on you
Hath some malignant demon hurled! no more
Can I, your daughter, share the galling yoke
Of servitude with your forlorn old age;
For like some lion's whelp, or heifer bred
Upon the mountains, hurried from your arms
Shall you behold me, and with severed head
Consigned to Pluto's subterraneous realms
Of darkness, there among the silent dead,
Wretch that I am, shall I be laid. These tears
Of bitter lamentation I for you,

For you, O mother, shed; but my own life
I heed not, nor the shame, nor fatal stroke,
For I in death a happier lot obtain.
   CHOR. To thee, O Hecuba, with hasty step
Behold Ulysses some new message brings.

ULYSSES, HECUBA, POLYXENA, CHORUS.

   ULY. Though I presume the counsels of our troops
And their decision are already known
To thee, O woman, yet must I repeat
Th' unwelcome tidings; at Achilles' tomb,
Polyxena, thy daughter, have the Greeks
Resolved to slay; me to attend the virgin
Have they commanded: but Achilles' son
Is at the altar destined to preside,
And be the priest. Know'st thou thy duty then?
Constrain us not to drag her from those arms
With violence, nor strive with me; but learn
The force of thy inevitable woes:
For there is wisdom, e'en when we are wretched,
In following reason's dictates.
   HEC.   Now, alas!
It seems a dreadful struggle is at hand,
With groans abounding and unnumbered tears.
I died not at the time I ought to die,
Neither did Jove destroy me; he still spares
My life, that I may view fresh woes, yet greater,
Wretch that I am, than all my former woes.
But if a slave, who not with bitter taunt,
Or keen reproach, her questions doth propose,
Might speak to freemen, now 'tis time for you
To cease, and give me audience while I ask——
   ULY. Allowed, proceed; for I without reluctance
Will grant thee time.
   HEC.   Remember you when erst
You came to Troy a spy, in tattered garb
Disguised, and from your eyes upon your beard
Fell tears extorted by the dread of death?
   ULY. I well remember: for by that event
My inmost heart was touched.
   HEC.   But Helen knew you,
And told me only.
   ULY.   I can ne'er forget
Into what danger I was fallen.
   HEC.   My knees
You in a lowly posture did embrace.
    ULY. And to thy garment clung with faltering hand.
    HEC. At length I saved and from our land dismissed you.
    ULY. Hence I the solar beams yet view.

HEC.   What language
Did you then hold, when subject to my power?
    ULY. Full many were the words which I devised
To save my life.
    HEC.   Doth not your guilt appear
From your own counsels? Though your tongue avows
The generous treatment you from me received
No benefit on me do you confer,
But strive to harm me. O ungrateful race
Of men, who aim at popular applause
By your smooth speeches; would to Heaven I ne'er
Had known you, for ye heed not how ye wound
Your friends, whene'er ye can say ought to win
The crowd. But what pretence could they devise
For sentencing this virgin to be slain?
Are they constrained by fate, with human victims,
To drench the tomb on which they rather ought
To sacrifice the steer? or doth Achilles
Demand her life with justice, to retaliate
Slaughter on them who slaughtered? But to him
Hath she done nought injurious. He should claim
Helen as victim at his tomb, for she
His ruin caused by leading him to Troy.
If it was needful that some chosen captive
Distinguished by transcendent charms should die,
We were not meant; for the perfidious daughter
Of Tyndarus is most beauteous, and her crimes
To ours at least are equal. Justice only
In this debate supports me: hear how large
The debt which 'tis your duty to repay
On my petition: you confess you touched
My hand, and these my aged cheeks, in dust
Grovelling a suppliant; yours I now embrace,
From you the kindness which I erst bestowed
Again implore, and sue to you: O tear not
My daughter from these arms, nor slay the maid:
Sufficient is the number of the slain.
In her I yet rejoice, in her forget
My woes; she, for the loss of many children,
Consoles me, I in her a country find,
A nurse, a staff, a guide. The mighty ought not
To issue lawless mandates, nor should they,
On whom propitious fortunes now attend,
Think that their triumphs will for ever last:
For I was happy once, but am no more,
My bliss all vanished in a single day.
Yet, O my friend, revere and pity me,
Go to the Grecian host, admonish them
How horrible an action 'twere to slay

These captive women whom at first ye spared,
And pitied when ye dragged them from the altars.
For by your laws 'tis equally forbidden
To spill the blood of freemen, or of slave.
Although you weakly argue, will your rank
Convince them: for the self-same speech, when uttered
By the ignoble, and men well esteemed,
Comes not with equal force.

    CHOR.   The human soul
Is not so flinty as to hear the woes
And plaintive strains thou lengthen'st out, nor shed
The sympathizing tear.

    ULY.   To me attend,
O Hecuba, nor through resentment deem
That from a foe such counsels can proceed:
I am disposed to save thee, and now hold
No other language: but will not deny
What I to all have said; since Troy is taken,
On the first warrior of the host who asks
A victim, should thy daughter be bestowed.
The cause why many cities are diseased
Is this: the brave and generous man obtains
No honourable distinction to exalt him
Above the coward. But from us, O woman,
Achilles claims such homage, who for Greece
Died nobly. Is not this a foul reproach,
If, while our friends yet live, we seek their aid,
But after death ungratefully forget
Past services? Should armed bands once more
Assemble, and renew the bloody strife,
Will not some hardy veteran thus exclaim:
"Shall we go forth to battle, or indulge
The love of life, now we have seen the dead
Obtain no honours?" While from day to day
I live, though I have little, yet that little
For every needful purpose will suffice.
But may conspicuous trophies o'er my grave
Be planted, for such tribute to my name
Will last to after-ages. If thou call
Thy sufferings piteous, hear what in reply
We have to urge; amidst the Grecian camp
Are many aged dames, as miserable
As thou art, with full many a hoary sire,
And weeping bride, torn from her valiant lord,
O'er whose remains hath Ida's dust been strewn.
Support thy woes: if with mistaken zeal
We have resolved to honour the deceased,
Our crime is ignorance: but ye barbarians
Pay no distinction to your friends, no homage

To the illustrious dead ; hence Greece prevails ;
But ye from your pernicious counsels reap
The bitter fruits they merit.

    CHOR.   Ah, what ills
Ever attend the captive state, subdued
By brutal violence, and forced t' endure
Unseemly wrongs.

    HEC.   Those words I vainly spoke
Thy slaughter to avert, in air were lavished ;
But, O my daughter, if thy power exceed
Thy mother's, like the nightingale send forth
Each warbled note, to save thy life, excite,
By falling at his knees, Ulysses' pity,
And on this ground, because he too hath children,
Entreat him to compassionate thy doom.

    POLYX. I see thee, O Ulysses, thy right hand
Beneath thy robe concealing, see thee turn
Thy face away, lest I should touch thy beard.
Be of good cheer; I'll not call down the wrath
Of Jove who guards the suppliant, but will follow
Thy steps, because necessity ordains
And 'tis my wish to die ; if I were loth,
I should appear to be an abject woman,
And fond of life : but what could lengthened life
Avail to me, whose father erst was lord
Of the whole Phrygian realm? Thus first I drew
My breath beneath the roofs of regal domes ;
Then was I nurtured with the flattering hope
That I should wed a monarch, and arrive
At the proud mansion of some happy youth.
Ill-fated princess, thus I stood conspicuous
Amid the dames and brightest nymphs of Troy,
In all but immortality a goddess ;
But now am I a slave, and the first cause
Which makes me wish to die, is that abhorred
Unwonted name ; else some inhuman lord
With gold perchance might purchase me, the sister
Of Hector, and full many a valiant chief,
Might make me knead the bread, and sweep the floor,
And ply the loom, and pass my abject days
In bitterness of woe : some servile mate
Might bring dishonour to my bed, though erst
I was deemed worthy of a sceptred king :
Not thus. These eyes shall to the last behold
The light of freedom. O ye shades receive
A princess. Lead me on then, O Ulysses,
And as thou lead'st despatch me, for no hope,
No ground for thinking, I shall e'er be happy,
Can I discern : yet hinder not by word

Or deed the steadfast purpose I have formed;
But, O my mother, in this wish concur
With me, that I may die ere I endure
Such wrongs as suit not my exalted rank.
For whosoe'er hath not been used to taste
Of sorrow, bears indeed the galling yoke,
Yet is he grieved, when he to such constraint
Submits his neck: but they who die may find
A bliss beyond the living; for to live
Ignobly were the utmost pitch of shame.

CHOR. A great distinction, and among mankind
The most conspicuous, is to spring from sires
Renowned for virtue; generous souls hence raise
To heights sublimer an ennobled name.

HEC. Thou, O my daughter, well indeed hast spoken;
Yet these exalted sentiments of thine
To me will cause fresh grief; but, if the son
Of Peleus must be gratified, and Greece
Avoid reproach, Ulysses, slay not her,
But me, conducting to Achilles' tomb,
Transpierce with unrelenting hand. I bore
Paris, whose shafts the son of Thetis slew.

ULY. Not thee for victim, O thou aged dame,
But her, Achilles' spectre hath demanded.

HEC. Yet slay me with my daughter; so shall earth,
And the deceased who claims these hateful rites,
A twofold portion drink of human gore.

ULY. Enough in her of victims; let no more
Be added: would to Heaven we were not bound
To offer up this one!

HEC. The dread behests
Of absolute necessity require,
That with my daughter I should die.

ULY. What mean'st thou?
I know no lord to counteract my will.

HEC. Her, as the ivy clings around the oak,
Will I embrace.

ULY. Not if to wiser counsels
Thou yield just deference.

HEC. I will ne'er consent
My daughter to release.

ULY. Nor will I go,
And leave her here.

POLYX. Attend to me, my mother,
And, O thou offspring of Laertes, treat
The just emotions of parental wrath
With greater mildness. But, O hapless woman,
Contend not with our conquerors. Would you fall
Upon the earth and wound your aged limbs,

Thrust from me forcibly, by youthful arms
Torn with disgrace away? Provoke not wrongs
Unseemly; O, my dearest mother, give
That much-loved hand, and let me join my cheek
To yours; for I no longer shall behold
The radiant orb of yonder sun. Now take
A last farewell, O you who gave me birth;
I to the shades descend.
  Hec.   But I the light
Am doomed to view, and still remain a slave.
  Polyx. Unwedded, reft of promised bridal joys.
  Hec. Thou, O my daughter, claim'st the pitying tear:
But I am a most miserable woman.
  Polyx. There shall I sleep among the realms beneath,
From you secluded.
  Hec.   What resource, alas!
For me, the wretched Hecuba is left?
Where shall I finish this detested life?
  Polyx. Born free, I die a slave.
  Hec.   I too, bereft
Of all my children.
  Polyx.   What commands to Hector,
Or to your aged husband, shall I bear?
  Hec. Tell them I of all women am most wretched.
  Polyx. Ye paps which sweetly nourished me——
  Hec.   Alas!
My child's untimely miserable fate.
  Polyx. Farewell, my mother, and my dear Cassandra.
  Hec. To others in that language speak; be theirs
The happiness thy mother cannot taste.
  Polyx. And thou, my brother Polydore, who dwell'st
Among the Thracians, famed for generous steeds——
  Hec. If yet he live; but this I greatly doubt,
Because I am in all respects so wretched.
  Polyx. He lives, and when the hour of death is come,
Will close your eyes.
  Hec.   I'm prematurely dead
While yet alive, bowed down to earth by woe.
  Polyx. Now bear me hence, Ulysses, o'er my face
Casting a veil: for ere I at the altar
Am slain, this heart is melted by the plaints
Of my dear mother, and my tears augment
Her sorrows. O thou radiant light; for still
Am I permitted to invoke thy name,
But can enjoy thee only till I meet
The lifted sword, and reach Achilles' tomb.
        [*Exeunt* Ulysses *and* Polyxena.
  Hec. I faint, my limbs are all unnerved; return,
My daughter, let me touch that hand once more,

Leave me not childless. O, my friends, I perish;
Ah, would to Heaven I could see Spartan Helen,
In the same state, that sister to the sons
Of Jove, for by her beauteous eyes was Troy,
That prosperous city, with disgrace o'erthrown.

CHORUS.

ODE.

I. 1.

Ye breezes, who the ships convey,
That long becalmed at anchor lay,
  Nor dared to quit the strand;
As the swift keel divides the wave,
Say whither am I borne a slave,
Ordained to tread the Doric land,
Or Phthia, where beset with reeds,
Apidanus, the sire of limpid rills,
Winding a-down the channelled hills,
  Waters the fruitful meads?

I. 2.

Or to that isle, with dashing oar
Impelled, shall I my woes deplore,
  And on the sacred earth,
Where first the palm and laurel rose,
Memorials of Latona's throes,
Which to the twins divine gave birth,
Teach the harmonious strain to flow;
With Delos' nymphs Diana's praise resound,
Her hair with golden fillet bound,
  And never-erring bow?

II. 1.

Or, pent in some Athenian tower,
Devoted to Minerva's power,
  On the robe's tissued ground
While, shadowed by my needle, spread
Expressive forms, in vivid thread,
Picture the goddess whirling round
Her chariot with unrivalled speed;
Or represent the Titan's impious crew,
Whom Jove's red lightnings overthrew,
  Those monsters doomed to bleed?

II. 2.

Alas! my sons, a valiant band,
My fathers, and my native land,

     Ye shared the general fate.
   Sacked by the Greeks, Troy's bulwarks smoke,
   But I, constrained to bear the yoke,
   Shall soon behold some foreign state,
   To ignominious bondage led;
And leaving vanquished Asia Europe's slave,
   Debarred an honourable grave,
     Ascend the victor's bed.

TALTHYBIUS, HECUBA, CHORUS.

TAL. Where, O ye Phrygian damsels, shall I find
The wretched Hecuba, who erst was queen
Of Ilion?
   CHOR.   Prostrate near you on the ground,
Wrapt in her mantle, there she lies.
   TAL.   Great Jove!
What shall I say? that thou from Heaven look'st down
Upon mankind, or have they rashly formed
A vain opinion, deeming that the race
Of gods exist, though fortune governs all?
Ha! was not this the queen of wealthy Phrygia,
And was not she the happy Priam's wife?
But her whole city by the hostile spear
Is now destroyed, while she a slave, bowed down
By age, and childless, stretched upon the ground,
Defiles with dust her miserable head.
Old as I am, yet gladly would I die
Rather than sink into abhorred disgrace.
Arise, unhappy woman, O lift up
That feeble body, and that hoary head.
   HEC. Away! O suffer this decrepit frame
To rest. Why move me! Whosoe'er thou art,
What mean'st thou? why dost thou molest th' afflicted?
   TAL. Talthybius: me, the herald of the Greeks,
O woman, Agamemnon hath despatched
To fetch you.
   HEC.   Com'st thou, by the Greeks ordained,
My friend, to slay me also at the tomb?
How welcome were such tidings; let us go,
With speed conduct me thither.
   TAL.   To inter
Your daughter, I invite you; both the sons
Of Atreus, and the assembled Grecian host,
Have sent me for that purpose.
   HEC.   Ah! what say'st thou?
Thou com'st not to inform me I must die,
But to unfold the most disastrous tidings.
Then art thou lost, my daughter, from the arms
Of thy fond mother torn; of thee, my child

Am I bereft. But how did ye destroy her,
Respectfully, or with the ruthless hand
Of hostile rage? Speak, though it wound my soul.
  TAL. A second time, in pity to your daughter,
You make me weep; for now while I relate
Her sufferings, tears bedew these swimming eyes,
Such as I shed when at the tomb she perished.
To view the sacrifice the Grecian host
Were all assembled: taking by the hand
Polyxena, on the sepulchral hillock
Achilles' son then placed her: I drew near,
Attended by the chosen youths of Greece,
To hold the tender victim, and prevent
Her struggles. But Achilles' son, uplifting
With both his hands a cup of massive gold,
Poured forth libations to his breathless sire;
And gave a sign to me, through the whole camp
Strict silence to proclaim. I in the midst
Stood up and cried: "Be mute, ye Greeks, let none
Presume to speak, observe a general silence."
The troops obeyed, and through their crowded ranks
Not e'en a breath was heard, while in these words
The chief expressed his purpose: "Son of Peleus,
My father, the propitiatory drops
Of these libations which invite the dead
Accept; O come and quaff the crimson blood
Of this pure virgin, whom to thee all Greece
And I devote; be thou benign, O grant us
Securely to weigh anchor, to unbind
Our halsers, and on all of us bestow
A happy voyage to our native land
From vanquished Troy." He ceased, and in his prayer
Joined the whole army, when the chief unsheathed
His golden-hilted sword, and gave a sign
To chosen youths of Greece to hold the virgin,
Which she perceived, and in these words addressed
The warriors: "O ye Argives, who laid waste
My city, willingly I die, let no man
Confine these arms, I with undaunted breast
Will meet the stroke. I by the gods conjure you
Release, and slay me as my rank demands
Like one born free; for I from mighty kings
Descend, and in the shades beneath should blush
To be accounted an ignoble slave."
Through all the host ran murmurs of assent,
And royal Agamemnon bade the youths
Release the virgin; they their monarch's voice,
Soon as they heard, obeyed; our lord's behests
The princess too revering, from her shoulder

Down to her waist rent off the purple robe,
Displayed her bosom like some statue formed
In exquisite proportion, and to earth
Bending her knee, in these affecting words
Expressed herself: "If at my breast thou aim
The wound, strike here; if at my neck, that neck
Is ready bared." Half willing, and half loth,
Through pity for the maid, he with keen steel
Severed the arteries; streams of blood gushed forth:
Yet even thus, though at her latest gasp,
She showed a strong solicitude to fall
With decency, while stood the gazing host
Around her: soon as through the ghastly wound
Her soul had issued, every Greek was busied
In various labours; o'er the corse some strewed
The verdant foliage, others reared a pyre
With trunks of fir: but he who nothing brought,
From him who with funereal ornament
Was laden, heard these taunts: "O slothful wretch,
Bear'st thou no robe, no garland, hast thou nought
To give in honour of this generous maid?"
Such their encomiums on thy breathless daughter.
You, of all women, who in such a child
Were happiest, now most wretched I behold.

CHOR. Fate, the behests of the immortal gods
Accomplishing, with tenfold weight hath caused
This dreadful curse to fall on Priam's house,
And on our city.

HEC.   'Midst unnumbered ills
I know not, O my daughter, whither first
To turn my eyes, for if on one I touch,
Another hinders me, and I again,
By a long train of woes succeeding woes,
To some fresh object am from thence called off;
Nor can I from my tortured soul efface
The grief thy fate occasions; yet the tale
Of thy exalted courage checks my groans,
Which else had been immoderate. No just cause
Have we for wonder, if the barren land
Cheered by Heaven's influence, with benignant suns
Yields plenteous harvests, while a richer soil
Deprived of every necessary aid
Bears weeds alone. But 'midst the human race
The wicked man is uniformly wicked,
The good still virtuous, nor doth evil fortune
Corrupt his soul; the same unsullied worth
He still retains. Is this great difference owing
To birth, or education? We are taught
What virtue is, by being nurtured well,

And he who thoroughly hath learnt this lesson,
Guided by the unerring rule of right,
Can thence discern what's base.—My soul in vain
Hath hazarded these incoherent thoughts.
But, O Talthybius, to the Greeks repair,
And strict injunctions give, that no man touch
My daughter's corse, but let the gazing crowd
Be driven away. For in a numerous host
Its multitudes break loose from all restraints,
The outrages of mariners exceed
Devouring flame, and whosoe'er abstains
From mischief, by his comrades is despised.
But, O my aged servant, take and dip
That urn in ocean's waves, and hither bring,
Filled with its water, that the last sad rites
To my departed daughter I may pay,
And lave the corse of that unwedded bride,
Of that affianced virgin : but alas !
Whence with such costly gifts as she deserves,
Her tomb can I adorn? My present state
Affords them not, but what it doth afford
Will I bestow, and from the captive dames
Appointed to attend me, who reside
Within these tents, some ornaments collect,
If, unobserved by their new masters, aught
They have secreted. O ye splendid domes,
Ye palaces once happy, which contained
All that was rich and fair ; O Priam thou
The sire, and I who was the aged mother
Of an illustrious race, how are we dwindled
To nothing, stripped of all our ancient pride !
Yet do we glory, some in mansions stored
With gold abundant, others when distinguished
Among the citizens by sounding titles.
Vain are the schemes which with incessant care
We frame, and all our boastful words are vain.
The happiest man is he who, by no ill
O'ertaken, passes through life's fleeting day.
                              [*Exit* HECUBA.

CHORUS.

ODE.

I.

By Heaven was my devoted head
  Menaced with impending ill,
What time the pines, whose branches spread
Their tutelary shade o'er Ida's hill,

Were laid by Phrygian Paris low,
  That his adventurous bark might stem the tide,
    From Sparta's coast to waft the fairest bride
On whom the solar beams their golden radiance throw.

II.

Surrounding labours were at hand
  Leagued with the behests of fate;
    Then did such madness seize the land,
As called down vengeance from a foreign state.
  The royal swain with dazzled eyes
Gave that decree, the source of all our woes,
  When from three rival goddesses he chose
Bright Venus, and pronounced that she deserved the prize.

III.

The spear and death hence raged around,
Hence were my mansions levelled with the ground;
  Staining with tears Eurotas' tide,
Too deeply grieved to share the victor's pride,
  The Spartan virgin too in vain
Bewails her favoured youth untimely slain,
    While, sprinkling ashes o'er their vest
    And hoary head, the matrons bend
  O'er their sons' urns; their groans to Heaven ascend,
They tear their cheeks, and beat their miserable breast.

ATTENDANT, CHORUS.

ATT. Where is the wretched Hecuba, my friends,
Who in her woes surpasses all, or male,
Or of the female race? her none can rob
Of her just claim, pre-eminence in grief.
  CHOR. With the harsh sounds of that ill-boding tongue,
O wretch, what mean'st thou? wilt thou never cease
To be th' unwelcome herald of affliction?
  ATT. Most grievous are the tidings which I bring
To Hecuba, nor easy were the task
In words auspicious to make known to mortals
Such dire calamities.
  CHOR.   From her apartment
She seasonably comes forth to give thee audience.

HECUBA, ATTENDANT, CHORUS.

ATT. O most unfortunate, whose woes exceed
All that the power of language can express,
My queen, you perish, doomed no more to view
The blessed light; of children, husband, city,
Bereft and ruined.
  HEC.   Nothing hast thou told

But what I knew, thou only com'st t' insult me:
Yet wherefore dost thou bring to me this corse
Of my Polyxena, o'er whom 'twas said
The Grecian host with pious zeal all vied
To heap a tomb?

ATT. She knows not, but laments
For the deceased Polyxena alone,
And to her recent woes is yet a stranger.

HEC. Ah, bring'st thou the inspired prophetic head,
And the dishevelled tresses of Cassandra?

ATT. You speak of one yet living, but bewail not
This the deceased: survey the naked corse
Of him whose death to you will seem most strange
And most unlooked for.

HEC. Ha, I see my son,
My dearest Polydore, whom he of Thrace
Beneath his roof protected. I am ruined;
Now utterly I perish. O my son,
For thee, for thee I wake the frantic dirge,
By that malignant demon which assumed
Thy voice, thy semblance, recently apprized
Of this calamity.

ATT. O wretched mother,
Know you then what was your son's fate?

HEC. A sight
Incredible and new to me is that
Which I behold: for from my former woes
Spring woes in long succession, and the day
When I shall cease to weep, shall cease to groan,
Will never come.

CHOR. The woes which we endure
Alas! are dreadful.

HEC. O my son, thou son
Of an ill fated mother, by what death
Didst thou expire? through what disastrous cause
Here liest thou prostrate? ah, what bloody hand——

ATT. I know not: on the shore his corse I found.

HEC. Cast up by the impetuous waves, or pierced
With murderous spear?

ATT. The surges of the deep
Had thrown it on the sand.

HEC. Alas! too well
I comprehend the meaning of the dream
Which to these eyes appeared: the spectre borne
On sable pinions no illusion proved,
When, O my son, thee, thee it represented
No longer dwelling in the realms of light.

CHOR. Instructed by that vision, canst thou name
The murderer?

HEC. 'Twas my friend, the Thracian king,
With whom in secrecy his aged sire
Had placed him.
CHOR. Ha! what mean'st thou? to possess
That gold by slaying him?
HEC. O, 'twas a deed
Unutterable, a deed without a name,
Surpassing all astonishment, unholy,
And not to be endured. Where now the laws
Of hospitality? Accursed man,
How cruelly hast thou with reeking sword
Transpierced this unresisting boy, nor heard
The gentle voice of pity!
CHOR. Hapless queen,
How hath some demon, thy malignant foe,
Rendered thee of all mortals the most wretched:
But I behold great Agamemnon come,
And therefore, O my friends, let us be silent.

AGAMEMNON, HECUBA, CHORUS.

AGA. Whence this delay? why go you not t' inter,
O Hecuba, your daughter, whom Talthybius
Directed that no Greek might be allowed
To touch? We therefore have with your request
Complied, nor moved the corse. But you remain
Inactive, which I wonder at, and come
To fetch you, for each previous solemn rite
That best might please, if aught such rites can please,
Have we performed. But ah, what Trojan youth
Do I behold lie breathless in the tent?
For that he was no Greek, the garb informs me
In which he's clad.
HEC. Thou wretch, for of myself
I speak, when thee, O Hecuba, I name;
What shall I do, at Agamemnon's knees
Fall prostrate, or in silence bear my woes?
AGA. Why weep, with face averted, yet refuse
T' inform me what hath happened? who is he?
HEC. But from his knees, if, deeming me a slave
And enemy, the monarch should repel me,
This would but make my sorrows yet more poignant.
AGA. I am no seer, nor can I uninformed
Trace out the secret purpose of your soul.
HEC. Am I mistaken then, while I suppose
A foe in him who doth not mean me ill?
AGA. If 'tis your wish I should not be apprized,
We both are of one mind; you will not speak,
And I as little am disposed to hear.
HEC. Without his aid no vengeance for my child

Can I obtain : yet why deliberate thus?
Prosper or fail I must take courage now.
O royal Agamemnon, by those knees
A suppliant I conjure you, by that beard,
And that right hand, victorious o'er your foes.

AGA. What do you wish for? To obtain your freedom?
This were not difficult.

HEC. No, give me vengeance
On yonder guilty wretch, and I am willing
To linger out the remnant of my life
In servitude.

AGA. Then why implore our aid?

HEC. For reasons you suspect not. Do you see
That breathless corse o'er which my tears I shed?

AGA. The corse I see; but cannot comprehend
What follows next.

HEC. Him erst I bore and nurtured.

AGA. Is the deceased, O miserable dame,
One of your children?

HEC. Not of those who fell
Beneath Troy's walls.

AGA. What! had you other sons?

HEC. Yes, him you see, born in an evil hour.

AGA. But where was he when Ilion was destroyed?

HEC. His father, apprehensive of his death,
Conveyed him thence.

AGA. From all the other children
Which then he had, where placed he this apart?

HEC. In this same region where his corse was found.

AGA. With Polymestor, sovereign of the land?

HEC. He, to preserve that execrable gold,
Was hither sent.

AGA. But, by what ruthless hand,
And how, was he despatched?

HEC. By whom beside?
The murderer was his friend, the Thracian king.

AGA. Was he thus eager? O abandoned wretch,
To seize the gold!

HEC. E'en thus; soon as he knew
Troy was o'erthrown.

AGA. But where did you discover
The body, or who brought it?

HEC. On the shore
This servant found it.

AGA. Or in quest of him
Or other task then busied?

HEC. To fetch water
To lave Polyxena's remains she went.

AGA. When he had slain him, it appears, his friend
Did cast him forth.
  HEC.   He to the waves consigned
The stripling's mangled corse.
  AGA.   O wretched woman,
Surrounded by immeasurable woes.
  HEC. I am undone; no farther ill remains
For me t' experience.
  AGA.   Ah! what woman e'er
Was born to such calamities?
  HEC.   Not one
Exists, whose sorrows equal mine, unless
You of Calamity herself would speak.
Yet hear the motive why I clasp your knees.
If I appear to merit what I suffer,
I must be patient; but if not, avenge
My wrongs upon the man who 'gainst his guest
Such treachery could commit, who, nor the gods
Of Erebus beneath, nor those who rule
In Heaven above regarding, this vile deed,
Did perpetrate, e'en he with whom I oft
Partook the feast, on whom I showered each bounty,
Esteeming him the first of all my friends;
Yet, when at Ilion's palace with respect
He had been treated, a deliberate scheme
Of murder forming, he destroyed my son,
On whom he deigned not to bestow a tomb,
But threw his corse into the briny deep.
Though I indeed am feeble, and a slave,
Yet mighty are the gods, and by their law
The world is ruled: for by that law we learn
That there are gods, and can mark out the bounds
Of justice and injustice; if such law
To you transmitted, be infringed, if they
Who kill their guests, or dare with impious hand
To violate the altars of the gods,
Unpunished 'scape, no equity is left
Among mankind. Deeming such base connivance
Unworthy of yourself, revere my woes,
Have pity on me, like a painter take
Your stand to view me, and observe the number
Of my afflictions; once was I a queen,
But now am I a slave; in many a son
I once was rich, but now am I both old
And of my children reft, without a city,
Forlorn, and of all mortals the most wretched.
But whither would you go? With you I seem
To have no interest. Miserable me!

Why do we mortals by assiduous toil,
And such a painful search as their importance
Makes requisite, all other arts attain,
Yet not enough intent on the due knowledge
Of that sole empress of the human soul
Persuasion, no rewards bestow on those
Who teach us by insinuating words
How to procure our wishes? who can trust
Hereafter in prosperity? That band
Of my heroic sons is now no more,
Myself a captive, am led forth to tasks
Unseemly, and e'en now these eyes behold
The air obscured by Ilion's rising smoke.
It might be vain perhaps, were I to found
A claim to your assistance on your love:
Yet must I speak: my daughter, who in Troy
Was called Cassandra, the prophetic dame,
Partakes your bed; and how those rapturous nights
Will you acknowledge, or to her how show
Your gratitude for all the fond embraces
Which she bestows, O king, or in her stead
To me her mother? In the soul of man
Th' endearments of the night, by darkness veiled,
Create the strongest interest. To my tale
Now listen: do you see that breathless corse?
Each act of kindness which to him is shown,
Upon a kinsman of the dame you love
Will be conferred. But, in one point my speech
Is yet deficient. By the wondrous arts
Of Dædalus, or some benignant god,
Could I give voice to each arm, hand, and hair,
And each extremest joint, they round your knees
Should cling together, and together weep,
At once combining with a thousand tongues.
O monarch, O thou light of Greece, comply,
And stretch forth that avenging arm to aid
An aged woman, though she be a thing
Of nought, O succour: for the good man's duty
Is to obey the dread behests of justice,
And ever punish those who act amiss.

CHOR. 'Tis wonderful, indeed, how all events
Happen to mortals, and the dread behests
Of fate, uncircumscribed by human laws,
Constrain us to form amities with those
To whom the most inveterate hate we bore,
And into foes convert our former friends.

AGA. To you, O Hecuba, your son, your fortunes,
And your entreaties, is my pity due.
I in obedience to the gods and justice

Wish to avenge you on this impious friend,
Could I appear your interests to espouse,
Without the troops suspecting that I slay
The Thracian monarch for Cassandra's sake:
My terrors hence arise; the host esteem
Him our ally, and the deceased a foe:
What though you held him dear, his fate, the loss
Of you alone, affects not the whole camp.
Reflect too, that you find me well disposed
To share your toils, and in your cause exert
My utmost vigour; but, what makes me slow,
Is a well-grounded fear of blame from Greece.

   HEC. Alas! there's no man free: for some are slaves
To gold, to fortune others, and the rest,
The multitude or written laws restrain
From acting as their better judgment dictates.
But since you are alarmed, and to the rabble
Yield an implicit deference, from that fear
I will release you; only to my schemes
Be privy, if some mischief I contrive
Against the murderer of my son: but take
No active part. If, when the Thracian suffers,
As he shall suffer, 'mongst the Greeks a tumult
Break forth, or they attempt to succour him,
Restrain them, without seeming to befriend
My interests. As for what remains, rely
On me, and I will manage all things well.

   AGA. How then? what mean you? With that aged hand
To wield a sword, and take away the life
Of that barbarian, or by drugs endued
With magic power? the help you need, what arts
Can furnish? what strong arm have you to fight
Your battles? whence will you procure allies?

   HEC. These tents conceal a group of Trojan dames.

   AGA. Mean you those captives whom the Greeks have seized.

   HEC. With them I on the murderer will inflict
Due punishment.

   AGA.   How can the female sex
O'er men obtain a conquest?

   HEC.   Numbers strike
A foe with terror, and the wiles of women
Are hard to be withstood.

   AGA.   They may strike terror,
But in their courage I no trust can place.

   HEC. What? did not women slay Ægyptus' sons,
And in their rage exterminate each male
From Lemnos? But leave me to find out means
How to effect my purpose. Through the camp

In safety this my faithful servant send;
And thou, when to my Thracian friend thou com'st,
Say, "Hecuba, erst Queen of Troy, invites
Thee and thy children, on thy own account,
No less than hers, because she to thy sons
And thee the self-same message must deliver."
The newly slain Polyxena's interment
Defer, O Agamemnon; in one flame
That when their kindred corses are consumed;
The brother with the sister, who demand
A twofold portion of their mother's grief
Together may be buried in one grave.
 AGA. These rites shall be performed, which could the
  troops
Set sail, I needs must have denied: but now,
Since Neptune sends not an auspicious breeze,
Expecting a more seasonable voyage,
Here must we wait. But may success attend you;
For 'tis the common interest of mankind,
Of every individual, every state,
That he who hath transgressed should suffer ill,
And fortune crown the efforts of the virtuous.
       [*Exit* AGAMEMNON.

CHORUS.

I. 1.

No more, O Troy, thy dreaded name
 Conspicuous in the lists of fame,
'Midst fortresses impregnable shall stand,
 In such thick clouds an armed host
 Pours terrors from the Grecian coast,
  And wastes thy vanquished land:
Shorn from thy rampired brow the crown
Of turrets fell; thy palaces o'erspread
 With smoke lie waste, no more I tread
Thy wonted streets, my native town.

I. 2.

I perished at the midnight hour,
 When, aided by the banquet's power,
Sleep o'er my eyes his earliest influence shed;
 Retiring from the choral song,
 The sacrifice and festive throng,
  Stretched on the downy bed
The bridegroom indolently lay,
His massive spear suspended on the beam,
 No more he saw the helmets gleam,
Or nautic troops in dread array.

II. 1.

While me the golden mirror's aid,
My flowing tresses taught to braid
In graceful ringlets with a fillet bound,
Just as I cast my robe aside,
And sought the couch ; extending wide
  Through every street this sound
  Was heard; " O when, ye sons of Greece,
This nest of robbers levelled with the plain,
  Will ye behold your homes again?
When shall these tedious labours cease?"

II. 2.

Then from my couch up starting, drest
Like Spartan nymph in zoneless vest,
At Dian's shrine an ineffectual prayer
  Did I address; for hither led,
  First having viewed my husband dead,
    Full oft I in despair,
As the proud vessel sailed from land,
Looked back, and saw my native walls laid low,
  Then fainting with excess of woe
At length lost sight of Ilion's strand.

III.

Helen that sister to the sons of Jove,
    And Paris Ida's swain,
  With my curses still pursuing,
  For to them I owe my ruin,
  Me they from my country drove,
  Never to return again,
  By that detested spousal rite
  On which Hymen never smiled,
No, 'twas some demon who with lewd delight
  Their frantic souls beguiled :
  Her may ocean's waves no more
  Waft to her paternal shore.

POLYMESTOR, HECUBA, CHORUS.

POLYM. For thee, O Priam, my unhappy friend,
And you, my dearest Hecuba, I weep,
Beholding your distress, your city taken,
Your daughter newly slain : alas! there's nought
To be relied on ; fame is insecure,
Nor can the prosperous their enjoyments guard
Against a change of Fortune, for the gods
Backward and forward turn her wavering wheel,
And introduce confusion in the world,
That we, because we know not will happen,

May worship them. But of what use are plaints
Which have no virtue to remove our woes?
If you my absence censure, be appeased,
For in the midst of Thracia's wide domains
I from these coasts was distant at the time
Of your arrival: soon as I returned,
When from the palace I was issuing forth,
This your attendant met me, and delivered
The message, hearing which, I hither came.

  HEC. O Polymestor, wretched as I am,
I blush to see thy face; because thou erst
In happier days didst know me, I with shame
Appear before thee in my present fortunes.
Nor can I look at thee with steadfast eyes:
But this thou wilt not deem to be a mark
Of enmity: the cause of such behaviour
Is only custom, which forbids our sex
To gaze on men.

  POLYM.   No wonder you thus act
Under such circumstances. But what need
Have you of me, and wherefore did you send
To fetch me from the palace?

  HEC.   I in private
A secret of importance would disclose
To thee and to thy children. From these tents
Give orders for thy followers to depart.

  POLYM. [*to his attendants, who retire.*]
Withdraw; this solitary spot is safe.
For you and the confederate Grecian host
Are all attached to me. But 'tis incumbent
On you t' inform me what my prosperous fortunes
Can yield to succour my unhappy friends!
For this is what I wish to do.

  HEC.   Say first,
If he, my son, whom this maternal hand
And his fond father in thy mansions placed,
My Polydore, yet live. I'll then pursue
My questions.

  POLYM.   Yes, in him you still are blest.

  HEC. How kind, how worthy of thyself that speech,
My dearest friend!

  POLYM.   What farther would you know?

  HEC. If haply yet the youth remember aught
Of me his mother.

  POLYM.   Much he wished to come
And visit you in private.

  HEC.   Is the gold
He brought from Troy preserved?

POLYM.   I keep it safe
In my own palace.
  HEC.   Keep it if thou wilt:
But covet not the treasures of thy friends.
  POLYM. I do not covet them; my utmost wish
Is to enjoy, O woman, what I have.
  HEC. Know'st thou then, what to thee and to thy sons
I want to say?
  POLYM.   I know not; till in words
Your thoughts are signified.
  HEC.   Bestow such love
On Polydore as thou receiv'st from me.
  POLYM. What is it that to me and to my children
You would disclose?
  HEC.   The spot, where deep in earth,
The ancient treasures of all Priam's house
Lie buried.
  POLYM.   Is this secret what you wish
Should to your son be mentioned?
  HEC.   Yes, by thee,
Because thou art a virtuous man!
  POLYM.   But wherefore
Did you require these children should be present?
  HEC. For them to know the secret, if thou die,
Will be of great advantage.
  POLYM.   You have spoken
Well and discreetly.
  HEC.   Know'st thou where at Troy
Minerva's temple stands?
  POLYM.   Is the gold there?
But by what mark shall I the spot distinguish?
  HEC. Above the surface rises a black stone.
  POLYM. Will you describe the place yet more minutely?
  HEC. The gold I in thy custody would place,
Which I from Ilion hither bring.
  POLYM.   Where is it?
Concealed beneath your garment?
  HEC.   'Midst a heap
Of spoils laid up within yon tents.
  POLYM.   Where mean you?
These are the Grecian mariners' abode.
  HEC. In separate dwellings have they placed the captives?
  POLYM. But how can we rely upon the faith
Of those within? doth no man thither come?
  HEC. There's not a Greek within; we are alone:
But enter thou these doors: for now the host,
Impatient to weigh anchor, would return
From Ilion to their homes. Thou with thy children

T' accomplish all the dread behests of fate,
Shalt thither go where thou hast lodged my son.
[*Exeunt* HECUBA *and* POLYMESTOR.

CHOR. Thou hast not yet received the blow,
But justice sure will lay thee low.
Like him who headlong from on high
Falls where no friendly haven's nigh,
Into the ocean's stormy wave,
Here shalt thou find a certain grave:
For twofold ruin doth impend
O'er him who human laws pursue,
And righteous gods indignant view:
Thee shall the hope of gain mislead,
Which prompts thee to advance with speed,
And Pluto's loathed abode descend:
Soon shalt thou press th' ensanguined strand,
Slain by a woman's feeble hand.

POLYM. [*within.*] Ah me, the light that visited these eyes
Is darkened.

SEMICHOR. Heard ye, O my friends, the shriek
Of yonder Thracian?

POLYM. [*within.*] Yet again, alas,
My children's foul and execrable murder!

SEMICHOR. My friends, some recent mischief hath within
Been perpetrated.

POLYM. [*within.*] Though your feet are swift,
Ye shall not 'scape, for through the walls I'll burst
My passage.

SEMICHOR. With a forceful hand, behold
He brandishes the javelin. Shall we rush
To seize him? This important crisis bids us
Assist our queen and Phrygia's valiant dames.

HEC. Now do thy worst, and from their hinges rend
Yon massive gates; no more canst thou impart
To those lost eyes their visual orbs, nor see
Thy sons, whom I have slain, to life restored.

HECUBA, CHORUS.

CHOR. Hast thou, my honoured mistress, caught the Thracian,
Over this treacherous friend hast thou prevailed,
And all thy threats accomplished?

HEC. Ye shall see him
Before the tent, without delay, deprived
Of sight, advancing with unsteady foot,
And the two breathless corses of his sons,
Whom I, assisted by the noblest matrons
Of Troy, have slain. Th' atonement he hath paid
To my revenge, is just. But now behold

He issues forth : I will retire and shun
The Thracian chief's unconquerable rage.

POLYMESTOR, HECUBA, CHORUS.

POLYM. Ah, whither am I going? wretched me!
Where am I? what supports me? With these hands
Groping my way like some four-footed beast,
How shall I turn me, to the right or left,
That I those murderous Phrygian dames may seize
Who have destroyed me? Impious and accurst
Daughters of Ilion, in what dark recess
Do they escape me? Would to heaven, O Sun,
Thou to these bleeding eyeballs could'st afford
A cure, that thou my blindness could'st remove.
But hush, I hear those women's cautious tread.
How shall I leap upon them? with their flesh
How shall I glut my rage, and for a feast
To hungry tigers cast their mangled bones,
In just requital of the horrid wrongs,
Which I from them, ah wretched me, have suffered?
But whither, by what impulse am I borne,
Leaving the corses of my sons exposed
To hellish Bacchanalians, as they lie
Torn by the dogs, and on the mountain's ridge
Cast forth unburied! Where shall I stand still?
Or whither shall I go? Like some proud bark
Towed into harbour, which contracts its sails;
I to that fatal chamber which contains
The corses of my murdered sons rush onward
With speed involuntary.
    CHOR.   Hapless man,
How art thou visited by woes too grievous
To be endured! but by dread Jove thy foe,
On him whose deeds are base, it is ordained
That the severest punishments await.
    POLYM. Rouse, O ye Thracians, armed with ponderous
        spears,
Arrayed in mail, for generous steeds renowned,
A hardy race, whom Mars himself inspires.
To you, O Grecian troops, and both the sons
Of Atreus, I with clamorous voice appeal:
Come hither, I implore you by the gods.
Do any of you hear me? Is there none
Who will assist? Why loiter ye? Those women,
Those captives have destroyed me. Horrid wrongs
Have I endured; ah me, the foul reproach!
But whither shall I turn, or whither go?
Through the aërial regions shall I wing
My swift career to that sublime abode

Where Sirius or Orion from his eyes
Darts radiant flames? or, to perdition doomed,
Shall I descend to Pluto's sable flood?
  CHOR. He merits pardon, whosoe'er assailed
By ills too grievous to be borne, shakes off
The loathed encumbrance of a wretched life.

AGAMEMNON, POLYMESTOR, HECUBA, CHORUS.

  AGA. Hearing thy shrieks I came. For Echo, child
Of craggy mountains, in no gentle note
Wafted those sounds tumultuous through the host.
Had we not known that by the Grecian spear
The towers of vanquished Phrygia are o'erthrown,
Such uproar would have caused no small alarm.
  POLYM. My dearest friend, soon as I heard your voice,
I instantly perceived 'twas Agamemnon.
See you my sufferings?
  AGA.   Wretched Polymestor!
Who hath destroyed thee? who bereaved of sight
Thy bleeding orbs, and those thy children slew?
Whoe'er the author of such deeds, his rage
Was dreadful sure 'gainst thee and 'gainst thy sons.
  POLYM. With the assistance of those captive dames,
Me Hecuba hath murdered, more than murdered.
  AGA. What mean'st thou? Are you guilty of the crime
With which he charges you? and have you dared
To perpetrate an action thus audacious?
  POLYM. Ah me! what said you? Is she near at hand?
Inform me where to find, that I may seize her,
And scatter wide to all the fowls of heaven
Her mangled corse.
  AGA.   Ha! what is thy design?
  POLYM. Allow me, I conjure you by the gods,
To grasp her with this frantic arm.
  AGA.   Desist,
And casting forth all rancour from thy heart,
Now plead thy cause; that, hearing both apart,
I with unbiassed justice may decide,
If thou these sufferings merit'st.
  POLYM.   I will speak.
There was one Polydore, the youngest son
Of those whom Hecuba to Priam bore;
Him erst removing from the Phrygian realm,
His sire to me consigned, that in my palace
He might be nurtured, when that hoary king
The fall of Troy suspected: him I slew:
But hear my motives for the deed, to prove
How justly and how prudently I acted,

Your enemy, that boy, if he survived
The ruin of his country, might, I feared,
Collect the scattered citizens of Troy,
And there again reside. I also feared,
That when the Greeks knew one of Priam's line
Was living, with a second fleet invading
The shores of Phrygia, they again might drain
Of their inhabitants our Thracian fields,
Involving us, their neighbours, in the vengeance
They on their foes at Ilion wreak. To us
Already hath such neighbourhood, O king,
Proved baneful. But, apprized of her son's fate,
Hecuba drew me hither, on pretence
She would inform me where in massive gold
The hidden treasures of old Priam's race
Beneath Troy's ruins were secured. Alone,
She with my children brought me to this tent,
That none beside might know. With bended knee,
While on a couch I sat, some on my left,
And others on my right, as with a friend,
Full many of the Trojan damsels took
Their places, holding up against the sun
My robe, the woof of an Edonian loom:
Some feigned t' admire it, others viewed my spear,
And stripped me of them both. From hand to hand
The matrons, seeming to caress my children,
Removed them far from their unhappy sire:
And after their fond speeches, in an instant,
(Could you believe it?) snatching up the swords,
Which they beneath their garments had concealed,
They stabbed my sons, whom while I strove to aid,
In hostile guise their comrades held my arms
And feet: if I looked up, they by the hair
Confined me; if I moved my hands, my struggles
Proved ineffectual, through the numerous band
Of women who assailed me, and to close
The scene of my calamity, accomplished
A deed with more than common horror fraught,
For they tore out my bleeding eyes, and fled.
But, like a tiger starting up, I chased
These ruthless fiends, and with a hunter's speed
Each wall examined, dashing to the ground,
And breaking what I seized. These cruel wrongs,
While I your interests study to maintain,
O Agamemnon, and despatch your foe,
Have I endured. To spare a long harangue,
The whole of what 'gainst woman hath been said
By those of ancient times, is saying now,
Or shall be said hereafter, in few words

Will I comprise; nor ocean's waves, nor earth,
Nurture so vile a race, as he who most
Hath with the sex conversed, but knows too well.
    CHOR. Curb that audacious virulence of speech,
Nor, by thy woes embittered, thus revile
All womankind; the number of our sex
Is great, and some there are, whom as a mark
To envy, their distinguished worth holds forth,
Though some are justly numbered with the wicked.
    HEC. O Agamemnon, never ought the tongue
To have a greater influence o'er mankind
Than actions; but whoever hath done well,
Ought to speak well; and he, whose deeds are base,
To use unseemly language, nor find means
By specious words to colour o'er injustice.
Full wise indeed are they to whom such art
Is most familiar: but to stand the test
Of time not wise enough; for they all perish,
Not one of them e'er 'scapes. These previous thoughts
To you, O mighty king, have I addressed.
But now to him I turn, and will refute
The fallacies he uttered. What pretence
Hast thou for saying, that to free the Greeks
From such a second war, and for the sake
Of Agamemnon, thou didst slay my son?
For first, O villain, the barbarian race
With Greece, nor will, nor ever can be friends.
What interest roused thy zeal? Didst thou expect
To form a nuptial union? Wert thou moved
By kindred ties, or any secret cause?
Greece with a fleet forsooth would have returned
To lay thy country waste. Who, canst thou think,
Will credit such assertions? If the truth
Thou wilt confess, gold and thy thirst of gain
Were my son's murderers. Why, when Troy yet flourished,
Why, when the city was on every side
Fenced by strong bulwarks, why, when Priam lived,
And Hector wielded a victorious spear,
Didst thou not, if thou hadst designed to act
In Agamemnon's favour, at the time
When thou didst nurture my unhappy son,
And in thy palace shelter, either slay,
Or to the Greeks surrender up the youth
A living prisoner? But when Ilion's light
Was utterly extinguished, when the smoke
Declared the city subject to our foes,
The stranger thou didst murder, at thy hearth
Who sought protection. To confirm thy guilt,
Now hear this farther charge: if thou to Greece

Hadst been a friend indeed, thou should'st have given
The gold thou say'st thou keep'st, not for thine own,
But Agamemnon's sake, among the troops
Who suffer want, and from their native land
Have for a tedious season been detained.
But thou from those rapacious hands e'en now
Canst not endure to part with it, but hoard'st it
Still buried in thy coffers: as became thee,
Hadst thou trained up my son, hadst thou to him
Been a protector, great is the renown
Thou would'st have gained; for in distress the good
Are steadfast; but our prosperous fortunes swarm
With friends unbidden. Hadst thou been in want,
And Polydore abounded, a sure treasure
To thee would he have proved: but now no longer
In him hast thou a friend; thou of thy gold
Hast lost th' enjoyment, thou thy sons hast lost,
And art thyself thus wretched. But to you,
O Agamemnon, now again I speak:
If you assist him, you will seem corrupt;
For you will benefit a man devoid
Of honour, justice, piety, or truth;
It might be said that you delight in evil;
But, I presume not to reproach my lords.

 CHOR. How doth a virtuous cause inspire the tongue
With virtuous language!

 AGA.   On a stranger's woes
Reluctant I pronounce, but am constrained;
For shame attends the man who takes in hand
Some great affair, and leaves it undecided.
Know then, to me thou seem'st not to have slain
Thy guest through an attachment to my cause,
Nor yet to that of Greece, but that his gold
Thou might'st retain: though in this wretched state
Thou speak to serve thy interests. Among you
Perhaps the murder of your guests seems light;
We Greeks esteem it base. If I acquit thee
How shall I 'scape reproach? Indeed I cannot:
Since thou hast dared to perpetrate the crime,
Endure the consequence.

 POLYM.   Too plain it seems,
Ah me! that, vanquished by a female slave,
Here shall I perish by ignoble hands.

 HEC. Is not this just for the atrocious deed
Which thou hast wrought?

 POLYM.   My children, wretched me!
And these quenched orbs.

 HEC.   Griev'st thou, yet think'st thou not
That I lament my son?

POLYM.   Malignant woman,
Do you rejoice in taunting my distress?
  HEC. In such revenge have not I cause for joy?
  POLYM. Yet not so hastily, when ocean's wave——
  HEC. Shall in a bark convey me to the shores
Of Greece?
  POLYM.   Shall whelm you in its vast abyss
Fall'n from the shrouds.
  HEC.   Raised thither by what impulse?
  POLYM. Up the tall mast you with swift foot shall climb.
  HEC. On feathered pinions borne, or how?
  POLYM.   With form
Canine endued, and eyeballs glaring fire.
  HEC. Whence didst thou learn that I such wondrous change
Shall undergo?
  POLYM.   Bacchus, the Thracian seer,
Gave this response.
  HEC.   To thee did he unfold
Nought of the grievous sufferings thou endur'st?
  POLYM. Then could you ne'er have caught me by your wiles.
  HEC. But on this change of being, after death,
Or while I yet am living, shall I enter?
  POLYM. After your death, and men shall call your tomb——
  HEC. By my new form, or what is it thou mean'st?
  POLYM. The sepulchre of that vile brute, an object
Conspicuous to the mariner.
  HEC.   I care not;
My vengeance is complete.
  POLYM.   Cassandra too,
Your daughter, must inevitably bleed.
  HEC.   Abomination! On thy guilty head
These curses I retort.
  POLYM.   Her shall the wife
Of Agamemnon slay, who sternly guards
His royal mansion.
  HEC.   Such a frantic deed
As this may Tyndarus' daughter ne'er commit!
  POLYM. She next uplifting the remorseless axe
Shall smite her lord.
  AGA.   Ha! madman, dost thou court
Thy ruin?
  POLYM. Slay me; for the murderous bath
Awaits you, when to Argos you return.
  AGA. Will ye not drag him from my sight by force?
  POLYM. Hear you with grief what I announce?
  AGA.   My followers,
Why stop ye not the miscreant's boding mouth?
  POLYM. This mouth be closed for ever: I have spoken.
  AGA. Will ye not cast him with the utmost speed

Upon some desert island, since he dares
To speak with such licentiousness? Depart,
O wretched Hecuba, and both those corses
Deposit in the grave. But, as for you,
Ye to your lord's pavilions must repair,
O Phrygian dames: for I perceive the gales
Rising to waft us homeward; may success
Attend the voyage to our native land!
And in our mansions may we find all well,
Freed from these dangers!
    CHOR.   To the haven go,
And to the tents, my friends, t' endure the toils
Our lords impose: for thus harsh fate enjoins.

HERCULES DISTRACTED.

PERSONS OF THE DRAMA.

AMPHITRYON.	LYCUS.
MEGARA.	IRIS.
CHORUS OF THEBAN OLD MEN.	A FIEND.
	MESSENGER.
HERCULES.	THESEUS.

SCENE.—BEFORE THE ALTAR OF JUPITER, AT THE ENTRANCE OF THE HOUSE OF HERCULES IN THEBES.

AMPHITRYON, MEGARA.

AMP. Is there on earth, a stranger to the man
Who shared the same auspicious nuptial bed
With Jove, Amphitryon born at Argos, sprung
From Perseus' son Alcæus, me the sire
Of Hercules? He in these regions dwelt,
Where from the soil a helmed crop arose;
Mars, a small number of that race, preserved,
Whose children's children people Cadmus' city.
Hence Creon king of Thebes, Menæceus' son,
Derives his birth, and Creon is the sire
Of this unhappy Megara, to grace
Whose hymeneal pomp, each Theban erst
Attuned the jocund lute, into my house
When Hercules conducted her. But leaving
This realm where I resided, and his consort
And kindred, my son chose to fix his seat
Within the walls of Argos, of that city
Erected by the Cyclops, whence I fled
Stained with Electryon's gore: but to alleviate
My woes, and in his native land obtain
A quiet residence, this great reward
He on Eurystheus promised to bestow,
That he would rid the world of every pest:
Harassed by Juno's stings, or envious fate,
With her conspiring: but, his other labours
Accomplished, he through Tænarus' jaws at length

Went to the house of Pluto, to drag forth
Into the realms of day hell's triple hound:
He thence returns not. But an old tradition
Among the race of Cadmus hath prevailed,
That Lycus, Dirce's husband, erst bore rule
Over this city, till Jove's sons, Amphion
And Zethus, who on milk-white coursers rode,
Became its sovereigns. Lycus' son who bears
His father's name, no Theban, but arriving
From the Eubœan state, slew royal Creon,
And having slain him, seized the throne, invading
The city with tumultuous broils convulsed.
But the affinity which we have formed
With Creon, seems to be my greatest curse:
For while my son stays in the realms beneath,
Lycus th' egregious monarch of this land
Would with the children of Alcides kill
His consort, by fresh murders to extinguish
The past, and kill me too (if one through age
So useless may be numbered among men),
Lest when the boys attain maturer age,
They should avenge their grandsire Creon's death.
But I (for my son left me here to tend
His children, and direct the house, since he
Entered the subterraneous realms of night),
With their afflicted mother, lest the race
Of Hercules should bleed, for an asylum
Have chosen this altar of protecting Jove,
Which my illustrious son for a memorial
Of his victorious arms did here erect,
When he in battle had subdued the Minyans.
But we, though destitute of every comfort,
Of food, drink, clothing, though constrained to lie
On the bare pavement, here maintain our seat,
For every hospitable door is barred
Against us, and we have no other hope
Of being saved. Some of our friends I see
Are faithless, and the few who prove sincere,
Too weak to aid us. Such is the effect
Of adverse fortune o'er the race of men;
May he to whom I bear the least attachment,
Never experience that unerring test
Of friendship.

MEG. Thou old man, who erst didst storm
The Taphian ramparts, when thou with renown
Didst lead the host of Thebes; the secret will
Of Heaven, how little can frail mortals know!
For to me too of no avail have proved
The fortunes of my father, who elate

With wealth and regal power (whence at the breasts
Of its possessors spears are hurled by those
Whose souls the lust of mad ambition fires),
And having children, gave me to thy son,
Joining a noble consort in the bonds
Of wedlock with Alcides, through whose death
These blessings are all fled. Now I, and thou,
Old man, are doomed to perish with the sons
Of Hercules, whom, as the bird extends
Her sheltering wings over her callow brood,
I guard. By turns they come and question me :
" O mother, whither is my father gone ?
What is he doing ? when will he return ?"
Though now too young sufficiently to feel
How great their loss, thus ask they for their sire.
I change the theme, and forge a soothing tale,
But am with wonder smitten when the doors
Creak on their massive hinges, and at once
They all start up, that at their father's knees
They may fall prostrate. But what hope hast thou
Of saving us, or what support, old man?
For I to thee look up. We from the bounds
Of these domains unnoticed cannot 'scape ;
Mightier than us, a watchful guard is placed
At every avenue, and in our friends
No longer for protection can we trust.
Explain thyself, if thou hast any scheme,
By which thou from impending death canst save us;
But let us strive to lengthen out the time,
Since we are feeble.

  AMP.   'Tis no easy task
In such a situation, O my daughter,
To form a sure and instantaneous judgment.

  MEG. What is there wanting to complete thy woes,
Or why art thou so fond of life ?

  AMP.   That blessing
I still enjoy, still cherish pleasing hopes.

  MEG. I also hope, old man : but it is folly
To look for what we never can attain.

  AMP. We by delaying might avert our fate.

  MEG. But I in this sad interval of time
Feel piercing anguish.

  AMP.   The auspicious gales
Of fortune, O my daughter, yet may waft
Both you and me out of our present troubles,
If e'er my son your valiant lord return.
But O be pacified yourself, and cause
Your children to dry up their streaming tears ;
With gentle language and delusive tales

Beguile them, though all fraudful arts are wretched.
For the disasters which afflict mankind
Are wearied out; the stormy winds retain not
Their undiminished force; nor are the blest
Perpetually blest: for all things change,
And widely differ from their former state.
The valiant man is he who still holds fast
His hopes; but to despair bespeaks the coward.

CHORUS, AMPHITRYON, MEGARA.

CHOR. Propped on my faithful staff, from home,
And from the couch of palsied age,
In melancholy guise I roam,
Constrained to chaunt funereal strains,
As the expiring swan complains,
A war of words alone I wage,
In semblance, but a flitting sprite,
An airy vision of the night.
I totter; yet doth active zeal
This faithful bosom still inspire.
Ye children who have lost your sire,
Thou veteran, and thou aged dame,
Doomed for thy lord these griefs to feel,
Whose Pluto's dreary mansions claim;
O weary not your tender feet.
Like steeds by galling harness bound,
To turn the ponderous mill around,
I would advance my friends to meet,
Yet are my utmost efforts vain,
This shattered frame I scarce sustain:
Draw near, O take this trembling hand,
And holding fast my robe, support
My steps, thy needful aid I court,
Because I am too weak to stand.
Lead on the chief, though now by years
Bowed down, who marshalled on the strand,
His comrades erst a hardy band;
With him in youth we launched our spears,
Nor then belied our native land.
See how their eyes dart liquid fire,
Those children emulate their sire;
But still hereditary fate,
Pursues with unrelenting hate
Their tender years, nor can their charms
Redeem them from impending harms.
What valiant champions of thy cause,
O Greece, thy violated laws,
When these thy great supports shall fail,
Torn from thy fostering land wilt thou bewail.

But I behold the monarch of the realm,
Tyrannic Lycus, who these doors approaches.

   Lycus, Amphitryon, Megara, Chorus.

 Lyc. This question (if I may) I to the sire
And consort of Alcides would propose
(But, as your king, I have a right to make
Any inquiries I think fit): How long
Seek ye to spin out life? What farther hope
Have ye in view, what succour to ward off
The stroke of death? Expect ye that the father
Of these deserted children, who lies stretched
Amid the realms beneath will thence return,
That ye bely your rank, and meanly utter
These clamorous plaints on being doomed to die?
Through Greece hast *thou* diffused an idle boast,
That Jove enjoyed thy consort, and begot
An offspring like himself; while *you* exulted
In being called wife to the first of heroes.
But what great action hath your lord performed,
In having slain that hydra at the lake,
Or the Nemæan lion whom with snares
He caught, and then did arrogantly boast
That he had strangled in his nervous arms?
Will these exploits enable you to vie
With me? and for such merit am I bound
To spare the sons of Hercules, who gained
A name which he deserved not? He was brave
In waging war with beasts, in nought beside,
With his left hand he never did sustain
The shield, nor faced he the protended spear,
But with his bow, that weapon of a dastard,
Was still prepared for flight: such arms afford
No proof of courage; but the truly brave
Is he who in the ranks where he is stationed
Maintains his ground, and sees with steadfast eye
Those ghastly wounds the missile javelin gives.
Old man, I act not thus through cruelty,
But caution; for I know that I have slain
Creon *her* father, and possess his throne.
These children therefore will not I allow
To live till they attain maturer years,
Lest they should punish me for such a deed.

 Amp. Jove will assert the cause of his own son.
But as for me, O Hercules, my care
Shall be to prove the folly of this tyrant:
For thy illustrious name I will not suffer
To be reproached. First from a hateful charge

(And that of cowardice I deem most hateful),
Calling the gods to witness, am I bound
To vindicate thy honour. I appeal
To Jove's own thunder, and th' impetuous steeds,
Which drew Alcides' chariot when he sped
Those winged arrows to transpierce the flanks
Of earth-born giants, and among the gods
Triumphant revelled at the genial board.
Go next to Pholoe's realm, thou worst of kings,
And ask the Centaurs' monstrous brood, what man
They judge to be most brave, whether that title
Belongs not to my son, who only bears,
As you assert, the semblance of a hero?
But should you question the Eubœan mount
Of Dirphys, where your infancy was nurtured,
It cannot sound your praise: you have performed
No glorious action for your native land
To testify, yet scorn that wise invention
The quiver fraught with shafts: attend to me
And I will teach you wisdom. By his arms
Encumbered, stands the warrior who is sheathed
In ponderous mail, and through the fears of those
Who fight in the same rank, if they want courage,
Loses his life; nor, if his spear be broken,
Furnished with nought but courage, from his breast
Can he repel the wound; but he who bends
With skilful hand the bow, hath this advantage,
Which never fails him: with a thousand shafts
He smites the foe, no danger to himself
Incurring, but securely stands aloof,
And wreaks his vengeance while they gaze around,
Without perceiving whence the weapon comes:
His person he exposes not, but takes
A guarded post: for what in war displays
The greatest prudence, is to vex the foe,
Nor rush at random on their pointed spears.
Such reasoning on the subject in debate
With yours indeed agrees not: but what cause
Have you for wishing to destroy these children?
How have they injured you? In one respect
I deem you wise, because you dread the race
Of valiant men, and feel yourself a coward:
Yet is it hard on us, if we must bleed
Your apprehensions to remove; you ought
To suffer all we would inflict, from us
Whose merit is superior far to yours,
Were Jove impartial. Would you therefore wield
The sceptre of this land, let us depart
As exiles from the realm, or you shall meet

With strict retaliation, when the gales
Of wavering fortune alter. O thou land
Of Cadmus (for to thee I now will speak,
But in reproachful accents), such protection
Afford'st thou to the sons of Hercules,
Who singly warring with the numerous host
Of Minyæ, caused the Thebans to lift up
Their free-born eyes undaunted? I on Greece
No praises can bestow, nor will pass over
In silence its base treatment of my son,
For 'twas its duty in these children's cause,
Bearing flames, pointed spears, and glittering mail,
To have marched forth, and recompensed the toils
Of their great father, who hath purged the sea
And land from all its monsters. Such protection
Nor doth the Theban city, O my children,
Nor Greece afford you ; but ye now look up
To me a feeble friend who can do nought,
But plead for you with unavailing words.
For all the vigour which I once possessed
Hath now deserted me ; old age assails
My trembling limbs and this decrepit frame.
Were I again endued with youthful strength,
I would snatch up my javelin, and defile
With gore the yellow ringlets on the head
Of that oppressor, whom his fear should drive
Beyond the most remote Atlantic bounds.
   CHOR. Are there not causes such as may provoke
Those who are virtuous to express their thoughts,
Though destitute of eloquence?
   LYC.   'Gainst me
Speak what thou wilt, for thou art armed with words,
But for injurious language by my deeds
Will I requite thee. Go, send woodmen, some
To Helicon, some to Parnassus' vale,
Bid them fell knotted oaks, and having borne them
Into the city, heap their ponderous trunks
Around the altar, and with kindled flames
Consume the bodies of this hated race ;
So shall they learn that Creon the deceased
No longer is the ruler of this land,
But that I wield the sceptre. As for you
Who thwart my counsels, O ye aged men,
Not for the sons of Hercules alone
Shall ye lament, but for those evil fortunes
Which ye and your own house are doomed to suffer :
But this shall ye remember, that to me,
Your monarch, ye are slaves.
   CHOR.   O ye the race

Of earth, whom Mars erst sowed, when he had torn
From the huge dragon's jaws th' envenomed teeth,
With those right hands why will ye not uplift
The staves on which ye lean, and with his gore
Defile the head of this unrighteous man,
Not born at Thebes, but in a foreign realm,
From inconsiderate youths who gains that homage
Which he deserves not? but in evil hour
O'er me shalt thou bear rule, nor shall my wealth
Acquired by many toils be ever thine:
Go, act the tyrant in Euboea's land,
From whence thou hither cam'st: for while I live,
The sons of Hercules thou ne'er shalt slay,
Nor is their mighty father plunged so deep
Beneath earth's surface, that he cannot hear
His children's outcries. Thou to whom this land
Owes its destruction dost possess the throne:
But he its benefactor is deprived
Of the rewards he merits. Me thou deem'st
Officious, for protecting those I love
E'en in the grave, where friends are needed most.
O my right arm, how dost thou wish to wield
The spear, but through enfeebling age hast lost
Thy vigour: else would I have quelled thy pride
Who dar'st to call me slave, and in this Thebes,
Where thou exult'st, with glory dwelt. A city
Diseased through mutiny and evil counsels
Is void of wisdom, or would ne'er have chosen
Thee for its lord.

MEG. Ye veterans, I applaud
Your zeal; for indignation at the wrongs
His friends endure becomes the virtuous friend.
But let not anger 'gainst your lord expose you
To suffer in our cause. My judgment hear,
Amphitryon, if to thee in aught I seem
To speak discreetly. I these children love
(And how can I help loving those I bore?)
For whom I have endured the painful throes
Of childbirth. And to die is what I think of
As of a thing most dreadful; but the man
Who with necessity contends I hold
An idiot. But let us, since die we must,
Not perish in the flames to furnish scope
Of laughter to our foes, which I esteem
An ill beyond e'en death: for much is due
To the unsullied honour of our house,
For thee who erst in arms hast gained renown,
To die with cowardice, were a reproach
Not to be borne. My lord, though I forbear

To dwell on his just praises, is so noble,
He would not wish these children saved, to bear
The imputation of an evil name:
For through the conduct of degenerate sons
Reproach oft falls on their illustrious sires;
And the examples which my husband gave me,
I ought not to reject. But view what grounds
Thou hast for hope, that I of these may form
A proper estimate. Dost thou expect
Thy son to issue from the realms beneath?
What chief deceased from Pluto's loathed abode
Did e'er return? Can we by gentle words
Appease this tyrant? No: we ought to fly
From fools who are our foes: but to the wise
And generous yield; for we with greater ease
May make a friend of him in whom we find
A sense of virtuous shame. But to my soul
This thought occurs, that we, the children's sentence,
By our entreaties, haply might obtain
Converted into exile: yet this too
Is wretched, at th' expense of piteous need
To compass our deliverance. For their friends
Avoid the face of guests like these, and look
No longer kindly on the banished man
After one day is over. Rouse thy courage,
And bleed with us, thee too, since death awaits.
By thy great soul, O veteran, I conjure thee.
Although the man who labours to repel
Evils inflicted by Heaven's wrath, is brave,
Yet doth such courage border upon frenzy:
For what the fates ordain, no god can frustrate.

  CHOR. While yet these arms retained their youthful strength,
Had any one insulted thee, with ease
Could I have quelled him; but I now am nothing:
On thee, Amphityron, therefore 'tis incumbent
To think how best thou may'st henceforth ward off
Th' assaults of fortune.

  AMP.   No unmanly fear,
No wish to lengthen out this life, prevents
My voluntary death: but I would save
The children of my son, though I appear
To grasp at things impossible. Behold
I bear my bosom to the sword; pierce, slay,
Or cast me from the rock. But I, O king,
For this one favour sue to you; despatch
Me and this hapless dame before the children,
Lest them we view, most execrable sight,
In death's convulsive pangs, to her who bore them,
And me their grandsire, shrieking out for aid.

But as for all beside, do what you list,
For we have now no bulwark which from death
Can save us.
    MEG.   I entreat one favour more,
Which to us both will equally be grateful.
Permit me in funereal robes to dress
My children; for that purpose be the gates
Thrown open (for the palace now is closed
Against us) that they from their father's house
This small advantage may obtain.
    LYC.   Your wishes
Shall be complied with. I my servants bid
Unbar the gates. Go in, bedeck yourselves;
The costly robes I grudge not: but no sooner
Shall ye have put them on, than I to you
Will come, and plunge you in the shades beneath.
                                           [*Exit* LYCUS.

    MEG. Follow your hapless mother, O my children,
To your paternal house, where, though our wealth
Be in the hands of others, our great name
We still preserve.
    AMP.   O Jove, 'twas then in vain
That thou didst deign to share my nuptial couch,
In vain too, of thy son have I been styled
The father, for thou hast not proved the friend
Thou didst appear to be. I, though a man,
Exceed in virtue thee a mighty god;
Because I to their foes have not betrayed
The sons of Hercules: but thou, by stealth,
Entering my chamber, to another's wife
Without permission cam'st; yet know'st not how
To save thy friends; thou surely art a god
Either devoid of wisdom, or unjust.
                   [*Exeunt* AMPHITRYON *and* MEGARA.

CHORUS.

ODE.

I. 1.

For Linus' death, by all the tuneful Nine
    Bewailed, doth Phœbus' self complain,
And loudly uttering his auspicious strain,
    Smite with a golden quill the lyre; but mine
        Shall be the task, while songs of praise
        I chaunt and twine the laureate wreath,
        His matchless fortitude t' emblaze,
Who sought hell's inmost gloom, the dreary shades beneath;

HERCULES DISTRACTED.

Whether I call the hero son of Jove,
　　Or of Amphitryon; for the fame
To which his labours have so just a claim,
Must e'en in death attract the public love:
In the Nemæan forest first he slew
　　　That lion huge, whose tawny hide
　　　And grinning jaws extended wide,-
　　　He o'er his shoulders threw.

I. 2.

The winged arrows whizzing from his bow,
　　Did on their native hills confound
The Centaurs' race with many a deadly wound:
Alcides' matchless strength doth Peneus know,
　　　Distinguished by his limpid waves,
　　　The fields laid waste of wide extent,
　　　With Pelion, and the neighbouring caves
Of Homoles, uprooting from whose steep ascent,
Tall pines that cast a venerable shade,
The monsters armed their forceful hands,
And strode terrific o'er Thessalia's lands:
Then breathless on th' ensanguined plain he laid
That hind distinguished by her golden horns,
　　　And still in Dian's temple seen
　　　His prize, to glad the huntress queen,
　　　Oenöe's walls adorns.

II. 1.

The chariot with triumphal ensigns graced
　　　Ascending, to his stronger yoke
He Diomedes' furious coursers broke,
Scorning the bit, in hateful stalls who placed
　　　By their fell lord, the flesh of man
　　　Raging devoured, accursed food;
　　　A stream from their foul mangers ran,
Filled with unholy gore, and many a gobbet crude.
O'er Hebrus' silver tide at the command
　　　Of Argos' unrelenting king
Eurystheus, he these captive steeds did bring,
Close to Anauros' mouth on Pelion's strand.
Inhuman Cycnus, son of Mars, next felt
　　　The force of his resounding bow,
　　　Unsocial wretch, the stranger's foe,
　　　Who in Amphanea dwelt.

II. 2.

Then came he to th' harmonious nymphs, that band
　　　Who in Hesperian gardens hold
Their station, where the vegetative gold
Glows in the fruitage; with resistless hand

To snatch the apple from its height;
The dragon wreathed his folds around
The tree's huge trunk, portentous sight,
In vain; that monster fell transfixed with many a wound.
Into those straits of the unfathomed main
    He entered, with auspicious gales,
Where feared the mariner t' unfurl his sails,
And fixing limits to the watery plain
His columns reared: then from the heavens' huge load
    The wearied Atlas he relieved,
    His arm the starry realms upheaved,
        And propped the gods' abode.

III. 1.

Foe to the Amazons' equestrian race
    He crossed the boisterous Euxine tide,
And gave them battle by Mæotis' side.
What friends through Greece collected he to face
    Hippolita, th' intrepid maid,
    That he the belt of Mars might gain,
    And tissued robe with golden braid.
Still doth exulting Greece the virgin's spoils retain,
    Lodged in Mycene's shrine, with gore imbrued,
    The dog of Lerna's marshy plain,
    Who unresisting multitudes had slain,
The hundred-headed hydra, he subdued,
Aided by fire, and winged shafts combined,
    These from his well-stored quiver flew,
    And triple-formed Geryon slew,
        Fierce Erythræa's hind.

III. 2.

But having finished each adventurous strife,
    At length in evil hour he steers
To Pluto's mansion, to the house of tears,
The goal of labour, there to end his life,
    Thence never, never to return;
    His friends dismayed forsake these gates,
    In hopeless solitude we mourn.
Hell's stern award is passed, the boat of Charon waits
    To their eternal home his sons to bear,
    Most impious lawless homicide!
For thee, O Hercules, thee erst his pride,
Thy sire now looks with impotent despair.
Had I the strength which I possessed of yore,
    I with my Theban friends, arrayed
    In brazen arms, thy sons would aid:
        But youth's blest days are o'er.

Clad in funereal vestments I behold
The children of Alcides erst the great,
With his loved wife and his decrepit sire
Conducting them.   O wretched me ! no longer
Can I restrain the fountain of these tears
Which gush incessant from my aged eyes.

   Megara, Amphitryon, Chorus.

 Meg. Come on.   What priest, what butcher is at hand
To slay these wretched children, or transpierce
My bosom ?   Now the victims stand prepared
For their descent to Pluto's loathed abode.
By force, my children, are we borne along
United in th' unseemly bands of death ;
Decrepit age with helpless infancy
And intermingled matrons.   O dire fate
Of me and of my sons, whom these sad eyes
Shall never more behold !   Alas ! I bore,
I nurtured you, to be the scorn, the sport,
Of our inveterate foes, and by their hands
To perish.   Each fond hope, which from the words
Of your departed father erst I formed,
Hath proved fallacious.   The deceased to *thee*
Allotted Argos, in Eurystheus' palace
Wert *thou* to dwell a mighty king, and wield
The sceptre of Pelasgia's fruitful land,
Then with the lion's hide himself had worn
Thy front he covered: *you* were to ascend
The throne of Thebes for brazen chariots famed,
Possessing my hereditary fields,
Such were the hopes of your exulting sire,
Who to *your* hand consigned that ponderous mace
Deceitful gift of Dædalus : on *thee*,
Thou little one, he promised to bestow
Oecalia, which his shafts had erst laid waste :
To you all three, these realms in threefold portions
Did he distribute ; for your father's views
Were all magnanimous : but I marked out
Selected consorts for you, and formed schemes
Of new affinities, from the domains
Of Athens, Sparta, and the Theban city ;
That binding up your cables, and secure
From the tempestuous deep, ye might enjoy
A happy life : these prospects now are vanished :
For to your arms hath changeful Fortune given
The Destinies to be your brides, while tears
Are your unhappy mother's lustral drops.
Your grandsire celebrates the nuptial feast,

O'er which he summons Pluto to preside,
The father of your consorts. But, alas!
Whom first of you my children, or whom last
To this fond bosom shall I clasp, on whom
Bestow a kiss, whom in my arms sustain?
How like the bee with variegated wings
Shall I collect the sorrows of you all,
And blend the whole together in a flood
Of tears exhaustless? O my dearest lord,
If any of those spirits who reside
In Pluto's realms beneath, can hear the voice
Of mortals, in these words to thee I speak:
O Hercules, thy father and thy sons
Are doomed to bleed; I perish too who erst
On thy account was by the world called happy.
Protect us, come, and to these eyes appear,
Though but a ghost; thy presence will suffice:
For these thy children's murderers, when with thee
Compared, are dastards.

    AMP.   To appease the powers
Of hell beneath, O woman, be thy care.
But lifting to the skies my suppliant hands,
I call on thee, O Jove, that, if thou mean
To be a friend to these deserted children,
Thou interpose without delay and save them,
For soon 'twill be no longer in thy power:
Thou oft hast been invoked; but all my prayers
Are ineffectual; die, it seems, we must.
But, O ye aged men, the bliss which life
Can yield is small, contrive then how to pass
As sweetly as is possible the hours
Which fate allots you, e'en from morn till night
Shaking off every grief: for Time preserves not
Our hopes entire, but on his own pursuits
Intent, deserts us, borne on rapid wings.
Look but on me, amid the sons of men
Conspicuous erst performing glorious deeds;
And yet hath Fortune in one single day
Taken all from me, like a feather wafted
Into the trackless air. I know not him
To whom collected stores of wealth or fame
Are durable. Farewell, for this, my comrades,
Is the last time ye shall behold your friend.

    HERCULES, MEGARA, AMPHITRYON, CHORUS.

    MEG. Ha! O thou aged man, do I behold
My dearest husband? How shall I find utterance?
    AMP. I know not, O my daughter; for I too
Am with amazement seized.

MEG.   This sure is he
Who as we heard was in the realms beneath;
Else doth some vision in the noontide glare
Delude our senses. But what frantic words
Were those I spoke as if 'twas all a dream?
This is no other than thy real son,
Thou aged man. Come hither, O my children,
Cling to your father's robe, with speed advance,
Quit not your hold, for ye in him shall find
An equal to our great protector Jove.
  HER. All hail, thou mansion, and thou vestibule
Of my abode; thee with what joy once more
Do I behold, revisiting the light.
Ha! what hath happened? I my children see
With garlands on their temples, and my wife
Amidst a throng of men, my father too
Weeping for some mischance. I'll go to them,
And ask the cause. What recent ill, O woman,
Hath happened to this house?
  MEG.   My dearest lord,
O thou who to thy aged father com'st
A radiant light, in safety hast thou reached,
At this important crisis, the abodes
Of those thou lov'st.
  HER.   What mean you by these words?
What tumults, O my sire, are we involved in?
  MEG. We are undone; but, O thou aged man,
Forgive, if I've anticipated that
Thou would'st have said to him: for in some points
Our sex are greater objects of compassion
Than males. I deem my children dead; I too
Am perishing.
  HER.   O Phœbus! with what preludes
Do you begin your speech?
  MEG.   My valiant brothers,
And aged sire, alas! are now no more.
  HER. Who slew them, how, or with what weapon?
  MEG.   Lycus,
The monarch of this city, was their murderer.
  HER. With arms did he oppose them, or prevail,
When foul sedition through the land diffused
Its pestilent contagion?
  MEG.   By revolt
He holds the sceptre of the Theban realm.
  HER. But wherefore hath this sudden panic reached
You and my aged sire?
  MEG.   He would have slain
Thy father, me, and these defenceless children.
  HER. What mean you? could he fear my orphan race?

MEG. Lest they hereafter might avenge the death
Of Creon.
    HER.   But what garb is this they wear,
Which suits some corse?
    MEG.   Already in these vestments
For our funereal rites are we arrayed.
    HER. And were ye on the point of perishing
By violence? Ah me!
    MEG.   Our friends desert us;
For we have heard that thou wert dead.
    HER.   Whence rose
This comfortless depression of the soul?
    MEG. Eurystheus' heralds the sad tidings bore.
    HER. But for what cause did ye forsake my house,
My sacred Lares?
    MEG.   From his bed thy sire
Was forcibly dragged forth.
    HER.   So void of shame
Was Lycus as to treat his age with scorn?
    MEG. Shame dwells not near the shrine of brutal force.
    HER. Were we thus destitute of friends when absent?
    MEG. What friends abide with him who is unhappy?
    HER. But did they scorn the battles which I fought
Against the Minyans?
    MEG.   I to thee repeat it,
Calamity is friendless and forlorn.
    HER. Will ye not cast from your dishevelled hair
These wreaths of Pluto? will ye not look up
To yon bright sun, and ope your eyes to view
Scenes far more pleasing than the loathsome shades
Of hell beneath? But I, for wrongs like these
Demand my vengeful arm, with speed will go
And overturn the house of that new king,
His impious head I to the ravenous hounds
Lopped from his trunk will cast, and each base Theban
Who with ingratitude repays my kindness
With this victorious weapon smite: my shafts
The rest shall scatter, till Ismenos' channel
Be choked up with the corses of the slain,
And Dirce's limpid fountain stream with gore.
For whom, in preference to my wife, my children,
And aged father, shall I aid? Farewell,
Ye labours which unwittingly I strove
T' accomplish, mindless of these dearest pledges;
In their defence I equally am bound
To yield up life, if for their father they
Were doomed to bleed. What! shall we call it noble
To war against the hydra or the lion,
And execute the mandates of Eurystheus,

HERCULES DISTRACTED.

If I avert not my own children's death?
No longer else shall I, as erst, be styled
Alcides the victorious.
    CHOR.   It is just
Parents should aid their sons, their aged sire,
And the dear partner of the nuptial bed.
    AMP. My son, this mighty privilege is yours,
To be the best of friends to those you love,
And a determined foe to those you hate.
But be not too impetuous.
    HER.   In what instance
Have I been hastier, O my honoured sire,
Than it becomes me?
    AMP.   To support his cause,
The king hath many, who in fact are poor,
Though fame accounts them rich; they raised a tumult,
And caused the ruin of the state, to plunder
Their neighbours; for the fortunes they possessed
Are through their own extravagance and sloth
Reduced to nothing. As the gates you entered,
These could not fail to see you: O beware
Lest since you by your foes have been perceived,
You perish when you least foresee your danger,
Oppressed by numbers.
    HER.   Though all Thebes beheld me,
I care not. But when I descried a bird
Of evil omen perched aloof, I knew
That there had some calamity befallen
My house, and therefore with presaging soul
In secrecy I entered these domains.
    AMP. Draw near with pious awe, my son, salute
The Lares, and display that welcome face
In your paternal mansions. For to drag
Your wife and children forth, with me your sire
To murder us, the king himself will come.
But all will prosper, if you here remain,
And a secure asylum will you find,
Nor through the city spread a loud alarm
Ere your designs succeed.
    HER.   Thus will I act,
For thou hast rightly spoken; I am entering
The palace. From the sunless caves beneath
Of Proserpine, after a long delay
Returning, first to our domestic gods
Will I be mindful to address my vows.
    AMP. Have you indeed then visited the house
Of Pluto, O my son?
    HER.   And thence the dog
With triple-head brought to these realms of light.

AMP. Conquered in battle, or on you bestowed
By hell's indulgent goddess?
   HER.   I prevailed
O'er him in combat, and have been so happy
As to behold the far-famed mystic orgies.
   AMP. But is the beast lodged in Eurystheus' palace?
   HER. Him Cthonia's groves and Hermion's walls confine.
   AMP. Knows not Eurystheus that you are returned
Into this upper world?
   HER.   He doth not know:
For I came first to learn what passes here.
   AMP. But wherefore in the realms beneath, so long
Did you remain?
   HER.   I there prolonged may stay,
My sire, to bring back Theseus from the shades.
   AMP. And where is he, gone to his native land?
   HER. He went to Athens, pleased with his escape
From the infernal regions. But attend
Your father to the palace, O my sons,
Which now ye enter in a happier state
Than when ye left it: but take courage, cease
To pour forth floods of tears; and, O my wife,
Collect thyself, let all thy terrors cease,
And loose my garments; for I have not wings,
Nor would I vanish from my friends. Alas!
Their hold they quit not, but cling faster still,
And faster to my vest. Because ye stand
Upon the verge of ruin, I will take
And bear you hence, as by the ship light boats
Are guided o'er the deep: for I refuse not
The care my children claim. Here all mankind
Are on a level, they of nobler rank
And mean condition, to their progeny
Bear equal love. The gifts of fortune vary,
Some have abundant wealth, and some are poor;
But the whole human race feels this attachment.
   [*Exeunt* HERCULES *and* MEGARA, *with the children.*

CHORUS.

ODE.

I.

Youth is light, and free from care
But now a burden on my head
Heavier than Ætna's rock, old age, I bear,
Before these eyes its sable veil is spread.

Not for the wealth of Asiatic kings,
Or heaps of gold that touched yon roof sublime,
Ere would I barter life's enchanting prime;
    Hence wealth a brighter radiance flings,
    And poverty itself can charm:
    But thou, curst dotage, art the sum
Of every fancied, every real harm;
May'st thou be plunged beneath the deep, nor come
To peopled town, or civilized abode,
Go wing thy distant flight along th' aërial road.

I. 2.

    Did the gods with sapient care
    Mete out their bounty to mankind,
The good, the gift of twofold youth should share
Unquestioned token of a virtuous mind,
Behold life's son its blest career renew,
While the degenerate sleep to wake no more.
We by these means distinctly might explore
    Their merits with as clear a view,
    As sailors, who each starry spark
    Enumerate that adorns the skies.
But now the gods have by no certain mark
Directed whom we for their worth should prize,
Whom shun as wicked: uninformed we live,
Revolving time hath nought but plenteous wealth to give.

II. 1.

    Mindful of its ancient themes,
    This faltering tongue shall ne'er refuse,
Oft as I wander by their haunted streams,
To blend each gentle grace and tuneful muse:
O may I dwell among the harmonious choirs,
My brows still circled with a laureate wreath!
Still shall the bard, a hoary veteran, breathe
    The strains Mnemosuné inspires:
    While memory wakes, I ne'er will cease
    Th' exploits of Hercules to sing;
Where Bromius yields the purple vine's increase,
Where Libyan pipes and the lute's sevenfold string
Are heard in dulcet unison; to praise
The Nine who aid the dance, I'll wake my choral lays.

II. 2.

    Delian virgins at the gate
    Assembled, festive pæans sing,
The triumphs of Latona's son relate,
And nimbly vaulting form their beauteous ring.

Into thy temple, by devotion led,
O Phœbus, will I raise my parting breath;
The swan thus warbles at the hour of death:
    Though hoary hairs my cheeks o'erspread.
    How great the hero's generous love,
    Whose merits aid our votive song,
Alcides the resistless son of Jove;
Those trophies, which to noble birth belong
By him are all surpassed, his forceful hand
Restoring peace, hath cleansed this monster-teeming land.

LYCUS, AMPHITRYON, CHORUS.

LYC. Forth from the portals at due season comes
Amphitryon; for 'tis long since ye were decked
In robes and trappings such as suit the dead.
But go, command the children and the wife
Of Hercules without these gates t' appear,
Because ye have engaged that ye will die
By your own hands.
    AMP.   You persecute, O king,
Me whom already fortune hath made wretched,
And with sharp taunts insult my dying race:
Although in power supreme, you ought to act
With moderation; but since you impose
This harsh necessity, we must submit,
And execute your will.
    LYC.   Where's Megara?
Where are the children of Alcmena's son?
    AMP. To me she seems, as far as I can guess,
From looking through the door——
    LYC.   What grounds hast thou
For this opinion?
    AMP.   In a suppliant posture
To sit before the Lares.
    LYC.   And implore them
With unavailing plaints to save her life.
    AMP. In vain too calls she on her lord deceased.
    LYC. But he is absent, he can ne'er return.
    AMP. Unless some god should raise him up again.
    LYC. Go thou, and from the palace lead her hither.
    AMP. 'Twould make me an accomplice in the murder,
If this I acted.
    LYC.   Since thy soul recoils,
I, whom such idle scruples cannot move,
Will with their mother bring the children forth.
Follow my steps, my servants, that at length
We may behold sweet peace succeed our toils.
                              [*Exit* LYCUS.

AMP. Depart: for to that place the Fates ordain
You now are on the road; perhaps the sequel
Will be another's province: but expect,
Since you have done amiss, to suffer vengeance.
He, O ye veterans, at a lucky hour
Enters the palace, for on ambushed swords
His feet will stumble, while the villain hopes
Those he would murder are too near at hand
To 'scape: but I will go to see him fall
A breathless corse: for when our foe endures
The just requital of his impious deeds,
There is a joy resulting from his death.
[*Exit* AMPHITRYON.

CHOR. Changed are our evil fortunes. To the shades
He who was erst a mighty king descends.
O justice, and ye dread vicissitudes
Of fate, ordained by Heaven!

1st SEMICHOR. Thou art at length
Gone thither, where by death thou for those taunts,
With which thou o'er the virtuous didst exult,
Shalt make atonement.

2nd SEMICHOR. My delight bursts forth
In floods of tears: for now is come that day
The tyrant deemed would never visit him.

1st SEMICHOR. But let us also look into the palace,
My aged friend, and mark if yonder miscreant
Be punished as I wish.

LYC. [*within*.] Ah me! ah me!

CHOR. That melody most grateful to mine ear
Beneath yon roofs commences; nor is death
Far distant; for these cries the monarch utters
Are but a prelude to the fatal stroke.

LYC. [*within*.] Ye realms of Cadmus, I through treachery
    perish!

2nd SEMICHOR. Others have perished by that bloody
    hand.
Since then the retribution thou endur'st
Is just, endure it bravely.

1st SEMICHOR. Where is he
Who uttered 'gainst the blest immortal powers
His foolish blasphemies, and called the gods
Too weak to punish him?

2nd SEMICHOR. That impious man
Is now no more. Yon vaulted roofs are silent,
Let us begin the harmonious choral lay;
For, as I wished, our comrades prove victorious.

Chorus.

ODE.

I. 1.

The sumptuous banquet, with th' enlivening dance
    Now every Theban shall employ;
    Dried are our tears, and past mischance
Yields to the lyre abundant themes of joy:
      Stretched low in dust the tyrant lies;
      But he, who by an ancient right
      Obtains the sceptre, is our king;
From Acheron's loathed stream behold him rise,
Revisiting the cheerful realms of light,
And hope, unlooked for, doth fresh transports bring.

I. 2.

The gods take cognizance of broken trust,
    Nor are they deaf to holy prayer.
    On gold and fortune, power unjust
Attends; man's reason is too weak to bear
      The joint temptations. Heaven at length,
      Whose kind protection we invoke,
      Deigning with pity to behold
Our woes, to the neglected laws their strength
Restoring, with vindictive fury broke
The sable car which bore the god of gold.

II. 1.

Now let the flowery wreath, the victor's pride,
    Adorn Ismenos; let each street employ
      The hours in dance and social joy;
Let Dirce from the silver wave arise,
And old Asopus' daughters by her side,
      Forsaking their paternal stream,
      Conspire to aid our rapturous theme,
And for Alcides claim the victor's prize.
Ye Pythian rocks, with waving forests crowned,
And seats of Helicon's melodious choir,
      Come every nymph, with cheerful sound,
Visit these walls which to the clouds aspire;
In helmed crop here warriors filled the plains,
Whose lineage undecayed from age to age remains.

II. 2.

O ye, the partners of one nuptial bed,
    Happy Amphitryon, sprung from mortal race,
      And Jove, who rushed to the embrace

Of bright Alcmena; for of thee aright,
Though erst, O Jove, I doubted, was it said
 Thou didst enjoy that beauteous dame;
 With the renown his triumphs claim,
Time through the world displays Alcides' might,
Emerged from grisly Pluto's realms abhorred,
Who quits the darksome caverns of the earth,
 To me a far more welcome lord,
Than yon vile tyrant of ignoble birth.
Now to the bloody strife we lift our eyes;
The vengeful sword is bared, if Justice haunt the skies.
 SEMICHOR. Ha! are we all by the same panic seized?
My aged friends, what spectre, hovering o'er
The palace, do I see? Those tardy feet
Raise from the ground, precipitate thy flight,
Be gone.—From me, O Pæan, mighty king,
Avert these evils.

   IRIS, A FIEND, CHORUS.

 IRIS. O, ye aged men,
Be not dismayed: the fiend whom ye behold
Is daughter of old Night, and I am Iris,
The gods' ambassadress. We are not come
To harm your city; for we only war
Against one man, who, sprung 'tis said from Jove
And from Alcmena: till he had performed
Severest labours, fate preserved his life;
Nor did his father Jove permit, or me,
Or Juno, e'er to hurt him: but, each toil
Eurystheus' hate enjoined, now he hath finished,
Those oft-polluted hands with recent gore
Will Juno stain, by urging him to slay
His children: in this scheme I too conspire.
Come on then, armed with a relentless heart,
Unwedded daughter of the pitchy Night;
Instil into that hero's breast such frenzy
As shall o'erturn his reason, and constrain him
To perpetrate this murder; his wild steps
Goad onward, throw the bloody cable forth,
That having sent this band of graceful sons,
Slain by their father's arm, adown the gulf
Of Acheron, th' effects of Juno's wrath
And mine, he may experience; for the gods
Would be mere things of no account, but great
Would be the power of man, if he escaped
Unpunished.
 FIEND. I from noble parents spring,
Night is my mother; and that blood which streamed
From the foul wound of Ouranus, my sire:

To me belongs this praise, I 'gainst my friend
No envious rancour feel, nor with delight
Invade them; but this counsel would suggest
To you and Juno, ere I see you rush
Into a fatal error, if my words
Can move you: he into whose house you send me
Is not obscure, or in the realms beneath,
Or yet among the gods: for when o'er lands,
Impervious erst, and o'er the stormy waves,
He had established peace, he to the gods
Their ancient honours, which by impious men
Had been abolished, singly did restore.
I therefore would dissuade you from contriving
'Gainst him these mischiefs.

    IRIS.   Blame not thou the schemes
Devised by Juno and by me.

    FIEND.   Your steps
Into a better path, from that which leads
To evil, would I turn.

    IRIS.   The wife of Jove
Sent thee not hither to act thus discreetly.

    FIEND. Witness, thou sun, reluctant I obey.
But if constrained to be the instrument
Of Juno's wrath and yours, I with such speed
As when the hounds obey the huntsman's voice,
Your signal will attend; nor shall the deep
Upheaving with a groan its troubled waves,
The earthquake, or the thunderbolt, whose blast
Is winged with fate, outstrip me, when I rush
Into the breast of Hercules: the gates
Will I burst open, and assail the house,
First causing his devoted sons to bleed;
Nor shall their murderer know that his own hand
Slew those whom he begot, till he is rescued
From the distraction I inspire. Behold
He at the barrier stands, and shakes his head,
And rolls in silence his distorted eyes,
Flaming with anger. To contain his breath
No longer able, like a bull, prepared
To make the terrible assault, he bellows,
And calls the Furies from the dire abyss
Of Tartarus. Thee I to a greater height
Of frenzy soon will rouse, and through thy soul
Cause my terrific clarion to resound.
O noble Iris, to Olympus' height
Now wing your swift career, while I, unseen,
Will enter the abodes of Hercules.

                        [*Exeunt* IRIS *and the* FIEND.

CHOR. Thou city, groan; thy choicest flower,
The son of Jove, is cropped: O Greece,
Thy benefactor's fatal hour
Impends. To thee for ever lost,
Assailed by that infernal pest,
The dauntless chief, deprived of peace,
Shall feel his agonizing breast
With horrible distraction tossed.
Hence in her brazen chariot went
The raging fiend, on mischief bent;
She urges with a scorpion goad
Her steeds along th' ethereal road.
That hundred-headed child of Night,
With all those hissing snakes around,
From her envenomed eyeballs bright
The Gorgon thus directs the wound.
Soon changed by Heaven's supreme decree,
Is man's short-lived felicity.
Ye infants, soon shall ye expire,
Slain by your own distracted sire.
Ah me! thy son, without delay,
Shall be left childless, mighty Jove;
For on his tortured soul shall prey
Yon fiend, and by the powers above
Vengeance commissioned to destroy.
O mansion erst the scene of joy!
To form a prelude to this dance,
Neither the cheering timbrel's sound,
Nor sportive Menades advance;
Here human gore shall stream around,
Instead of that refreshing juice,
Which Bacchus' purple grapes produce.
Away, ye children, danger's nigh,
For he who wakes this hostile strain,
Traces your footsteps as ye fly;
Nor will the fiend with fruitless rage,
A war beneath those mansions wage.
Alas! we sink o'erwhelmed with woe,
My tears shall never cease to flow.
I wail the grandsire hoar with age,
The mother too who bore that train
Of lovely children, but in vain.
Lo, what a tempest shakes the wall,
And makes th' uprooted mansion fall!
What mean'st thou, frantic son of Jove?
The hellish uproar thou dost raise,
Filling the palace with amaze,
Is such as vexed the realms above,

Till issuing with victorious might,
Pallas invincible in fight
The huge Enceladus oppressed,
And piled all Ætna on his breast.

MESSENGER, CHORUS.

MES. O ye whose heads are whitened o'er with age!
CHOR. Why dost thou call me with so loud a voice?
MES. Atrocious are the mischiefs which have happened
Within the palace.
CHOR.   I need now call in
No other seer. The boys are slain. Ah me!
MES. Indulge your groans, for such events as these
Demand them.
CHOR.   By a foe, e'en by the hand
Of their own sire, in whom that foe they found.
MES. No tongue can utter woes beyond what we
Have suffered.
CHOR.   What account hast thou to give
Of the dire fate the father on his sons
Inflicted? Sent by the avenging gods,
Say why such mischiefs visited this house,
And how the children miserably fell.
MES. To purify the house were victims brought
Before Jove's altar, after Hercules
Had slain and cast the monarch of this land
Forth from these doors. Beside the victor stood
His band of graceful children, with his sire
And Megara. The sacred vase was borne
Around the altar: from ill-omened words
We all abstained. But while Alcmena's son
In his right hand a kindled torch sustained,
Ready to dip it in the lustral water,
He made a silent stand; on this delay
The children steadfastly observed their sire,
But he no longer was the same; his eyes
Were seized with strong convulsions, from their fibres
Blood started forth, his bearded cheeks with foam
Were covered: he midst bursts of laughter wild
Cried: "Wherefore need I kindle, O my father,
The fire for sacrifice, ere I have slain
Eurystheus, in a double toil engaged,
When I at once might better finish all?
Soon as I hither bring Eurystheus' head,
These hands which reek already with the gore
Of Lycus, will I cleanse. Pour forth those waters
Upon the ground, and cast your urns away.
Who brings my bow, my club? I to Mycene
Will go: let spades and levers be prepared,

That I from their foundations may o'erturn
Those walls which with the plummet and the line
The Cyclops reared." Then eager to depart,
Although he had no chariot, yet he talked
As if he had one, fancying that he mounted
The seat, and with his hand as with a thong
Drove the ideal steeds. His servants laughed,
And at the same time trembled; till one cried
(As on each other they with eager eyes
Were gazing), "Doth my master sport with us,
Or is he frantic?" Meanwhile through the palace
Backward and forward he with hasty step
Was walking: but no sooner did he reach
That spacious hall, where at the genial board
The men are wont t' assemble, than he said
That he was come to Nisus' ancient city,
And to th' imperial dome: and on the floor,
As if reclining at the genial board,
Bade us set forth the banquet. But the pause
Which intervened was short, ere he exclaimed,
That he was traversing the Isthmian rocks
O'ergrown with woods; then casting off his mantle
He strove though there was no antagonist
With whom to strive, proclaimed himself the victor,
The name of that imaginary foe
Announcing, over whom he had prevailed:
But 'gainst Eurystheus he anon did utter
Menaces the most horrible, and talk
As if he at Mycene had been present.
His father strove to hold his vigorous arm,
And said to him; "What mean you, O my son?
What wanderings into distant realms are these?
Hath not the blood of him you have just slain
Distracted you?" Then for Eurystheus' sire
Mistaking his own father, as he strove
To touch his hand, repelled the trembling suppliant:
Against his sons, the quiver and the bow,
Thinking to slay the children of Eurystheus,
He next made ready; they with terror smitten
Ran different ways; the first beneath the robes
Of his unhappy mother skulked; a second
Flew to the shade the lofty column formed:
Under the altar quivering like a bird,
The last concealed himself: their mother cried,
"What mean'st thou, O thou father, would'st thou slay
Thy sons?" Aphitryon too, that aged man,
And all the servants shrieked. But round the pillar
The boy pursuing, he at length turned short,
And meeting him, as foot to foot they stood,

Transfixed his liver with a deadly shaft;
Supine he fell, and with his streaming gore
Distained the sculptured pillars, at whose base
He breathed his last. But, with a shout, Alcides
Uttered these boasts : " One of Eurystheus' brood
Slain by this arm, for the inveterate hate
His father bore me, to atone, here lies
A breathless corse." Against another then,
Who to the basis of the altar fled,
And hoped to 'scape unseen, he bent his bow;
But ere he gave the wound, the wretched youth
Fell at his father's knees, stretched forth his hands
To touch his chin, or twine around his neck,
And cried : " O spare my life, my dearest sire,
Yours, I am yours indeed; nor will you slay
Eurystheus' son." But he with glaring eyes
Looked like a Gorgon, while the boy pressed on
So close, he had no scope to aim the shaft,
But as the smith the glowing anvil smites,
Full on his auburn tresses he discharged
The ponderous mace, the crashing bones gave way.
Scarce had he slain the second, when he ran
To butcher his third son o'er both their corses :
But the unhappy mother in her arms
Caught up, into an inner chamber bore
The child, and closed the doors : but he, as if
He had indeed been at the Cyclops' city,
With levers from their hinges forced them, pierced
His wife and offspring with a single shaft,
And then to slay his aged father rushed
With speed impetuous : but a spectre came,
Which to our eyes the awful semblance bore
Of Pallas brandishing her pointed spear,
And threw a rocky fragment at the breast
Of Hercules, which checked his murderous frenzy,
And plunged him into sleep. Upon the ground
Headlong he fell, where 'midst the ruins lay,
Rent from its pedestal a broken column :
But rallying from our flight, we, by his sire
Assisted, to the pillar bound him fast
With thongs, that on his wakening from this trance
He might commit no more atrocious deeds.
There doth he taste an inauspicious sleep,
First having slain his children and his consort.
I know no mortal more completely wretched.
[*Exit* MESSENGER.

CHOR. There was a murder in the Argive land
Most wondrous and unparalleled through Greece
In days of yore, which the confederate daughters

Of Danaus perpetrated; but their crimes
By the dire fate of Progne's only son
Were far surpassed. I of a bloody deed
Now speak which they committed, they whose voice
Equals the Muses' choir; but thou who spring'st
From Jove himself, hast in thy frenzy slain
All thy three sons; for them what groans, what tears,
What invocations to the shades beneath,
Or songs shall I prepare to soothe the rage
Of grisly Pluto? Shivered on the ground
The portals of that lofty mansion view,
Behold the corses of the children stretcht
Before their miserable sire, whose senses,
Since he hath slain them, in profoundest sleep
Are buried. Mark those knotty cords around
The brawny limbs of Hercules, entwined
And to the columns in the palace fixed.
But old Amphitryon, like a bird who wails
Over its callow brood, with tardy step
Comes hither in the bitterness of grief.

AMPHITRYON, CHORUS.

The Palace gates thrown open, discover HERCULES *stretched on the ground and sleeping.*

AMP. Ye aged Thebans, will ye not be silent,
Will ye not suffer him dissolved in sleep
His miseries to forget?
    CHOR.   These tears, these groans,
To you, O venerable man, I pay,
To those slain children, and the chief renowned
For his victorious conflicts.
    AMP.   Farther still
Retire; forbear, forbear those clamorous sounds,
Lest his repose ye break, and from a trance
The sleeper rouse.
    CHOR.   How dreadful was this slaughter!
AMP. Ha! ha! begone, for he in wild confusion
Is starting up. Why will ye not lament,
Ye aged men, in a more gentle tone?
Lest roused from sleep he burst his chains, destroy
The city, smite his sire, and with the ground
Lay these proud mansions level.
    CHOR.   This I hold
Impossible.
    AMP.   Be silent, I will mark
Whether he breathe: O let me place my ear
Still closer.
    CHOR.   Sleeps he?

AMP.   An accursed repose,
Alas! he tastes, who hath his consort slain,
And slain his sons with that resounding bow.
  CHOR. Now wail.
  AMP.   I wail those children's fate.
  CHOR.   Your son,
Alas! old man, our equal pity claims.
  AMP. Observe strict silence, for again he rises
And turns around: I will conceal myself
Beneath that roof.
  CHOR.   Be of good cheer: night seals
The eyelids of your son.
  AMP.   Mark, mark me well,
I am so wretched that without reluctance
I can bid life adieu: but if he kill
Me too who am his father, guilt on guilt
Shall he accumulate, and join the stings
Of parricide to those which from the Furies
Who haunt him, he already doth endure.
  CHOR. Better you then had died, when you prepared
T' avenge the slaughtered brothers of Alcmena,
And stormed the fortress of the Taphian isle.
  AMP. Fly, leave the palace instantly; avoid
That frantic man, who from his sleep is roused,
For adding soon fresh slaughter to the past,
With Bacchanalian transport shall he range
Through Cadmus' city.
  CHOR.   Why hast thou, O Jove,
Hated thy son so bitterly, and plunged him
Into this sea of troubles?
  HER. [*waking.*]   Ha! I breathe,
And view each wonted object, air, and earth,
And these bright solar beams. Into what storm,
What dreadful perturbation of the soul
Have I been plunged! all heated I transpire,
Not from my lungs, but from my feverish heart.
Behold me! wherefore am I bound with chains,
Like a disabled ship towed into haven,
And by this youthful chest and nervous arm
Joined to a broken pillar? Here I sit
Contiguous to the corses of the slain;
My winged shafts lie scattered on the ground,
With that unerring bow which erst I bore
In war to guard me, and with care preserved.
Sent by Eurystheus, am I then arrived
A second time at the drear shades beneath?
Neither the rock of Sisyphus, nor Pluto,
Nor Ceres' sceptred daughter, do I see.
I sure am stricken senseless with amazement,

And know not where I am. But ho! what friend
Is near, or at a distance, who will come
To give me information? For each object
Which I was erst acquainted with seems strange.

AMP. Shall I approach this scene of my afflictions
Ye aged men?

CHOR.   I will attend your steps,
Nor meanly in calamity betray you.

HER. Why dost thou weep, my sire, and veil those
    eyes,
Retiring far from thy beloved son?

AMP. My son—for though unhappy, you are mine.

HER. But what calamity do I endure
That causes thee to shed these tears?

AMP.   Your woes
Are such, that any god, if he endured
The same, would groan.

HER.   This hath a dreadful sound:
But you, my fortunes have not yet explained.

AMP. Because if you your senses have recovered,
Yourself behold them.

HER.   .   Tell me what thou mean'st—
If to my charge thou lay'st some recent crime.

AMP. If you no longer to the powers of hell
Are subjected, the truth will I unfold.

HER. Alas! how darkly thou again allud'st
To what my soul suspects.

AMP.   Your looks I watch
To see if reason wholly be restored.

HER. I recollect not that I e'er was frantic.

AMP. [*to the* CHORUS.]
Shall I unbind the shackles of my son,
Or how must we proceed?

HER.   Say who was he
That bound me? for with scorn have I been treated.

AMP. Thus much of your afflictions may you know:
Forbear all farther questions.

HER.   Is thy silence
Sufficient then to teach me what I wish
To learn?

AMP.   O Jove, dost thou behold the curses
Hurled on thy son from envious Juno's throne?

HER. What dire effects of her inveterate rage
Have I endured?

AMP.   Of that vindictive goddess
No longer think: but to your own afflictions
Attend.

HER. Alas! I utterly am ruined!
What farther ill wouldst thou disclose?

AMP.   See there
The corses of your murdered children lie.
　HER. Alas! what dreadful objects strike these eyes!
　AMP. My son, against your progeny you waged
An inauspicious war.
　HER.   Why talk of war?
Who slew them?
　AMP.   You, your arrows, and the cause
Of all these mischiefs, that remorseless goddess.
　HER. What mean'st thou, or what crime have I committed,
My father, O thou messenger of ill?
　AMP. By frenzy urged. But you such questions ask,
As I with grief must answer.
　HER.   Have I murdered
My consort also?
　AMP.   All these deeds of horror
That single arm did perpetrate.
　HER.   Alas!
A cloud of griefs surrounds me.
　AMP.   For this cause
Your fortunes I lament.
　HER.   Have I demolished
My own house too, with Bacchanalian rage
Inspired?
　AMP.   The whole of what I know amounts
To this, that you are most completely wretched.
　HER. Where did this fatal madness seize me first?
　AMP. As round the altar, you, a flaming brand,
To expiate the foul murder which distains
Your hands, were bearing.
　HER.   Ah! why lengthen out
A guilty life, when of my dearest children
I am become the murderer? Why delay
To leap from the high rock, or with a sword
Transpierce this bosom, on myself their blood
Avenging? or t' avert that infamy
Which waits me, shall I rush into the flames?
But Theseus comes to bar these desperate counsels,
My kinsman and my friend; in a true light
To him shall I appear, and the pollution
I have incurred by slaying my own sons
Will be conspicuous to my dearest comrade.
What shall I do? or where can I find out
A solitude impervious to my woes?
On rapid wings, O could I mount, or plunge
Into the nether regions of the earth?
Give me a veil to darken o'er my head.
For 'tis with shame I think on the offence
Caused by this deed: but to myself alone

Ascribing the defilement of their blood,
I wish not to contaminate the guiltless.

THESEUS, AMPHITRYON, HERCULES, CHORUS.

   THE. An armed squadron of Athenian youths
I hither bring, who near Asopus' stream
Are stationed to assist your son in battle.
For to the city of Erectheus' race
A rumour came, that Lycus, having seized
The sceptre of this land, is waging war
'Gainst you. O aged man, I to repay
The benefits which Hercules conferred
On me, whom from the deary shades beneath
In safety he redeemed, on your behalf
Attend, if of this arm, or of my troops,
Ye need the help. But, ha, what means the floor
With weltering corses heaped? hath my design
Proved ineffectual? am I then arrived
Too late to remedy the dreadful mischiefs
Which have already ta'en effect? who slew
Those children, or whose consort was the dame
Whom I behold? for where the boys are laid,
No signs appear of any battle fought:
But sure I of some other recent ill
Now make discovery.
   AMP.   O thou goddess, throned
Upon that hill where verdant olives spring.
   THE. Why speak you to me in this piteous tone,
And with such prelude?
   AMP.   Grievous are the ills
Which we endure through Heaven's severe behest.
   THE. What boys are they o'er whose remains you weep?
   AMP. Them did my miserable son beget,
And when begotten slay, this impious murder
He dared to perpetrate.
   THE.   Express yourself
In more auspicious terms.
   AMP.   I wish t' obey
Th' injunctions thou hast given.
   THE.   What dreadful words
Are these which you have uttered!
   AMP.   In a moment
Were we undone.
   THE.   What mean you, what hath happened?
   AMP. This frenzy seized him sprinkled with the venom,
Which from the hundred-headed hydra flowed.
   THE. Such Juno's wrath. But who, O aged man,
Stands 'mong the dead?

AMP. My son, my valiant son,
Inured to many toils, who in that war
Where earth's gigantic brood were slain, advanced
Among the gods to the Phlegræan field
Armed with his buckler.
THE. Ah, what mighty chief
Was e'er so wretched?
AMP. Scarcely shalt thou know
A man with greater labours vexed, and doomed
To wander through more regions.
THE. But why veils he
Beneath that robe his miserable head?
AMP. Because thy presence, friendship's sacred ties
Added to those of kindred, and the gore
Of his slain children, fill his soul with shame.
THE. I with his griefs am come to sympathize;
Uncover him.
AMP. That garment from your eyes
Remove, display your visage to the sun.
It ill becomes my dignity to weep:
Yet I a suppliant strive to touch your beard,
Your knees, your hand, and shed these hoary tears.
O curb your soul, my son, whose fierceness equals
That of the lion, else 'twill hurry you
To bloody impious rage, and make you add
Mischiefs to mischiefs.
THE. Ho! on thee I call,
On thee, who to that seat of misery seem'st
Fast riveted; permit thy friends to see
Thy face: for darkness hath no cloud so black
As to conceal thy woes. Why dost thou wave
Thy hand and point to those whom thou hast slain,
Lest by this converse I pollute myself?
I am not loth to share thy woes; I erst
Was happy (which my soul is ever bound
To recollect with gratitude) when thou
From hell's loathed gloom, the mansion of the dead,
Didst safely bear me to the realms of light.
For I abhor th' attachment of those friends
Which time impairs, him too who would enjoy
Their better fortunes, but refuse to sail
In the same bark with those who prove unblest.
Rise up, unveil thy miserable head
And look on me. A noble mind sustains
Without reluctance what the gods inflict.
HER. Did you, O Theseus, see me slay my children?
THE. I heard, and now behold the ills thou speak'st of.
HER. Then why didst thou uncover to the sun
My guilty head?

THE. Why not? canst thou, a man,
Pollute the gods?
HER. Avaunt, O wretch, avaunt,
For I am all contagion.
THE. To a friend
No mischief from his friend can be transmitted.
HER. Your conduct I applaud, nor will deny
That I have served you.
THE. I who erst received
Those favours at thy hands, now pity thee.
HER. I am indeed an object of your pity,
From having slain my sons.
THE. For thee I weep,
Because to me thou heretofore wert kind
When vexed by other ills.
HER. Did you e'er meet
With those who were more wretched?
THE. Thy afflictions
Are of such giant bulk, that they to heaven
Reach from this nether world.
HER. Hence am I ready
For instant death.
THE. Canst thou suppose the gods
Regard thy threats?
HER. Self-willed are they and cruel,
And I defy the gods.
THE. Restrain thy tongue,
Lest thou by uttering such presumptuous words
Increase thy sufferings.
HER. I with woes am fraught
Already, nor remains there space for more.
THE. But what design'st thou? whither art thou borne
With frantic rage?
HER. In death will I return
To those abodes beneath, whence late I came.
THE. Thou speak'st the language of a vulgar man.
HER. Exempt from all calamity yourself,
On me these admonitions you bestow.
THE. Are these fit words for Hercules to use,
Who many toils endured?
HER. I had not suffered
Thus much, if any bounds had circumscribed
My labours.
THE. Benefactor of mankind,
And their great friend?
HER. From them no aid I find;
But Juno triumphs.
THE. Greece will not permit thee
To perish unregarded.

HER.   Hear me now,
That I with reason your advice may combat;
To you will I explain both why it is
And long hath been impossible for me
To live; and first, because from him, I spring,
Who, having slain the father of Alcmena,
Defiled with murder, wedded her who bore me.
When thus the basis of a family
Is laid in guilt, the children must be wretched.
But Jove (or some one who assumed the name
Of Jove) begot me; hence to Juno's hate
Was I obnoxious. Yet, O let not this
Offend thine ear, old man, for thee, not Jove,
I deem my real sire. While yet I hung
An infant at the breast, Jove's wife by stealth
Sent snakes into my cradle to destroy me.
But after I attained the bloom of manhood,
Of what avail were it, should I recount
The various labours I endured, what lions,
What typhons with a triple form, what giants,
Or what four-footed centaurs, who in crowds
Rushed to the battle, by this arm were slain?
How I despatched the hydra too, that monster
With heads surrounded, branching out anew,
And having suffered many toils beside,
Went to the mansions of the dead, to bring
Hell's triple-headed dog into the realms
Of light, for thus Eurystheus had enjoined?
But I at last, wretch that I am, this murder
Did perpetrate, and my own children slay,
That to their utmost summit I might raise
The miseries of this house. My fate is such
That in my native Thebes I must not dwell:
But if I here continue, to what temple
Or friends can I repair? for by such curses
I now am visited, that none will dare
To speak to me. To Argos shall I go?
How can I, when my country drives me forth?
To any other city should I fly,
The consequence were this: with looks askance
I should be viewed as one well known, and harassed
With these reproaches by malignant tongues:
"Is not this he, the son of Jove, who murdered
His children and his consort? from this land
Shall not th' accursed miscreant be expelled?"
To him who was called happy once, such change
Is bitterness indeed: as for the man
Whose sufferings are perpetual, him, when wretched,
No kinsman pities. I to such a pitch
Of woe shall come, I deem, at length, that earth,

Uttering a voice indignant, will forbid me
To touch its surface, ocean, o'er its waves,
And every river, o'er its streams, to pass.
I shall be like Ixion then, with chains
Fixed to the wheel. 'Twere better that no Greek
With whom I in my happier days conversed
Should see me more. What motive can I have
For living? or to me of what avail
Were it to keep possession of this useless
And this unholy being? flushed with joy,
Let Jove's illustrious consort, in the dance,
Strike with her sandals the resplendent floor
Of high Olympus: for she now hath gained
Her utmost wish, and from his basis torn
The first of Grecian warriors. Who can pray
To such a goddess, who, with envy stung,
Because Jove loved a woman, hath destroyed
The benefactors of the Grecian realm,
Those blameless objects of her hate?

THE. This mischief
Springs from no god except the wife of Jove.
Well dost thou judge, in saying that 'tis easier
To give thee wholesome counsel, than endure
Such agonies. But no man 'scapes unwounded
By fortune, and no god; unless the songs
Of ancient bards mislead. Have not the gods
Among themselves formed lawless marriages?
Have they not bound in ignominious chains
Their fathers, to obtain a throne? In heaven
Yet dwell they, and bear up beneath the load
Of all their crimes. But what canst thou allege,
If thou, frail mortal as thou art, those ills
Immoderately bewail'st to which the gods
Without reluctance yield? from Thebes retire,
Since thus the laws ordain; and follow me
To Pallas' city: when thy hands are there
Cleansed from pollution, I to thee will give
A palace, and with thee divide my wealth.
The presents which the citizens to me
Appropriated, when twice seven blooming victims
I by the slaughter of the Cretan bull
Redeemed, on thee will I bestow. For portions
Of land are through the realm to me assigned:
These, while thou liv'st henceforth shall by thy name
Be called: but after death, when to the shades
Of Pluto thou descend'st, with sacrifice
And with the sculptured tomb, shall Athens grace
Thy memory. For her citizens have gained
This fairest wreath from every Grecian state,

By yielding succour to the virtuous man
Their glories are augmented: and to thee
Will I repay with gratitude the kindness
Which thou deserv'st for saving me; for thou
Hast need of friends at present: but no friend
Is wanted when the gods confer renown;
For, if he wills, Jove's aid is all-sufficient.
 Her. You hold a language foreign to my griefs.
But I suppose not that the gods delight
In lawless nuptials, that their hands are bound
With galling chains, nor did I e'er believe,
Nor can I be convinced, that one bears rule
Over another. For a deity
If he be truly such, can stand in need
Of no support. But by some lying bard
Those miserable fables were devised.
Although I am most wretched, yet I thought
I might be charged with cowardice for leaving
These realms of light. For he who bears not up
'Gainst adverse fortune, never can withstand
The weapon of his foe. I am resolved
To wait for death with firmness: to your city
Meantime will I retreat, and am most grateful
For your unnumbered gifts. Unnumbered labours
Have I been erst acquainted with; from none
Did I e'er shrink, these eyes did never stream
With tears, nor thought I that I e'er should come
To such a pitch of meanness as to weep:
But now, it seems, must Fortune be obeyed.
I am content. Thou, O my aged sire,
Behold'st my exile, thou in me behold'st
The murderer of my children: to the tomb
Consign their corses with funereal pomp,
And o'er them shed the tributary tear:
For me the laws allow not to perform
This office. Let their mother, e'en in death,
Clasp to her breast, and in her arms sustain,
Our wretched offspring, whom in evil hour
I slew reluctant. But when thou with earth
Hast covered them, thy residence still keep
Here in this city, miserably indeed,
Yet on thy soul lay this constraint, to bear
With me the woes which I most deeply feel.
The very sire, ye children, who begot,
Murdered you; no advantage ye derive
From what this arm by all my labours gained,
And from your father's triumphs no renown.
Have not I slain thee too who didst preserve
My bed inviolate, and o'er my house
Long watch with patient care? Ah me! my wife,

My sons : but how much more to be lamented
Am I myself, from them for ever torn ?
Ye melancholy joys of kisses lavished
On their remains, and ye my loathed companions,
The weapons which I still retain, but doubt
Whether to keep or dash them to the ground ;
For they, while at my side they hang, will seem
To utter these reproachful words : " With us
Thy consort and thy children hast thou slain,
Yet thou the very instruments preserv'st
Which were their murderers." After such a charge
Can I still bear them ? what can I allege ?
But stripping off those arms with which through Greece
I have achieved full many glorious deeds,
Shall I expose myself to those who hate me,
And die ignobly ? I must not abandon
But keep them still, though sorrowing. Aid me, Theseus,
In this one enterprise ; to Argos go
And for your friend obtain the great reward
Promised for dragging from the shades of hell
That execrable hound : lest if by you
Deserted, I through grief for my slain children
Should come to some calamitous end. Thou realm
Of Cadmus, and ye citizens of Thebes,
With tresses shorn, in concert weep ; the tomb
Of my slain children visit, there bewail,
In one funereal dirge, the dead, and me ;
For smitten with the same dire scourge of fate
By Juno, we all perish.
   THE.   Hapless man,
Arise ; enough of tears.
   HER.   I cannot rise,
These limbs are now grown stiff.
   THE.   Calamity
Subdues the valiant.
   HER.   Would I were a stone,
Insensible to sufferings !
   THE.   Cease these plaints ;
And to the friend who comes to serve thee, give
Thy hand.
   HER.   But let me not wipe off the blood
Upon your garments.
   THE.   Wipe it off, nor scruple,
For I object not.
   HER.   Of my sons bereft,
In you the likeness of a son I find.
    THE. Fling round my neck thine arm : I'll lead the way.
    HER. A pair of friends : though one of us be wretched.
Such, O my aged father, is the man
We ought to make a friend.

THE.   His native realm
Produces an illustrious progeny.
   HER. Turn me around, that I may see my sons.
   THE. Hoping such philtre may thy griefs appease.
   HER. This earnestly I wish for, and would clasp
My father to this bosom.
   AMP.   Here, lo, here!
For what my son desires, to me is grateful.
   THE. Of all the labours thou didst erst achieve,
Hast thou thus lost the memory?
   HER.   All those ills
Were less severe than what I now experience.
   THE. Should any one behold thee grown unmanly,
He could not praise thee.
   HER.   Though to you I seem
Degraded to an abject life, I trust
That I my former courage shall resume.
   THE. Where now is the illustrious Hercules?
   HER. What had you been, if still you in the shades
Had miserably dwelt?
   THE.   Then sunk my courage
Beneath the meanest of the human race.
   HER. Why then persist in saying that my woes
Have quite subdued me?
   THE.   Onward!
   HER.   Good old man,
Farewell.
   AMP.   Farewell too, O my son.
   HER.   My children
Inter as I directed.
   AMP.   O, my son,
But who will bury me?
   HER.   I.
   AMP.   When will you
Come hither?
   HER.   After thou hast for my children
Performed that pious office.
   AMP.   How?
   HER.   I'll fetch thee
From Thebes to Athens.—Bear into the palace
My children's corses which pollute the ground.
But as for me, who have disgraced and plunged
My house in ruin, I will follow Theseus,
Towed like a battered skiff. Whoe'er prefers
Wealth or dominion to a steadfast friend,
Judges amiss.
   CHOR.   Most wretched, drowned in tears,
Reft of our great protector, we depart.

The Children of Hercules.

PERSONS OF THE DRAMA.

Iolaus.	Demophoon.
Copreus.	Macaria.
Chorus of Athenian	Alcmena.
Old Men.	Messenger.
Eurystheus.	

SCENE.—Before the Altar of Jupiter, in the Forum at Marathon, a City in the Athenian Dominions.

Iolaus.

Long have I held this sentiment: the just
Are born the streams of bounty to diffuse
On all around them; while the man whose soul
Is warped by interest, useless in the State,
Untractable and harsh to every friend,
Lives only for himself; in words alone
This doctrine I imbibed not. Through a sense
Of virtuous shame and reverence for my kindred
When I in peace at Argos might have dwelt,
I singly shared the toils of Hercules,
While he on earth remained; but now he dwells
In heaven, I guard his children, though protection
Be what I need myself. For when their sire
Forsook this nether world, Eurystheus strove
Immediately to slay us; but I 'scaped
From that oppressor's fangs, and though to me
Lost is my country, I have saved my life.
But we poor vagabonds, from city fly
To some fresh city, ever forced to change
Our dwelling; for Eurystheus deems it meet
To add this wrong to former wrongs, he sends
His heralds wheresoe'er he hears we settle,
And claims and drives us forth from every land;
No slight resentment from the Argive realm
Against our friends denouncing, he reminds them
Of his own prosperous fortunes; when they see

My weakness, and these little ones bereft
Of their great father, to superior might
They crouch, and force the suppliant to depart.
But with the exiled race of Hercules
A voluntary exile, I partake
Their evil fortunes, steadfastly resolved
Not to betray them; by malignant tongues
It never shall be said, "Oh, mark these orphans!
Since their sire's death their kinsman Iolaus
Protects them not." But, exiled from all Greece,
On reaching Marathon and the domain
Subject to the same rulers, here we sit
Before the altars of the gods, and sue
For their assistance. In this region dwell
Two sons of Theseus, I am told, by lot
Who portion out this realm, they from Pandion
Descend, and to these children are allied.
We therefore undertook our present journey
To the Athenian realm; two aged guides
Conduct the hapless wanderers; my attention
Is to the boys devoted; but Alcmena,
Entering the adjacent temple, in her arms
Tenderly clasps the female progeny
Of her departed son. Amid the crowd
We fear to introduce these tender virgins,
Or place them at the altars of the gods.
But Hyllus and his brothers, more mature
In years, inquire in what far distant land
A fortress for our future residence
We yet can find, if we from these domains
By force should be expelled. My sons, come hither,
Cling to this garment; for to us I see
Eurystheus' herald coming, by whose hate,
We wanderers, banished from each friendly realm,
Are still pursued. Thou, execrable miscreant,
Perish thyself, and perish he who sent thee:
For to the noble father of these children
Oft hath that tongue enjoined severest toils.

COPREUS, IOLAUS.

Cop. What, think'st thou unmolested to enjoy
This pleasant seat, and have thy vagrant steps
Entered at length a city prompt to fight
Thy battles? for the man who will prefer
Thy feeble arm to that of great Eurystheus,
Exists not. Hence! why in these useless toils
Dost thou persist? thou must return to Argos
Where they have doomed thee to be stoned.

IOL.   Not thus:
For in this altar shall I find protection,
And this free country on whose soil we tread.
   Cop. Wilt thou constrain me then to have recourse
To violence?
   IOL.   With forceful hand, nor me
Nor these poor children shalt thou hence expel.
   Cop. Ere long shalt thou perceive that thou hast uttered
Erroneous prophesies.
   IOL.   This ne'er shall be
Long as I live.
   Cop.   Depart, for I will seize them
'Gainst thy consent, and to Eurystheus' power
Surrender up, for they to him belong.
   IOL. Aid me, ye ancient citizens of Athens,
For we, though suppliants, forcibly are torn
E'en from Jove's public altar, and the wreaths
Twined round our sacred branches are polluted;
Shame to your city, insult to the gods.

CHORUS, IOLAUS, COPREUS.

   CHOR. What clamorous voices from yon altars rise?
What mischiefs are impending?
   IOL.   See a man
Burdened with age, wretch that I am! lie prostrate.
   CHOR. Who threw thee down? what execrable hand——
   IOL. 'Tis he, O stranger, he who to your gods
Yielding no reverence, strives with impious force
E'en now, to drag me from this hallowed seat
Before Jove's altar.
   CHOR.   He! But from what land
Cam'st thou, old man, to this confederate state
Formed of four cities? From the distant coast
Of steep Euboea did ye ply your oars?
   IOL. The life I lead, O stranger, is not that
Of vagrant islanders; but in your realm
From famed Mycene's bulwarks I arrive.
   CHOR. Among thy countrymen, old man, what name
Thou bear'st, inform me.
   IOL.   Ye perchance knew somewhat
Of Iolaus, great Alcides' comrade,
A name not quite unnoticed by renown.
   CHOR. I formerly have heard of him: but say
Who is the father of that infant race,
Whom with thy arm thou guid'st?
   IOL.   These are the sons
Of Hercules, O strangers, they, to you,
And to your city, humble suppliants come.

CHOR. On what account, inform me; to demand
An audience of the state?
  IOL.   That to their foes
They may not be surrendered up, nor torn
Forcibly from the altars of your gods,
And carried back to Argos.
  COP.   But thy lords
Who bear rule over thee, and hither trace
Thy steps, will ne'er be satisfied with this.
  CHOR. O stranger, 'tis our duty to revere
The suppliants of the gods: with forceful hand
Shall no man drag thee from this holy spot,
This seat of the immortal powers; dread justice
Shall guard thee from the wrong.
  COP.   Out of your land
The vagrant subjects of Eurystheus drive,
As I admonish; and this hand shall use
No violence.
  CHOR.   How impious is that city
Which disregards the helpless stranger's prayer!
  COP. 'Twere best to interfere not in these broils,
And to adopt some more expedient counsels.
  CHOR. You, therefore, to the monarch of this realm
Should have declared your errand, ere thus far
You had proceeded: but with brutal force
These strangers from the altars of the gods
Presume not to convey, and to this land
Of freedom yield due reverence.
  COP.   But what king
Rules this domain and city?
  CHOR.   Theseus' son,
Renowned Demophoon.
  COP.   Better I with him
This contest could decide: for all I yet
Have spoken, is but a mere waste of words.
  CHOR. Behold, he hither comes in haste, and with him,
To hear this cause, his brother Acamas.

  DEMOPHOON, IOLAUS, COPREUS, CHORUS.

  DEM. Since by thy speed, old man, thou hast outstripped
Thy juniors, and already reached the shrine
Of Jove, inform me what event hath caused
This multitude t' assemble.
  CHOR.   There the sons
Of Hercules in suppliant posture sit,
And with their wreaths, as you behold, O king,
Adorn the altar; that is Iolaus,
The faithful comrade of their valiant sire.
  DEM. How needed their distress these clamorous shrieks?

THE CHILDREN OF HERCULES.

CHOR. [*turning towards* COPREUS.]
He raised the uproar, when by force he strove
To bear them hence, and on his knees, to earth
Threw the old man, till I for pity wept.

DEM. Although he in the habit which he wears
Adopts the mode of Greece, such deeds as these
Speak the barbarian. But without delay
On thee it is incumbent now to tell me
The country whence thou cam'st.

COP. I am an Argive;
Thus far to solve your question: but from whence
I come, and on what errand, will I add;
Mycene's king, Eurystheus, sends me hither
To fetch these vagrants home: yet I, O stranger,
Will with abundant justice, in my actions,
As well as words, proceed; myself an Argive,
I bear away these Argives, I but seize
The fugitives who from my native land
Escaped, when by the laws which there prevail
They were ordained to bleed. We have a right,
Because we are the rulers of the city,
To execute the sentence we enact
'Gainst our own subjects. To the sacred hearths
Of many other states when they repaired,
We urged the self-same reasons, and none ventured
To be the authors of their own destruction.
But haply they in you may have perceived
A foolish tenderness, and hither come,
Desperate themselves, you also to involve
In the same perils, whether they succeed
Or fail in the emprise: for they no hope
Can cherish, while you yet retain your reason,
That you alone, in all the wide extent
Of Greece, whose various regions they have traversed,
Should pity those calamities which rise
But from their own imprudence. Now compare
Th' alternative proposed; by sheltering them
In these dominions, or allowing us
To bear them hence, what gain may you expect?
Side but with us, these benefits are yours:
Eurystheus' self, and Argos' numerous troops,
Will aid this city with their utmost might;
But if, by their seducing language moved,
Ye harbour groundless pity for their woes,
Arms must decide the strife. Nor vainly think
We will desist till we have fully tried
The temper of our swords. But what excuse
Have ye to plead? Of what domains bereft
Are ye provoked to wage a desperate war

With the Tirynthian Argives? What allies
Will aid you? What pretext can ye allege
To claim funereal honours for the slain?
The curses of your city will await
Such conduct; for the sake of that old man,
Whom I may justly call a tomb, a shadow,
And those unfriended children, should you step
Into the yawning gulf. Suppose the best
Which possibly can happen, that a prospect
Of future good hence rises; distant hopes
Fall short of present gain. In riper years
Ill can these youths be qualified to fight
Against the Argive host (if this elate
Your soul with hope), and ere that wished event
There is a length of intermediate time
In which ye may be ruined; but comply
With my advice; on me no gift bestow,
Let me but take what to ourselves belongs,
Mycene shall be yours. But oh, forbear
To act as ye are wont, nor form a league
With those of no account, when mightier friends
May be procured.

 DEM.   Who can decide a cause
Or ascertain its merits till he hear
Both sides distinctly?

 IOL.   In your land, O king,
This great advantage, freedom of reply
To the malignant charge against me urged,
I find, and no man, as from other cities,
Shall drive me hence. But we have nothing left
For which it now behoves us to contend
With him, nor aught, since that decree hath passed,
To do with Argos; from our native land
We are cast forth. In this distressful state,
How can he drag us back again with justice
As subjects of Mycene, to that realm
Which hath already banished us? We there
Are only foreigners. But why should he
Whom Argos dooms to exile, by all Greece
Be also exiled? Not by Athens sure;
For ne'er will Athens from its blest domains
Expel the race of Hercules, appalled
By Argos' menaced wrath. For neither Trachis,
Nor is that city of Achaia here,
Whence thou by boasting of the might of Argos
In words like those which thou hast uttered now,
These suppliants didst unjustly drive away
Though seated at the altars. If thy threats
Here too prevail, no longer shall we find

Freedom, not e'en in Athens; but I know
Full well the generous temper of its sons,
And rather would they die. For to the brave
Shame is a load which renders life most hateful.
Enough of Athens—for immoderate praise
Becomes invidious; I remember too
How oft I have been heretofore distressed
By overstrained encomiums. But on you
How greatly 'tis incumbent to protect
These children will I show, since o'er this land
You rule; for Pittheus was the son of Pelops,
From Pittheus Æthra sprung, from Æthra Theseus
Your father; from your ancestors to those
Of your unhappy suppliants I proceed;
Alcides was the son of thundering Jove
And of Alcmena; from Lysidice,
Daughter of Pelops, did Alcmena spring,
One common grandsire gave your grandame birth,
And theirs; so near in blood are you to them;
But, O Demophoon, what beyond the ties
Of family you to these children owe
Will I inform you, and relate how erst
With Theseus in one bark I sailed, and bore
Their father's shield, when we that belt, the cause
Of dreadful slaughter, sought; and from the caves
Of Pluto, Hercules led back your sire.
This truth all Greece attests. They in return
From you implore this boon, that to their foes
They may not be surrendered up, nor torn
By force from these your tutelary gods,
And banished from this realm. For to yourself
'Twere infamous and baneful to your city
Should suppliants, exiles, sprung from ancestors
The same with yours (ah, miserable me!)
Behold, behold them!) with a forceful arm
Be dragged away. But to your hands, and beard,
Lifting these hallowed branches, I entreat you
Slight not Alcides' children, undertake
Their cause; and, oh, to them become a kinsman,
Become a friend, a father, brother, lord,
For better were it to admit these claims,
Than suffer them to fall beneath the rage
Of Argive tyrants.
    CHOR.   I with pity heard
Their woes, O king, but now I clearly see
How noble birth to adverse fortune yields;
For though they spring from an illustrious sire,
Yet meet they with afflictions they deserve not.
    DEM. Three powerful motives urge me, while I view

The misery which attends you, not to spurn
These strangers; first dread Jove, before whose altars
You with these children sit; next kindred ties,
And services performed in ancient days,
Give them a claim to such relief from me
As from their godlike father mine obtained;
And last of all that infamy which most
I ought to loathe; for if I should permit
A foreigner this altar to despoil,
I in a land of freedom shall no longer
Appear to dwell, but to surrender up,
Through fear, the suppliants to their Argive lords,
In this extreme of danger. Would to heaven
You had arrived with happier auspices;
But tremble not lest any brutal hand
Should from this hallowed altar force away
You and the children. Therefore go thou back
To Argos, and this message to Eurystheus
Deliver; tell him too if there be aught
Which 'gainst our guests he can allege, the laws
Are open; but thou shalt not drag them hence.

 Cop. Not if I prove that it is just, and bring
Prevailing reasons?

 Dem.   How can it be just
To drive away the suppliant?

 Cop.   Hence no shame
Shall light on me, but ruin on your head.

 Dem. Should I permit thee to convey them hence
In me 'twere base indeed.

 Cop.   Let them be banished
From your domains, and I elsewhere will seize them.

 Dem. Thou fool, who deem'st thyself more wise than
Jove!

 Cop. All villains may, it seems, take refuge here.

 Dem. This altar of the gods, to all affords
A sure asylum.

 Cop.   In a different light,
This to Mycene's rulers will appear.

 Dem. Am not I then the monarch of this realm?

 Cop. Offer no wrong to them, if you are wise.

 Dem. Do ye then suffer wrong when I refuse
To violate the temples of the gods?

 Cop. I would not have you enter on a war
Against the Argives.

 Dem.   Equally inclined
Am I to peace, yet will not I yield up
These suppliants.

 Cop.   Hence am I resolved to drag
Those who belong to me.

DEM.   Thou then to Argos
Shalt not with ease return.
  COP.   Soon will I make
Th' experiment and know.
  DEM.   If thou presume
To touch them, thou immediately shalt rue it.
  COP. I by the gods conjure you not to strike
A herald.
  DEM.   Strike I will, unless that herald
Learn to behave discreetly.
  CHOR.   Go. And you,
O king, forbear to touch him.
  COP.   I retire:
For weak in combat is a single arm.
But I again shall hither come, and bring
A host of Argives armed with brazen spears:
Unnumbered warriors wait for my return.
The king himself, Eurystheus, is their chief;
He on the borders of Alcathous' realm
Waits for an answer. He in glittering mail,
Soon as he hears your arrogant reply,
To you, your subjects, this devoted realm,
And all its wasted forests will appear,
For we in vain at Argos should possess
A band so numerous of heroic youths,
If we chastised not your assuming pride.   [*Exit* COPREUS.
  DEM. Away, detested miscreant; for I fear not
Thy Argos: and thou ne'er, by dragging hence
These suppliants, shalt disgrace me: for this city
As an appendage to the Argive realm
I hold not, but its freedom will maintain.
  CHOR. 'Tis time each sage precaution to exert,
Ere to the confines of this land advance
The troops of Argos: for Mycene's wrath
Is terrible in combat, and more fierce
Than heretofore will they invade us now.
For to exaggerate facts beyond the truth
Is every herald's custom. To his king,
How many specious tales do you suppose
Of the atrocious insults he endured,
He will relate, and add how he the loss
Of life endangered?
  IOL.   To the sons devolve
No honours which exceed the being born
Of an illustrious and heroic sire,
And wedding into virtuous families.
But on that man no praise will I bestow,
Who by his lusts impelled, among the wicked
A nuptial union forms; hence to his sons

Disgrace, instead of pleasure, he bequeaths.
For noble birth repels adversity
Better than abject parentage. When sinking
Under the utmost pressure of our woes,
We find these friends and kinsmen, who alone
Amid the populous extent of Greece
Stand forth in our behalf. Ye generous youths,
Now give them your right hands, and in return
Take those of your protectors : O my sons,
Draw near : we have made trial of our friends.
If ye again behold your native walls,
Possess the self-same mansions, and the honours
Which your illustrious father erst enjoyed ;
These deem your saviours and your friends, nor wield
Against their fostering land the hostile spear.
On your remembrance let these benefits
Be ever stamped, and hold this city dear;
For they deserve your reverence, who from us
Repel so great a nation, such a swarm
Of fierce Pelasgian troops : and, though they see
Our poverty and exile, have refused
To yield us up, or banish from their realm.
Both while I live, and after the cold grave
Receives me at the destined hour, my friend,
I with loud voice your merits will applaud,
Approaching mighty Theseus, and my words
Shall soothe your father's ear when I recount
With what humanity you have received us,
And how protected the defenceless sons
Of Hercules : by your illustrious birth
Distinguished, you the glories of your sire
Through Greece maintain : sprung from a noble lineage,
Yet are you one among that chosen few
Who in no instance deviate from the virtues
Of your great ancestry : although 'mid thousands
Scarce is a single instance to be found
Of those who emulate their father's worth.

CHOR. This country, in a just and honest cause,
Is ever prompt to succour the distressed.
Hence in its friends' behalf hath it sustained
Unnumbered toils, and now another conflict
I see impending.

DEM.   Rightly hast thou spoken,
And in such toils I feel a conscious pride.
These benefits shall never be forgotten ;
But an assembly of the citizens
I instantly will summon, and arrange
A numerous squadron, to receive the onset
Of fierce Mycene's host, first sending spies

To meet them, lest they unawares assail us.
For the bold warrior, who without delay
Goes forth to battle, keeps the foe aloof.
I also will collect the seers, and slay
The victims; but do you, old man, meanwhile
Enter the palace with these children, leaving
Jove's altar: for my menial train are there,
Who will with fond solicitude attend you,
Although I am not present: but go in.

IOL. I will not leave the altar; on this seat
We suppliants will remain, and pray to Jove,
That prosperous fortunes may attend your city.
But when you from this conflict are with glory
Released, we to your palace will repair;
Nor are the gods, who war on our behalf,
O king, inferior to the gods of Argos.
For o'er that city, Jove's majestic consort,
Juno, but here Minerva doth preside.
This I maintain, that nought ensures success
Beyond the aid of mightier deities,
Nor will imperial Pallas be subdued. [*Exit* DEMOPHOON.

CHORUS.
ODE.

I.

Boast as thou wilt, and urge thy proud demand,
    This nation disregards thy ire,
    Thou stranger from the Argive land.
    Nor can thy sounding words control
    The steadfast purpose of my soul:
    Great Athens, by her lovely choir
    Distinguished, shall unstained preserve
Her ancient glory, nor from virtue swerve;
But thou, devoid of wisdom, dost obey
The son of Sthenelus, the tyrant's impious sway,

II.

Who com'st amidst an independent state,
    In nought inferior to the strength
    Of Argos, and with brutal hate
    Dar'st, though a foreigner, to seize
    The exiles, who our deities
    Implore, and in these realms at length
    From their distress obtain a shield:
Thou e'en to sceptred monarchs will not yield,
Yet no just plea thy subtle tongue hath found.
How can such conduct warp the man whose judgment's
    sound?

III.

Peace is the object of my dear delight:
  But thou, O tyrant, thou whose breast
Well may I deem by frenzy is possest,
If 'gainst this city thou exert thy might,
Pant'st after trophies which thou ne'er shalt gain.
  Bearing targe and brazen lance
  Others with equal arms advance.
O thou, who fondly seek'st th' embattled plain,
  Shake not these turrets, spare the haunt
Of every gentle grace.—Thou wretch, avaunt.

DEMOPHOON, IOLAUS, CHORUS.

IOL. Why com'st thou hither, O my son, with eyes
Expressive of affliction? from the foe
What recent information canst thou give?
Do they delay their march, are they at hand,
Or bring'st thou any tidings? for the threats
That herald uttered sure will be accomplished.
Blest in the favour of the gods, the tyrant
Exults, I know, and arrogantly deems
That he o'er Athens shall prevail; but Jove
Chastises the presumptuous.
  DEM.   Argos comes
With numerous squadrons, and its king Eurystheus,
Myself beheld him. It behoves the man
Who claims the merit of an able chief,
Not to depend upon his spies alone
To mark the foe's approach. But with his host
He hath not yet invaded these domains,
But halting on yon mountain's topmost ridge
Observes (I from conjecture speak) the road
By which he may lead forth his troops to battle,
And where he in this realm with greatest safety
May station them. Already have I made
Each preparation to repel their onset.
The city is in arms, the victims stand
Before the altars, with their blood t' appease
The wrath of every god, and due lustrations
Are sprinkled by the seers, that o'er our foes
We may obtain a triumph, and preserve
This country. Every prophet who expounds
The oracles, convening, have I searched
Into each sage response of ancient times,
Or public or concealed, on which depends
The welfare of the realm. In all beside
Differ Heaven's mandates: but one dread behest

Runs through the several auspices, to Ceres
They bid me sacrifice some blooming maid
Who from a nobler sire derives her birth.
Zeal have I shown abundant in your cause,
But will not slay my daughter, nor constrain
Any Athenian citizen to make
Such an abhorred oblation: for the man
Exists not, who is so devoid of reason,
As willingly to yield his children up
With his own hands. But what afflicts me most
Is this: tumultuous crowds appear; some cry,
'Tis just that we the foreign suppliants aid,
But others blame my folly. If no means
Can be devised to satisfy them all,
Soon will a storm of civil war arise.
See thou to this, and think of some expedient,
How ye and how this country may be saved,
Without the citizens' calumnious tongues
My fame assailing. For I rule not here
With boundless power, like a barbarian king;
Let but my deeds be just, and in return
Shall I experience justice.
    CHOR.   Will not Jove
Suffer this city to exert its courage,
And aid these hapless strangers as we wish?
    IOL. Our situation, O my sons, resembles
That of the mariners, who having 'scaped
The storm's relentless fury, when in sight
Of land, are from the coast by adverse winds
Driven back into the deep. Thus from this realm
Just as we reach the shore, like shipwrecked men,
Are we expelled. O inauspicious Hope,
Why didst thou soothe me with ideal joy,
Although it was ordained that thou should'st leave
Thy favours incomplete? The king deserves
At least to be excused, if he consent not
To slay his subjects' daughters; to this city
My praise is due, and if the gods would place me
In the same prosperous fortunes, from my soul
Your benefits should never be effaced.
But now, alas! no counsel can I give
To you, my children. Whither shall we turn?
What god have we neglected? To what land
Have we not fled for shelter? We must perish,
We shall be yielded up. My being doomed
To die, I heed but for this cause alone,
That by my death I shall afford delight
To our perfidious foes. But, O my sons,
For you I weep, I pity you, I pity

EURIPIDES.

Alcmena, aged mother of your sire,
Oh, most unhappy in a life too long!
I too am wretched, who unnumbered toils
Have fruitlessly endured; it was ordained,
It was ordained, alas! that we should fall
Into the hands of our relentless foes,
And meet a shameful, miserable death.
Know you, what still remains for you to do,
On my behalf? For all my hopes of saving
The children are not vanished. In their stead
Me to the Argive host surrender up,
O king, and rush not into needless danger,
Yet save these children. To retain a love
Of life becomes me not; I yield it up
Without regret. It is Eurystheus' wish
The rather to seize me, and to expose
To infamy, because I was the comrade
Of Hercules; for frenzy hath possessed
His soul. The wise man, e'en in those he hates,
Had rather find discretion than a want
Of understanding; for a foe endued
With sense will pay due reverence to the vanquished.

CHOR. Forbear, old man, thus hastily to blame
This city; for to us though it might prove
More advantageous, yet to our disgrace
Would it redound, should we betray our guests.

DEM. A generous, but impracticable, scheme
Is that thou hast proposed: for Argos' king
In quest of thee no squadrons hither leads.
What profit to Eurystheus from the death
Of one so old as thou art could arise?
He wants to murder *these:* for to their foes
The rising blossoms of a noble race,
To whom the memory of their father's wrongs
Is present, must be dreadful: for all this
He cannot but foresee. But if thou know
Of any other counsel more expedient,
Adopt it; for my soul hath been perplexed,
Since that oracular response I heard
Which fills me with unwelcome apprehensions.
[*Exit* DEMOPHOON.

MACARIA, IOLAUS, CHORUS.

MAC. Deem not that I, O strangers, am too bold
Because I from my chamber venture forth;
This is my first request: for silence, joined
With modesty and a domestic life,
Is woman's best accomplishment. I heard
Your groans, O Iolaus, and advanced

Though not appointed by our house to act
As their ambassadress ; in some degree
Yet am I qualified for such an office,
I have so great an interest in the weal
Of these my brothers; on my own account
I also wish to hear if any ill,
Added to those you have already suffered,
Torture your soul.
   IOL.   Not now for the first time,
On thee, O daughter, most of all the children
Of Hercules my praise can I bestow :
But our ill-fated house, just as it seemed
Emerging from its past disgraces, sinks
Afresh into inextricable ruin.
The king informs us, that the seers, whose voice
Expounds the will of heaven, have signified
No bull nor heifer, but some blooming maid
Who from a noble sire derives her birth,
Must be the victim, if we would redeem
The city and ourselves from utter ruin ;
Here then are we perplexed : for his own children
He says he will not sacrifice, nor those
Of any of his subjects. Though to me
Indeed he speaks not plainly, in some sort
He intimates, that if we by no means
Can extricate ourselves from these distresses,
We must find out some other land to flee to,
For he this realm would from destruction save.
   MAC. May we indulge the hope of our escape
Upon these terms ?
   IOL.   These only : in all else
With prosperous fortunes crowned.
   MAC.   No longer dread
The spear of Argos, for myself, old man,
Am ready, ere they doom me to be slain,
And here stand forth a voluntary victim.
For what could we allege on our behalf,
If Athens condescend to undergo
Dangers so great, while we who have imposed
These toils on others, though within our reach
Lie all the means of being saved, yet shrink
From death ? Not thus : we should provoke the laugh
Of universal scorn, if, with loud groans,
We suppliants, at the altars of the gods,
Should take our seats, and prove devoid of courage,
From that illustrious father though we spring.
How can the virtuous reconcile such conduct ?
This to our glory would forsooth redound
(O may it never happen !) when this city

Is taken, should we fall into the hands
Of our triumphant foes, when after all
Some noble maid reluctant must be dragged
To Pluto's loathed embrace. But from these realms
Cast forth, should I become an abject vagrant,
Must I not blush when any one inquires,
"Why came ye hither with your suppliant branches
Too fond of life? Retreat from these domains,
For we no aid to cowards will afford."
But if when these are dead, my single life
Be saved, I cannot entertain a hope
That I shall e'er be happy: through this motive
Have caused full many to betray their friends.
For who with a deserted maid will join,
Or in the bonds of wedlock, or desire
That I to him a race of sons should bear?
I therefore hold it better far to die,
Than to endure, without deserving them,
Such foul indignities, as can seem light
To her alone, who, from a noble race
Like mine, descends not: to the scene of death
Conduct, with garlands crown me, and prepare
If ye think fit, th' initiatory rites;
Ye hence the foe shall conquer: for this soul
Shrinks not with mean reluctance. I engage
For these my brothers, and myself, to bleed
A willing victim; for with ease detached
From life, I have imbibed this best of lessons,
To die with firmness in a glorious cause.

CHOR. Alas! what language shall I find, t' express
My admiration of the lofty speech
I from this virgin hear, who for her brothers
Resolves to die? What tongue can utter words
More truly generous; or what man surpass
Such deeds as these?

IOL. Thou art no spurious child,
But from the godlike seed of Hercules,
O daughter, dost indeed derive thy birth.
Although thy words are such as cannot shame,
Thy fate afflicts me. Yet will I propose
What may with greater justice be performed.
Together call the sisters of this maid,
And to atone for the whole race, let her
On whom th' impartial lot shall fall, be slain;
But without such decision 'tis not just
That thou should'st die.

MAC. I will not die as chance
The lot dispenses; for I hence should forfeit
All merit: name not such a scheme, old man.

If me ye will accept, and of my zeal
Avail yourselves, I gladly yield up life
Upon these terms, but stoop not to constraint.
    IOL. The speech thou now hast uttered soars beyond
What thou at first didst say, though that was noble:
But thou thy former courage dost surpass
By this fresh instance of exalted courage,
The merit of thy former words, by words
More meritorious. Daughter, I command not,
Nor yet oppose thy death: for thou by dying
Wilt serve thy brothers.
    MAC.   You in cautious terms
Command me: fear not, lest on my account
You should contract pollution: for to die
Is my free choice. But follow me, old man,
For in your arms would I expire: attend,
And o'er my body cast the decent veil:
To dreadful slaughter dauntless I go forth,
Because I from that father spring, whose name
With pride I utter.
    IOL.   At the hour of death
I cannot stand beside thee.
    MAC.   Grant but this,
That when I breathe my last, I may be tended
By women, not by men.
    IOL.   It shall be thus,
O miserable virgin: for in me
'Twere base, if I neglected any rite
That decency enjoins, for many reasons;
Because thy soul is great, because 'tis just,
And of all women I have ever seen,
Because thou art most wretched. But from these
And from thy aged kinsman, if thou wish
For aught, to me thy last behests address.
    MAC. Adieu, my venerable friend, adieu!
Instruct these boys in every branch of wisdom,
And make them like yourself, they can attain
No higher pitch; strive to protect them still,
And for their sake that valued life prolong;
Your children we, to you our nurture owe.
Me you behold, mature for bridal joys,
Dying to save them. But may ye, my band
Of brothers who are here, be blest, and gain
All those advantages, which to procure
For you, the falchion shall transpierce my breast.
Revere this good old man, revere Alcmena
Your father's aged mother, and these strangers.
Should ye be ever rescued from your woes,
Should gracious Heaven permit you to revisit

Your native land, forget not to inter,
With such magnificence as I deserve,
Your benefactress, for I have not proved
Deficient in attention to your welfare,
But die to save our family. To me
These monumental honours shall suffice
Instead of children, or the virgin state,
If there be aught amid the realms beneath,
But 'tis my wish there may not: for if grief
On us frail mortals also there attend,
I know not whither any one can turn:
For by the wise hath death been ever deemed
The most effectual cure for every ill.

  IOL. O thou, distinguished by thy lofty soul,
Be well assured thy glory shall outshine
That of all other women; both in life
And death, shalt thou be honoured by thy friends.
But ah, farewell! for with ill-omened words
I tremble lest we should provoke the goddess,
Dread Proserpine, to whom thou now art sacred.
                                       [*Exit* MACARIA.
My sons I perish: grief unnerves my frame;
Support and place me in the hallowed seat:
And, O my dearest children, o'er my face
Extend this garment: for I am not pleased
With what is done: yet, had not Heaven's response
Found this completion, we must all have died;
For we must then have suffered greater ills
Than these, which are already most severe.

CHORUS.

ODE.

In just proportion, as the gods ordain,
    Is bliss diffused through life's short span,
    Or sorrow portioned out to man:
    No favoured house can still maintain
    From age to age its prosperous state,
For swift are the vicissitudes of fate,
    Who now assails pride's towering crest,
    Now makes the drooping exile blest.
    From destiny we cannot fly;
    No wisdom can her shafts repel;
But he who vainly dares her power defy
    Compassed with endless toils shall dwell.
    Ask not from Heaven with impious prayer,
    Blessings it cannot grant to man,
    Nor waste in misery life's short span
    O'erwhelmed by querulous despair.

The nymph goes forth to meet a noble death,
　　Her brothers and this land to save,
　　And fame, with tributary breath
　　Shall sound her praises in the grave.
　　For dauntless virtue finds a way
Through labours which her progress would delay.
　　Such deeds as these, her father grace,
　　And add fresh splendour to her race,
But if with reverential awe thou shed
　　Over the virtuous dead
A tear of pity, in that tear I'll join,
　　Inspired with sentiments like thine.

SERVANT, IOLAUS, CHORUS.

SER. Ye children, hail! but where is Iolaus,
That aged man; and hath your grandame left
Her seat before the altar?
　　IOL.　　　　　　　Here am I,
If aught my presence can avail.
　　SER.　　　　　　　On earth
Why art thou stretched, what means that downcast look?
　　IOL. Domestic cares have harrowed up my soul.
　　SER. Lift up thy head, arise.
　　IOL.　　　　　　　I am grown old,
And all my strength is vanished.
　　SER.　　　　　　　But to thee
I bring most joyful tidings.
　　IOL.　　　　　　　Who art thou?
Where have I seen thee? I remember not.
　　SER. Hyllus' attendant, canst thou not distinguish
These features?
　　IOL.　　　　　　O my friend, art thou arrived
To snatch me from despair?
　　SER.　　　　　　　Most certainly:
Moreover the intelligence I bring
Will make thee happy.
　　IOL.　　　　　　Thee I call, come forth,
Alcmena, mother of a noble son,
And listen to these acceptable tidings:
Full long thy soul, for those who now approach,
Was torn with grief, lest they should ne'er return.

ALCMENA, SERVANT, IOLAUS, CHORUS.

ALC. Whence with your voice resounds this echoing dome,
O Iolaus, is another herald
From Argos come, who forcibly assails you?
My strength indeed is small, yet be assured
Of this, presumptuous stranger, while I live
Thou shalt not bear them hence. May I no more

Be deemed the mother of that godlike son,
When I submit to this. But if thou dare
To touch the children, with two aged foes
Ignobly wilt thou strive.
    IOL.   Be of good cheer,
Thou hoary matron, banish these alarms;
No herald with a hostile message comes
From Argos.
    ALC.   Why then raised you that loud voice,
The harbinger of fear?
    IOL.   That from the temple
Thou might'st come forth, and join us.
    ALC.   What you mean
I comprehend not. Who is this?
    IOL.   He tells us
Thy grandson marches hither.
    ALC.   Hail, O thou
Who bear'st these welcome tidings? but what brings him
To these domains? Where is he? What affairs
Prevented him from coming hither with thee,
To fill my soul with transport?
    SER.   He now marshals
The forces which attend him.
    ALC.   In this conference
Am I no longer then allowed to join?
    IOL. Thou art: but 'tis my business to inquire
Into these matters.
    SER.   Which of his transactions
Say art thou most solicitous to know?
    IOL. The number of the troops he leads?
    SER.   Is great,
I cannot count them.
    IOL.   The Athenian chiefs
Are sure apprized of this.
    SER.   They are apprized,
And the left wing is formed.
    IOL.   Then the whole host
Arrayed in arms is ready for the battle.
    SER. The victims to a distance from the ranks
Already are removed.
    IOL.   But at what distance
Is the encampment of the Argive warriors?
    SER. So near that we their leader can distinguish.
    IOL. What is he doing; marshalling our foes?
    SER. This we conjecture: for I could not hear
His voice: but I must go; for I my lord
Will not abandon when he nobly braves
The dangers of the field.
    IOL.   I too with thee

Will join him; for the same are our intentions,
As honour bids us, to assist our friends.
　SER. Unwisely hast thou spoken.
　IOL. 　　　　　　　　With my friends
Shall not I then the stubborn conflict share?
　SER. That strength which erst was thine is now no more.
　IOL. Can I not pierce their shields?
　SER. 　　　　　　　　Thou may'st: but first,
More likely, fall thyself.
　IOL. 　　　　　No foe will dare
To meet me face to face.
　SER. 　　　　　By thy mere looks,
With that debilitated arm, no wound
Canst thou inflict.
　IOL. 　　　My presence in the field
Will to our troops give courage, and augment
Their number.
　SER. 　　　Of small service to thy friends
Will thy appearance prove.
　IOL. 　　　　　Detain me not:
I for some glorious action am prepared.
　SER. Thou hast the will to act, but not the power
　IOL. I will not be reproached for loitering here,
Say what thou wilt beside.
　SER. 　　　　　But without arms
How wilt thou face yon warriors sheathed in mail?
　IOL. The various implements of war are lodged
Beneath these roofs; with freedom will I use,
And if I live, return them; if I die,
The god will not demand them back again.
Go then into the temple, and reach down
Those martial trappings from the golden nails
On which they hang, and bring them to me swiftly.
For this were infamous, while some are fighting,
If others loiter slothfully behind. 　　[*Exit* SERVANT.
　CHOR. Time hath not yet debased that lofty soul
'Tis vigorous, though thy body be decayed.
Why should'st thou enter on these fruitless toils,
Which only injure thee, and to our city
Can be of little service? on thy age
Should'st thou reflect, and lay aside attempts
That are impossible, for by no arts
The long-lost force of youth canst thou regain.
　ALC. What schemes are these? distempered in your mind,
Me and my children mean you to abandon?
　IOL. The battle is man's province: to thy care
Them I consign.
　ALC. 　　　But if you die, what means
Have I of being saved?

IOL.   The tender care
Of the surviving children of thy son.
  ALC. Should they too meet with some severe mishap,
Which may the gods forbid.
  IOL.   These generous strangers
Will not betray thee; banish every fear.
  ALC. In them I trust: I have no other friend.
  IOL. Jove too, I know, is mindful of thy toils.
  ALC. I will not speak in disrespectful terms
Of Jove: but whether he his plighted troth
Have kept, full well he knows.
  SER. [*returning.*]   Thou here behold'st
The brazen panoply, now haste to sheathe
Thy limbs in mail; the battle is at hand,
And Mars detests a loiterer: if thou fear
Accoutrements so ponderous, to the field
Advance disarmed, nor till thou join the ranks
Wear these unwieldly trappings; for meantime
I in my hands their burden will sustain.
  IOL. Well hast thou spoken; with those arms attend me
Ready for the encounter, place a spear
In my right hand, and under my left arm
Hold me, and guide my steps.
  SER.   Shall I conduct
A warrior like a child?
  IOL.   I must tread sure,
Else 'twere an evil omen.
  SER.   Would thy power
Equalled thy zeal.
  IOL.   Haste: greatly 'twill afflict me
If, left behind, I cannot join the fray.
  SER. Slow are thy steps, and hence thou deem'st I move not.
  IOL. Behold'st thou not the swiftness of my pace?
  SER. Thou to thyself I see appear'st to hasten,
Although thou gain'st no ground.
  IOL.   When in the field
Thou seest me, thou wilt own I speak the truth.
  SER. What great exploit achieving? I could wish
That thou might'st prove victorious.
  IOL.   Through his shield
Some foe transfixing.
  SER.   We at length may reach
Th' embattled plain, but this I greatly fear.
  IOL. Ah, would to heaven, that thou, my withered arm,
Again wert vigorous, as in former days
Thee I remember, when thou didst lay waste
The Spartan realms with Hercules; thus fight
My battles now, and singly will I triumph
Over Eurystheus, for that dastard fears

To face the dangers of th' embattled field:
Too apt in our ideas to unite
Valour with wealth, yet to the prosperous man
Superior wisdom falsely we ascribe.
    [*Exeunt* IOLAUS *and* SERVANT.

CHORUS.

ODE.

I. 1.

O fostering Earth, resplendent Moon,
Who gladd'st the dreary shades of night,
And thou, enthroned at broadest noon,
Hyperion, 'midst exhaustless light,
To me propitious tidings bring,
Raise to the skies a festive sound,
And waft the gladsome notes around,
Till, from the palace of our king,
They echo through Minerva's fane:
My house, my country, to maintain
Against the ruthless spoiler's pride,
Menaced because this realm extends
Protection to its suppliant friends,
I with the sword our contest will decide.

I. 2.

Although there seem just cause for dread,
When cities like Mycene blest,
Whose triumphs fame hath widely spread
Enter this region to invest
Our bulwarks, harbouring ruthless hate.
Think, O my country, think what shame,
Should we reject the suppliant's claim
Appalled by Argos' haughty state.
Resistless Jove shall aid the spear
I brandish unappalled by fear;
The tribute of eternal praise
From all that breathe, to him is due:
Nor magnified by our weak view
Shall men above the gods their trophies raise.

II. 1.

Descend with venerable mien,
O thou our guardian and our queen,
For on thy fostering soil we stand,
These walls were reared by thy command,

Drive from our menaced gates the lawless host,
　　Suppress that Argive tyrant's boast;
For if by you unaided, is this hand
　　Too weak their fury to withstand.

II. 2.

Thee, O Minerva, we adore,
Thy altar ever streams with gore:
We on each moon's concluding day
To thee our public homage pay;
Through every fane harmonious numbers sound,
　　Sweet minstrelsy then breathes around,
And th' echoing hills their nightly dance repeat
　　As the nymphs move with agile feet.

SERVANT, ALCMENA, CHORUS.

SER. O royal dame, the message that to you
I bring, is both concise, and what reflects
On me abundant glory to relate,
In fight have we prevailed, and trophies reared
On which the armour of your foes is hung.
　　ALC. This day hath brought thee hither, O my friend,
Thy freedom for such tidings to receive:
But one anxiety there still remains
To which thou leav'st me subject; much I fear
For the important lives of those I love.
　　SER. They live, and have obtained from all the host
The greatest fame.
　　ALC.　　　　　And Iolaus too,
My aged friend?
　　SER.　　　　Yet more, he hath performed
Through the peculiar favour of the gods
Exploits most memorable.
　　ALC.　　　　　What glorious deed
Hath he achieved in fight?
　　SER.　　　　From an old man,
He is grown young again.
　　ALC.　　　　Thou speak'st of things
Most wonderful. But first, how fought our friends
With such success, I wish thee to inform me.
　　SER. All that hath passed, at once will I relate
When, to each other in the field opposed,
We had arranged both armies, and spread forth
The van of battle to its full extent,
Hyllus alighting from his chariot, stood
In the midway 'twixt either host, and cried:
"Thou leader of the Argive troops, who com'st
With hostile fury to invade this land,
Thy interests recommend what I propose,

Nor can Mycene suffer from the loss
If thou deprive her of a single warrior;
Therefore with me encounter hand to hand,
And if thou slay me, seize and bear away
The sons of Hercules; but if thou die,
My palace and hereditary rank
Permit me to enjoy." The troops assented,
And praised what he had spoken as the means
Of finishing their labours, and a proof
Of his exalted courage. But Eurystheus
Unmoved by reverence for th' assembled host
Who heard the challenge, and with terror smitten,
Forgot the general's part, nor dared to face
The lifted spear, but acted like a dastard:
Yet he who was thus destitute of courage
Came to enslave the sons of Hercules.
Hyllus again retreated to his rank;
The prophets too, when they perceived no peace
Could be effected by a single combat,
Without delay the blooming virgin slew,
Auspicious victim, from whose pallid lips
Her trembling spirit fled. The lofty car
Some mounted, o'er their sides while others flung
Their bucklers to protect them. To his host,
Meantime the king of Athens, in a strain
Worthy of his exalted courage, spoke:
"Ye citizens, the land to which ye owe
Your nourishment and birth, now claims your aid."
Equally loth to sully the renown
Of Argos and Mycene, in like terms
The foe besought his partners of the war
Their utmost vigour to exert. No sooner
Had the loud signal by Etruria's trump
Been given, than they in thickest battle joined.
Think with what crash their brazen shields resounded,
What groans and intermingled shouts were heard!
First through our lines the host of Argos burst,
And in their turn gave way: then foot to foot,
And man to man opposed, in stubborn conflict
We all persisted: multitudes were slain;
But in this language either chief his troops
Encouraged: " O ye citizens of Athens,
O ye who till the fruitful Argive field,
Will ye not from your native land repel
The foul disgrace?" But with our utmost efforts
Scarce could we put to flight the Argive host.
When Iolaus saw young Hyllus break
The ranks of battle, he with lifted hands
Entreated him to place him in his car,

Then seized the reins, and onward in pursuit
Of the swift coursers of Eurystheus drove.
As to the sequel; from report alone
Let others speak, I tell what I have seen:
While through Pallenè's streets he passed, where rise
Minerva's altars, soon as he descried
The chariot of Eurystheus, he a prayer
Addressed to blooming Hebe, and to Jove,
That for that single day he might recover
The pristine vigour of his youth, and punish
His foes as they deserve. You now shall hear
What a miraculous event ensued;
Two stars 'bove Iolaus' chariot stood,
And overshadowed it with gloomy clouds,
Which, by the wise 'tis said, were Hercules
Your son, and blooming Hebe: from that mist
Which veiled the skies, the chief grown young again,
Displayed his vigorous arms, and near the rocks
Of Scyron, seized Eurystheus in his car.
Binding his hands with chains, he hither brings
The Argive tyrant, a distinguished prize,
Who once was happy; but on all mankind
Loudly inculcates by his present fortunes
This lesson: not too rashly to ascribe
Felicity to him who in appearance
Is prosperous, but to wait till we behold
His close of life; for fortune day by day
Doth waver.

 CHOR. Thou great author of success,
O Jove, at length am I allowed to view
The day, by which my terrors are dispelled.

 ALC. 'Twas late indeed, when thou, O Jove, didst look
On my afflictions; yet am I to thee
Most grateful for the kindness thou hast shown me.
And though I erst believed not that my son
Dwells with the gods, I clearly know it now.
Now, O my children, ye from all your toils
Shall be set free, and of Eurystheus, doomed
With shame to perish, burst the galling yoke,
Behold your father's city, the rich fields
Of your inheritance again possess,
And sacrifice to your paternal gods,
From whom excluded, in a foreign land
Ye led a wandering miserable life.
But with what sage design yet undisclosed,
Hath Iolaus spared Eurystheus' life,
Inform me: for to us it seems unwise
Not to avenge our wrongs when we have caught
Our enemies.

SER. He through respect to you
Hath acted thus, that you might see the tyrant
Vanquished, and rendered subject to your power,
Not by his own consent, but in the yoke
Bound by necessity; for he was loth
To come into your presence, ere he bleed,
And suffer as he merits. But farewell,
O venerable matron, and remember
The promise you first made when I began
These tidings, and, oh, set me free: for nought
But truth should from ingenuous lips proceed.
[*Exit* SERVANT.

CHORUS.

ODE.

I. 1.

To me the choral song is sweet,
When the shrill flute and genial banquet meet,
If Venus also grace the festive board:
   I taste a more refined delight
  Now I behold my friends (transporting sight!)
  To unexpected happiness restored.
For in this nether world, eventful Fate,
And Saturn's offspring Time, full many a change create.

I. 2.

Follow the plain and beaten way,
From Justice, O my country, never stray,
Nor cease the powers immortal to revere.
   To heights scarce short of frenzy rise
  The errors of that mortal, who denies
  Assent to truths confirmed by proofs so clear.
Jove's power by signal judgments is descried,
Oft as his vengeance blasts the towering crest of pride.

II. 1.

In heavenly mansions with the blest,
Thy son, O venerable dame, doth rest;
He hath confuted those invidious tales,
   That to loathed Pluto's house he came
  Soon as he perished in that dreadful flame:
  He under roofs of burnished gold regales,
  On the soft couch of lovely Hebe placed;
Them two, both sprung from Jove, O Hymen, thou hast graced.

II. 2.

Events, which strike man's wondering eyes,
From a variety of causes rise.
For fame relates how Pallas saved the sire,
 And from her city far renowned,
Her race, protection have the children found;
She hath suppressed th' o'erweening tyrant's ire,
Whose violence no laws could ere control;
Curse on such boundless pride, that fever of the soul.

MESSENGER, EURYSTHEUS, ALCMENA, CHORUS.

MES. Your eyes indeed behold, O royal dame,
Yet shall this tongue declare that we have brought
Eurytheus hither, unexpected sight,
Reverse of fortune his presumptuous soul
Foresaw not, this oppressor little deemed
That he should ever fall into your hands,
When from Mycene, by the Cyclops' toil
Erected, he those squadrons led, and hoped
With pride o'erweening to lay Athens waste;
But Heaven our situation hath reversed:
And therefore with exulting Hyllus joins
The valiant Iolaus, in erecting
Trophies to Jove the author of our conquest.
But they to you commanded me to lead
This captive, wishing to delight your soul:
For 'tis most grateful to behold a foe
Fall'n from the height of gay prosperity.

ALC. Com'st thou, detested wretch? at length hath Justice
O'ertaken thee? First hither turn thy head,
And dare to face thine enemies: for, dwindled
Into a vassal, thou no longer rul'st.
Art thou the man (for I would know the truth)
Who didst presume to heap unnumbered wrongs,
Thou author of all mischief, on my son
While yet he lived, wherever now resides
His dauntless spirit? For in what one instance
Didst thou not injure him? At thy command,
Alive he travelled to th' infernal shades;
Thou sent'st, and didst commission him to slay
Hydras and lions. Various other mischiefs,
Which were by thee contrived, I mention not,
For an attempt to speak of them at large
Would be full tedious. Nor was it enough
For thee to venture on these wrongs alone,
But thou, moreover, from each Grecian state
Me and these children hast expelled, though seated
As suppliants at the altars of the gods,

Confounding those whose locks are grey through age
With tender infants. But thou here hast found
Those who were men indeed, and a free city
Which feared thee not. Thou wretchedly shalt perish,
And pay this bitter usury to atone
For all thy crimes, whose number is so great
That it were just thou more than once shouldst die.
  MES. You must not kill him.
    ALC.   Then have we in vain
Taken him captive. But what law forbids
His being slain?
  MES.   The rulers of this land
Consent not.
    ALC.   Is it not by them esteemed
A glorious action to despatch our foes?
  MES. Not such as they have seized alive in battle.
  ALC. Is Hyllus satisfied with this decree?
  MES. He, in my judgment, will forsooth act rightly,
If he oppose what Athens shall enjoin.
  ALC. The captive tyrant ill deserves to live,
Or longer view the sun.
  MES.   In this first instance
They did amiss, when by their swords he died not.
  ALC. Is it not just that he should suffer still?
  MES. He who will slay him is not to be found.
  ALC. What shall I say if some adventurous hand——
  MES. If you do this, you will incur great censure.
  ALC. I love this city, I confess: but no man,
Since he is fall'n into my power, shall force
This prisoner from me: let them call me bold
And more presumptuous than becomes a woman,
I am resolved to execute my purpose.
  MES. Full well I know the hatred which you bear
To this unhappy man is terrible,
And such as merits pardon.
    EUR.   Be convinced
Of this, O woman, that I cannot flatter,
Nor to preserve this wretched life say aught,
Whence they may brand me with a dastard's name.
For I with much reluctance undertook
This contest; near in blood am I to thee,
And of that race whence sprung thy son Alcides.
But whether I consented, or was loth,
Me Juno caused by her immortal power
To harbour this dire frenzy in my breast.
Since I became his foe, since I resolved
Upon this strife, much mischief I devised,
And brooded o'er it many a tedious night,
That after I had wearied out and slain

Those I abhorred, I might no longer lead
A life of fear: for well I knew thy son
Was no mere cipher, but a man indeed:
Though strong my hate, on him will I confer
The praise he merits from his valiant deeds.
But after he was dead, was I not forced,
Because I was a foe to these his sons,
And knew what bitter enmity 'gainst me
They from their sire inherited, to leave
No stone unturned, to slay, to banish them,
And plot their ruin? Could I have succeeded
In these designs, my throne had stood secure.
If thou my prosperous station hadst obtained,
Wouldst thou not have attempted to hunt down
The lion's whelps, instead of suffering them
At Argos unmolested to reside?
Thou canst prevail on no man to give credit
To such assertions: therefore, since my foes
Forbore to slay me, when prepared to lose
My life in battle, by the laws of Greece,
If I now die. my blood will fix a stain
Of lasting guilt on him who murders me.
This city hath discreetly spared my life,
More influenced by its reverence for the gods
Than by the hatred which to me it bears.
My answer to the charges thou hast urged
Against me, having heard, esteem me now
A suppliant, and though wretched, still a king,
For such is my condition: though to die
I wish not, yet can I without regret
Surrender up my life.
  CHOR.   To you, Alcmena,
A little wholesome counsel would I give,
This captive monarch to release, since such
The pleasure of the city.
  ALC.   If he die,
And to the mandates of th' Athenian realm
I still submit, what mischief can ensue?
  CHOR. 'Twere best of all. But how can these two things
Be reconciled?
  ALC.   I will inform you how
This may with ease be done. I, to his friends,
When slain will yield him up, and with this land
Comply in the disposal of his corse:
But he shall die to sate my just revenge.
  EUR. Destroy me if thou wilt; to thee I sue not:
But on this city, since it spared my life
Through pious reverence, and forbore to slay me,
Will I bestow an ancient oracle

Of Phœbus, which in future times shall prove
More advantageous than ye now suppose;
For after death, so have the Fates decreed,
My corse shall ye inter before the temple
Of the Pallenian maid: to you a friend
And guardian of your city, shall I rest
Beneath this soil for ever; but a foe
To those who spring from this detested race
When with their armies they invade this land
Requiting with ingratitude your kindness:
Such strangers ye protect. But thus forewarned,
Why came I hither? Through a fond belief
That Juno was with far superior power
To each oracular response endued,
And that my cause she ne'er would have betrayed.
On me waste no libations, nor let gore
Be poured forth on the spot of my interment,
For I to punish these their impious deeds,
Will cause them with dishonour to return:
From me shall ye receive a double gain,
For you I will assist, and prove to them
Most baneful e'en in death.

   ALC.   Why are ye loth
To slay this man, if what ye hear be true,
That welfare to this city hence will spring,
And your prosperity? For he points out
The safest road. Alive he is a foe,
But after he is dead will prove a friend.
Ye servants bear him hence, and to the dogs
Cast forth without delay his breathless corse:
Think not, presumptuous wretch, that thou shalt live
Again t' expel me from my native land.

   CHOR. With this am I well pleased. My followers, go.
For hence in our king's sight shall we stand guiltless.

RHESUS.

PERSONS OF THE DRAMA.

Chorus of Trojan
    Sentinels.
Hector.
Æneas.
Dolon.
A Shepherd.
Rhesus.

Ulysses.
Diomede.
Paris.
Minerva.
The Muse.
The Charioteer of
    Rhesus.

SCENE.—Before Hector's Tent at the Gates of Troy.

Chorus, Hector.

Chor. Let some swift sentinel to Hector's tent
Go and inquire if any messenger
Be yet arrived, who recent tidings bears
From those, who during the fourth nightly watch
Are by the host deputed. On your arm
Sustain your head, unfold those low'ring eyelids,
And from your lowly couch of withered leaves,
O Hector, rise, for it is time to listen.

    Hec. Who comes? art thou a friend? pronounce the watch-
        word.
Who are ye, that by night approach my bed?
Speak out.

    Chor.   We guard the camp.

    Hec.   Why com'st thou hither
With this tumultuous haste?

    Chor.   Be of good cheer.

    Hec. I am. Hast thou discovered in the camp
This night some treachery?

    Chor.   None.

    Hec.   Why then deserting
The post where thou art stationed, dost thou rouse
The troops, unless thou through this midnight gloom
Bring some important tidings? know'st thou not
That near the Argive host we under arms
Take our repose.

CHOR.   Prepare your brave allies:
Go to their chambers, bid them wield the spear,
Rouse them from slumber, and despatch your friends
To your own troop; caparison the steeds.
Who bears the swift alarm to Pantheus' son?
Who to Europa's offspring, Lycia's chief?
Where are the priests who should inspect the victims?
Who leads the light-armed squadron to the field?
And where are Phrygia's archers? Let each bow
Be strung.
    HEC.   Thy tidings are in part alarming,
In part thou giv'st us courage, though thou speak
Nought plainly. By the terrifying scourge
Of Pan hast thou been smitten, that thou leav'st
Thy station to alarm the host? Explain
These clamorous sounds. What tidings shall I say
Thou bring'st? Thy words are many, but their drift
I comprehend not.
    CHOR.   All night long, O Hector,
The Grecian camp hath kindled fires, the torches
Amid their fleet are blazing, and the host
Tumultuous rush to Agamemnon's tent,
At midnight calling on the king t' assemble
A council: for the sailors never yet
Were thus alarmed. But I, because I fear
What may ensue, these tidings hither bring,
Lest you should charge me with a breach of duty.
    HEC. Full seasonably thou com'st, although thou speak
Words fraught with terror: for these dastards hope
They in their barks shall from this shore escape
Ere I discover them: their kindled fires
Prove this suspicion. Thou, O partial Jove,
Hast robbed me of my triumph, like the prey
Torn from the lion, ere I have destroyed
With this avenging spear the Grecian host.
Had not the sun withdrawn his radiant beams,
I the successful battle had prolonged
Till I had burnt their ships, and hewn a way
Through their encampments, and in slaughter drenched
My bloody hand. I would have fought by night
And taken my advantage of the gales
Sent by auspicious fortune: but the wise,
And seers who knew the will of Heaven, advised me
To wait but till to-morrow's dawn appeared,
And then sweep every Grecian from the land.
But now no longer will they stay to prove
The truth of what my prophets have foretold:
For cowards in the midnight gloom are brave.
Instantly therefore through the host proclaim

RHESUS. 119

These orders: "Take up arms, and rouse from sleep;"
Pierced through the back as to the ships he flies,
So shall full many a dastard with his gore
Distain the steep ascent; the rest fast bound
In galling chains shall learn to till our fields.

CHOR. O Hector, ere you learn the real fact,
You are too hasty: for we know not yet
That they are flying.

HEC. Wherefore then by night
Are those fires kindled through the Grecian camp?

CHOR. I am not certain, though my soul full strongly
Suspects the cause.

HEC. If thou fear this, thou tremblest
At a mere shadow.

CHOR. Such a light ne'er blazed
Before among the foes.

HEC. Nor such defeat
In battle, did they e'er till now experience.

CHOR. This have you done; look now to what remains.

HEC. I give this short direction: take up arms
Against the foe.

CHOR. Behold! Æneas comes:
Sure, from his haste, some tidings, which deserve
His friends' attentive ear, the warrior brings.

ÆNEAS, HECTOR, CHORUS.

ÆNE. What mean the watch, O Hector, who by night
Were to their stations in the camp assigned,
That they, with terror smitten, at your chamber
In a nocturnal council have assembled?
And why is the whole army thus in motion?

HEC. Put on thy arms, Æneas.

ÆNE. What hath happen'd?
Are you informed that in this midnight gloom
The foe hath formed some stratagem?

HEC. They fly!
They mount their ships.

ÆNE. What proof have you of this?

HEC. All night their torches blaze; to me they seem
As if they would not wait to-morrow's dawn:
But, kindling fires upon their lofty decks,
They sure fly homeward from this hostile land.

ÆNE. But why, if it be thus, prepare your troops
For battle?

HEC. As they mount the deck, this spear
Shall overtake the dastards; I their flight
Will harass: for 'twere base, and prejudicial
As well as base, when Heaven delivers up

The foe into our hands, to suffer those
Who wronged us to escape without a conflict.
　ÆNE. Ah! would to Heaven you equally stood foremost
In wisdom, as in courage: but one man
By bounteous Nature never was endued
With knowledge universal: various gifts
Doth she dispense, to you the warrior's palm,
To others sapient counsels: now you hear
Their torches blaze, you thence infer the Greeks
Are flying, and would lead the troops by night
Over the trenches: but when you have passed
The yawning fosse, should you perceive the foes
Instead of flying from the land, resist,
With dauntless courage, your protended spear,
If you are vanquished, to these sheltering walls
You never can return: for in their flight
How shall the troops o'er slanting palisades
Escape, or, how the charioteer direct
Over the narrow bridge his crashing wheels?
If you prevail, you have a foe at hand,
The son of Peleus, from your flaming torches
Who will protect the fleet, nor suffer you
Utterly to destroy the Grecian host
As you expect; for he is brave. Our troops
Let us then leave to rest from martial toils,
And sleep beside their shields. That we despatch
Amid the foe some voluntary spy,
Is my advice: if they prepare for flight,
Let us assail the Greeks; but if those fires
Are kindled to ensnare us, having learned
The enemy's intentions, let us hold
A second council on this great emprise.
Illustrious chief, I have declared my thoughts.

CHORUS.

I.

These counsels I approve: thy wayward scheme,
　　O Hector, change, and think the same:
　　For perilous commands I deem,
Given by the headstrong chief, deserve our blame.
　　Why send not to the fleet a spy,
Who may approach the trenches, and descry
With what intent our foes upon the strand
　　Have kindled many a flaming brand?

　HEC. Ye have prevailed, because ye all concur
In one opinion: but depart, prepare
Thy fellow-soldiers, for perhaps the host

RHESUS.

May by the rumours of our nightly council
Be put in motion. I will send a spy
Among the Greeks ; and if we learn what schemes
They have devised, the whole of my intentions
To thee will I immediately reveal
In person. With confusion and dismay
But if the foe precipitate their flight,
Give ear, and follow where the clanging trump
Summons thee forth, for then I cannot wait,
But will this night attack the Grecian host,
Storm their entrenchments, and destroy their fleet.

   ÆNE. Despatch the messenger without delay.
For you now think discreetly, and in me
Shall find, when needed, in your bold emprise
A firm associate.   [*Exit* ÆNEAS.
   HEC.   What brave Trojan, present
At this our conference, as a spy will go
T' explore the Grecian navy ? to this land
What generous benefactor will arise ?
Who answers ? for I singly cannot serve
The cause of Troy and its confederate bands
In every station.
   DOL.   For my native realm,
Facing this danger, to the fleet of Greece
I as a spy will go ; and when I've searched
Into the progress of our foes, return :
But I on these conditions undertake
The toilsome enterprise——
   HEC.   Thou well deserv'st
Thy name, and to thy country art a friend,
O Dolon ; for this day thy father's house,
Which is already noble, thou exalt'st
With double fame.
   DOL.   I therefore ought to strive :
But after all my labours let me reap
A suitable reward. If gain arise
From the performance of the task enjoined,
We feel a twofold joy.
   HEC.   This were but just :
I contradict thee not : name thy reward ;
Choose what thou wilt, except the rank I bear.
   DOL. Your rich domains I wish not to possess.
   HEC. To thee a daughter of imperial Priam
In marriage shall be given.
   DOL.   With my superiors
I will not wed.
   HEC.   Abundant gold is ours,
If thou prefer this stipend.
   DOL.   My own house

With wealth is furnished, I am far remote
From want.
  Hec.   What then dost thou desire that Troy
Contains?
  Dol.   When you have conquered the proud Greeks,
Promise to give me——
  Hec.   I will give thee all
That thou canst ask, except my royal captives.
  Dol. Slay them; I seek not to withhold your arm
From cutting off the vanquished Menelaus.
  Hec. Is it thy wish, Oïleus' son to thee
Should be consigned?
  Dol.   The hands of princes, nurtured
Effeminately, are not formed to till
The stubborn soil.
  Hec.   From which of all the Greeks
Taken alive wouldst thou receive his ransom?
  Dol. Already have I told you, that at home
I have abundant riches.
  Hec.   Thou shalt choose
Among our spoils.
  Dol.   For offerings let them hang
High in the temples of the gods.
  Hec.   What gift
Greater than these canst thou from me require?
  Dol. Achilles' steeds: for when I stake my life
On Fortune's die, 'twere reasonable to strive
For such an object as deserves my toils.
  Hec. Although thou in thy wishes to possess
Those steeds hast interfered with me: for sprung
From an immortal race themselves immortal
They bear Pelides through the ranks of war,
Neptune, 'tis said, the king of ocean, tamed them
And gave to Peleus: I, who prompted thee
To this emprise, will not bely thy hopes,
But to adorn thy noble father's house,
On thee Achilles' generous steeds bestow.
  Dol. This claims my gratitude: if I succeed,
My courage will for me obtain a palm,
Such as no Phrygian ever won before:
Nor should you envy me, for joys unnumbered
And the first station in the realm, are yours.
             [*Exit* Hector.
      Chorus.
       II.

  The danger's great, but great rewards allure
   Thee, generous youth, t' assert thy claim,
    Thrice blest if thou the gift procure,
  Yet will thy toils deserve immortal fame:

Th' allies of kings let grandeur tend,
　May Heaven and Justice thy emprise befriend,
　For thou already seem'st to have acquired
　　　All that from man can be desired.

　　DOL. I am resolved to go: but my own doors
First must I enter, and myself attire
In such a garb as suits my present scheme,
Thence will I hasten to the Argive fleet.
　　CHOR. What other dress intend'st thou to assume
Instead of that thou wear'st?
　　DOL. 　　　　　　Such as befits
My errand and the stealth with which I travel.
　　CHOR. We ought to gain instruction from the wise.
What covering hast thou chosen for thy body?
　　DOL. I to my back will fit the tawny hide
Of a slain wolf, will muffle up my front
With the beast's hairy visage, fit my hands
To his fore-feet, thrust into those behind
My legs, and imitate his savage gait;
Approaching undiscovered by the foe,
The trenches and the ramparts that defend
The navy: but whenever I shall come
To desert places, on two feet I mean
To travel: such deception have I framed.
　　CHOR. May Hermes, Maïa's offspring, who presides
O'er well-conducted fallacies, assist
Thy journey thither, and with safety lead
Thy homeward steps! for well thou understand'st
The business; there is nought which yet thou need'st
But good success.
　　DOL. 　　　　I shall return in safety,
And having slain Ulysses, or the son
Of Tydeus, bring to you their ghastly heads;
For omens of assured success are mine:
Then say that Dolon reached the Grecian fleet.
These hands distained with gore, my native walls
Will I revisit ere the sun arise. 　　　[*Exit* DOLON.

　　　　　　CHORUS.

　　　　　　　ODE.

　　　　　　　I. I.

　　O thou, who issuing with majestic tread
　From Delian, Lycian, or Thymbræan fanes,
　Twang'st thy unerring bow; on Phrygia's plains,
　Apollo, thy celestial influence shed,
　　　Hither come with nightly speed,
　　　The enterprising chief to lead

Through mazes undiscovered by our foes;
 Aid thy loved Dardanian line,
 For matchless strength was ever thine,
Constructed by thy hand Troy's ancient bulwarks rose.

I. 2.

Speed Dolon's journey to the Grecian fleet,
Let him espy th' entrenchments of their host;
Again in triumph from the stormy coast
Conduct the warrior to his native seat;
 May he mount that chariot drawn
 By steeds that browsed the Phthian lawn
When our brave lord, the Mars of Greece, hath slain;
 Coursers of unrivalled speed,
 Which erst to Eacus' seed
To Peleus, Neptune gave who rules the billowy main.

II. 1.

His country, his paternal walls, to save,
The generous youth explores the anchored fleet:
From me such worth shall due encomiums meet.
How few with hardy bosoms stem the wave,
 When Hyperion veils his face,
 And cities tremble on their base!
At this dread crisis Phrygian heroes rise,
 Mysian chiefs, uncurbed by fear,
 Brandish with nervous arm the spear,
Curst be the lying tongue that slanders my allies.

II. 2.

In savage guise now Dolon stalks arrayed,
With step adventurous o'er the hostile ground:
What Grecian chief shall feel the deadly wound,
While the wolf's hide conceals his glittering blade?
 Weltering first in crimson gore,
 May Menelaus rise no more;
Next may the victor, Agamemnon's head
 Bear to Helen, stung with grief
 At her affinity to that famed chief
Who in a thousand ships to Troy his squadrons led.

A Shepherd, Hector, Chorus.

Shep. Most gracious monarch, may I ever greet
My lords with tidings such as now I bring!
 Hec. Full oft misapprehension clouds the soul
Of simple rustics: to thy lord in arms
Thou of thy fleecy charge art come to speak

At this unseemly crisis: know'st thou not
My mansion, or the palace of my sire?
There ought'st thou to relate how fare thy flock.
   SHEP. We shepherds are, I own, a simple race,
Yet my intelligence deserves attention.
   HEC. Such fortunes as befall the fold, to me
Relate not, for I carry in this hand
The battle and the spear.
   SHEP.   I too am come
Such tidings to unfold; for a brave chief,
Your friend, the leader of a numerous host,
Marches to fight the battles of this realm.
   HEC. But from what country?
   SHEP.   Thrace, and he is called
The son of Strymon.
   HEC.   Didst thou say, that Rhesus
Hath entered Ilion's fields?
   SHEP.   You comprehend me,
And have anticipated half my speech.
   HEC. Why doth he travel over Ida's hill,
Deserting that broad path where loaded wains
With ease might move?
   SHEP.   I have no certain knowledge;
Yet may we form conjectures; 'tis a scheme
Most prudent, with his host to march by night
Because he hears the plain with hostile bands
Is covered: but us rustics he alarmed,
Who dwell on Ida's mount, the ancient seat
Of Ilion's first inhabitants, by night
When through that wood, the haunt of savage beasts
The warrior trod: for with a mighty shout
The Thracian host rushed on, but we, our flocks,
With terror smitten, to the summit drove,
Lest any Greek should come to seize the prey,
And waste your crowded stalls: till we discovered
Voices so different from the Hellenian tribes,
That we no longer feared them. I advanced,
And in the Thracian language made inquiry
Of the king's vanguard, as they moved along
To explore a passage for the host, what name
Their leader bore, sprung from what noble sire,
To Ilion's walls he came, the friend of Priam.
When I had heard each circumstance I wished
To know, I for a time stood motionless,
And saw majestic Rhesus, like a god,
High in his chariot, drawn by Thracian steeds
Whiter than snow, a golden beam confined
Their necks, and o'er his shoulders hung a shield
Adorned with sculptures wrought in massive gold;

Like that which in Minerva's Ægis flames,
Bound on the courser's front, a brazen Gorgon
Tinkled incessant with alarming sound.
The numbers of an army so immense
I cannot calculate; the horse were many,
Many the ranks of troops with bucklers armed,
And archers; and a countless multitude,
Like infantry in Thracian vests arrayed
Brought up the rear. Such is th' ally who comes
On Troy's behalf to combat; nor by flight,
Nor by withstanding his protended spear,
Can Peleus' son escape him.

CHOR. When the gods
Are to a realm propitious, each event
Is easily converted into bliss.

HEC. Since I in battle prosper, and since Jove
Is on our side, I shall have many friends;
But those we need not who in former time
Our toils partook not, with malignant blast
When on the sails of Ilion Mars had breathed.
Rhesus hath shown too plainly what a friend
He is to Troy, for to the feast he comes,
Yet was he absent when the hunters seized
Their prey, nor did he share the toils of war.

CHOR. You justly scorn such friends; yet, O receive
Those who would aid the city.

HEC. We who long
Have guarded Ilion can defend it now.

CHOR. Are you persuaded you have gained already
A triumph o'er the foes?

HEC. I am persuaded,
And when to-morrow's sun the heaven ascends
This shall be proved.

CHOR. Beware of what may happen;
Jove oft o'erthrows the prosperous.

HEC. I abhor
These tardy succours.

SHEP. O, my lord, 'twere odious,
Should you reject with scorn the proffered aid
Of our allies: the sight of such a host
Will strike the foe with terror.

CHOR. Since he comes
But as a guest, not partner in the war,
Let him approach your hospitable board,
For little thanks are due from Priam's sons
To such confederates.

HEC. Prudent are thy counsels,
Thou too hast rightly judged: and in compliance
With what the messenger hath said, let Rhesus

Refulgent in his golden arms draw near,
For Ilion shall receive him as her friend.
[*Exit* SHEPHERD.

CHORUS.

ODE.

I. 1.

Daughter of Jove, forbear to wreak
 Impending vengeance, though the tongue,
O Nemesis, its boastful strain prolong:
I the free dictates of my soul will speak.
Thou com'st, brave son of that illustrious spring,
Thou com'st thrice welcome to our social hall:
At length doth thy Pierian mother bring
Her favoured child, while ling'ring in his fall,
Adorned by many a bridge, thee with paternal call

I. 2.

Doth Strymon summon to the field : of yore
 When he the tuneful Muse addressed,
A gliding stream he sought her snowy breast,
Thee, lovely youth, the yielding goddess bore :
To us thou com'st a tutelary power
Yoking thy coursers to the fervid car :
O Phrygia! O my country! at this hour
Hastes thy deliverer glittering from afar,
Him may'st thou call thy Jove, thy thunderbolt of war.

II. 1.

While swiftly glides th' unheeded day,
 Again shall Troy without control
Chant the young loves, and o'er the foaming bowl
The sportive contest urge 'midst banquets gay ;
But Atreus' sons desponding cross the wave,
And sail from Ilion to the Spartan strand.
Accomplish what thy friends foretold, O save
 These menaced walls by thy victorious hand,
Return with laurels crowned, and bless thy native land.

II. 2.

To dazzle fierce Pelides' sight,
 Before him wave thy golden shield
Obliquely raised, that meteor of the field,
Vault from thy chariot with unrivalled might,
And brandish with each dexterous hand a lance ;
Whoever strives with thee shall ne'er return
To Argive fanes, and join Saturnia's dance,
 He by the spear of Thrace in combat slain,
Shall lie a breathless corse on Troy's exulting plain.

Hail, mighty chief! ye Thracian realms, the mien
Of him ye bore speaks his exalted rank.
Observe those nervous limbs with plated gold
Incased, and hearken to those tinkling chairs
Which on his shield are hung. A god, O Troy,
E'en Mars himself, from Strymon's current sprung,
And from the Muse, brings this auspicious gale.

RHESUS, HECTOR, CHORUS.

RHE. Thou brave descendant of a noble sire,
Lord of this realm, O Hector, I accost thee
After a tedious absence, and rejoice
In thy success, for to the turrets reared
By Greece, thou now lay'st siege, and I am come
With thee those hostile bulwarks to o'erthrow,
And burn their fleet.
 HEC.   Son of the tuneful Muse,
And Thracian Strymon's stream, I ever love
To speak the truth, for I am not a man
Versed in duplicity; long, long ago,
Should you have come to succour Troy, nor suffered,
Far as on you depended, by our foes
This city to be ta'en. You cannot say
That uninvited by your friends you came not,
Because you marked not our distress. What heralds,
What embassies to you did Phrygia send,
Beseeching you, the city to protect,
What sumptuous presents did she not bestow?
But you, our kinsman, who derive your birth
From a barbarian stem, to Greece betrayed
Us, a barbarian nation, though from ruling
Over a petty state, by this right arm
I raised you to the wide-extended throne,
When round Pangæum and Pæonia's realm
Rushing upon the hardiest Thracian troops
I broke their ranks of battle, and subdued
The people to your empire: but you spurn
My benefits, nor come with speed to succour
Your friends in their distress. Though they who spring not
From the same ancestors, observed our summons;
Of whom full many in yon field of death
Have tombs heaped o'er them, a most glorious proof
Of faith unshaken; others under arms
Their chariots mount, and steadfastly endure
The wintry blasts, the parching flames of heaven,
Nor on a gay convivial couch reclined
Like you, O Rhesus, drain the frequent bowl.
That you may know I yet can stand alone,

Such conduct I resent; this to your face
I speak.
    RHE. I also am the same: my language
Is plain and honest; I am not a man
Of mean duplicity. My soul was tortured
With greater anguish far than thou couldst feel,
Because I was not present in this land;
But Scythia's tribes who near our confines dwell
Made war against me just as I to Troy
Was journeying; I had reached the Euxine shore
To sail with Thracia's host, the Scythian blood
There stained our spears, and my brave troops expired
'Midst intermingled slaughter: this event
Hindered my reaching Troy, and aiding thee
In battle. Having conquered them, and taken
For hostages their children, them I bound
To pay me annual tribute; with my fleet
Then crossed the Hellespont, and marched on foot
Through various realms, nor, as thou proudly say'st,
Drained the intoxicating bowl, nor slept
Beneath a gilded roof, but to such blasts
As cover with thick ice the Thracian wave,
Or through Pæonia howl, was I exposed
Wrapped in this mantle many a sleepless night.
But I, though late, am in due season come:
For this is the tenth year since thou hast waged
An ineffectual war, day after day
By thee is idly lavished, while the die
Of battle 'twixt the Argive host and thine
Spins doubtful ere it fall. But it for me
Will be sufficient that the sun once mount
The heavens, while I their bulwarks storm, invade
Their fleet, and slay the Greeks. To my own home
I the next day from Ilion will return,
Thy toils soon ending: let no Trojan bear
A shield: for with this spear will I subdue
The boasters, though 'twas late ere I arrived.
    CHOR. My soul this language doth approve,
  Such friends as thou art sent by Jove,
  But humbly I that god beseech,
  To pardon thy presumptuous speech.
  The navy launched from Argos' strand,
  Though freighted with a daring band,
  Neither in former times, nor now
  Contained a chief more brave than thou.
  How shall Achilles' self withstand,
  Or Ajax meet, thy vengeful hand?
  O may the morn with orient ray
  Exhibit that auspicious day,

When thou the victor's prize shalt gain
And dye with crimson gore the plain.

RHE. Soon with exploits like these will I atone
For my long absence: but, with due submission
To Nemesis, I speak; when from the foe
We have delivered this beleaguered city
And seized their spoils for offerings to the gods;
With thee to Argos will I go, invade,
And ravage with victorious arms, all Greece,
To teach them in their turn what 'tis to suffer.

HEC. Could I escape from the impending stroke,
And with that safety which we erst enjoyed
These walls inhabit, I to Heaven should pay
Full many a grateful vow: but as for Argos,
As for the Grecian states, to lay them waste
By arms were far less easy than you speak of.

RHE. Is it not said the bravest chiefs of Greece
Came hither?

HEC.   Them I hold not in contempt,
But long have kept at bay.

RHE.   When these are slain,
We therefore each obstruction have removed.

HEC. Forbear to think of distant prospects now,
While our immediate interests lie neglected.

RHE. Art thou so tame as to endure such wrongs
Without retorting them?

HEC.   While I maintain
What I possess, my empire is sufficient.
But freely take your choice, or in the left
Or the right wing, or centre of our host
Display your shield, and range your troops around.

RHF. I singly will encounter all our foes,
O Hector; but if thou esteem it base
Not to assist me when I burn their fleet,
Because thou hast already toiled so long,
Oppose me to Achilles in the front
Of battle.

HEC.   We at him no spear must aim.

RHE. Yet was I told he sailed for Troy.

HEC.   He sailed,
And still is here, but angry with the chiefs,
Refuses to assist them.

RHE.   In the camp
Of Greece, say who is second in renown?

HEC. Ajax, I deem, and Tydeus' son are equal
To any; but most fluent in his speech,
And with sufficient fortitude inspired,
Is that Ulysses, from whom Troy hath suffered
Insults the most atrocious; for by night,

Entering Minerva's fane, he stole her image,
And bore it to the Grecian fleet: disguised
In tattered vest, that vile impostor next
Entered the gates, and cursed the Argive host,
Sent as a spy to Ilion; having slain
The sentinels, he through the gates escaped,
And in some fraudful scheme is ever found:
At the Thymbræan temple is he stationed
Hard by our ramparts, we in him contend
With a most grievous pest.

RHE.   The valiant man
Is never mean enough to slay his foes
By stealth, he loves to meet them face to face;
But, as for him, the recreant chief thou nam'st,
Who lurking with a thievish purpose frames
These dark contrivances, as through the gates
I sally forth to combat, I will seize him;
Driven through his back, my spear shall leave the miscreant
Food for the vultures, for the impious robber
Who spoils the temples of the gods deserves
No better fate.

HEC.   Now choose, for it is night,
The spot for an encampment: I will show you
A separate quarter where your troops must sleep.
But mark me well, Apollo is the watchword;
In case of an emergency, announce
This signal to the Thracian host.   [*Exit* RHESUS.
                              Extend
The watch beyond the lines, and there receive
Dolon our spy, who sallied forth t' explore
The navy of our foes; if he be safe
He, by this time, the trenches must approach.
                              [*Exit* HECTOR.

CHORUS.

I.

Who comes this rampart to defend?
The times assigned us sentinels is o'er;
Yon fading constellation shines no more
Now the seven Pleiades the heaven ascend.
  In ether view the eagle glide.
  Wake! what means this long delay?
  Rise and watch; now dawns the day:
  Saw ye the moon diffuse her radiance wide?
  Aurora is at hand: but at the gate
(For Dolon sure returns) what faithful guard shall wait?
  SEMICHOR. To whom did the first watch belong?
  SEMICHOR.   'Tis said
Choræbus, son of Mygdon, is their chief.

SEMICHOR. Who in his room was stationed?
SEMICHOR. The Pæonians
Called from their tent Cilicia's hardy troops.
SEMICHOR. The Mysians summoned us.
SEMICHOR. Haste, let us seek
The fifth division of the watch, and rouse
Lycia's brave warriors as by lot ordained.

CHORUS.

II.

Hark! couched on her ill-omened nest,
Fell murderess of her son, in varied strains
Near Simois' banks the nightingale complains:
What sounds melodious heave her throbbing breast!
    The flocks on Ida wont to feed
    Still browse o'er that airy height,
    Soothing the cold ear of night,
Hark to the murmurs of the pastoral reed.
Sleep on our closing eyelids gently steals;
Sweet are its dews when morn her earliest dawn reveals.
SEMICHOR. But wherefore doth not he draw near whom
    Hector
Sent to explore the fleet?
SEMICHOR. He hath so long
Been absent that I tremble.
SEMICHOR. If he fell
Into some ambush, and is slain, we soon
Shall have sufficient cause for fear.
SEMICHOR. But haste,
Rouse Lycia's warriors as by lot ordained. [*Exit* CHORUS.

ULYSSES, DIOMEDE.

ULY. Heard'st thou, O Diomede, the sound of arms,
Or in these ears did empty murmurs ring?
DIO. No; but the steely trappings which are linked
To yonder chariots, rattled, and I too
With vain alarm was seized, till I perceived
The coursers, who their clanging harness shook.
ULY. Beware, lest in this gloom of night thou stumble
Upon the sentinels.
DIO. Though in the dark
We tread, I with such caution will direct
My steps as not to err.
ULY. But, should'st thou wake them,
Thou know'st the watchword of their host.
DIO. I know
It is Apollo; this I heard from Dolon.
ULY. Ha! I perceive our foes have left these chambers.

DIO. Here, Dolon told us, is the tent of Hector:
'Gainst him I wield this javelin.
    ULY.   What hath happened?
Is the whole squadron too elsewhere removed?
    DIO. Perchance they too 'gainst us may have contrived
Some stratagem.
    ULY.   For Hector now is brave
Since he hath conquered.
    DIO.   How shall we proceed?
For in this chamber him we cannot find,
And all our hopes are vanished.
    ULY.   To the fleet
Let us in haste return: for him some god
Protects, and crowns him with triumphant wreaths:
We must not strive 'gainst Fortune's dread behests.
    DIO. Then to Æneas will we go, or Paris
That Phrygian most abhorred, and with our swords
Lop off their heads.
    ULY.   But how, in darkness wrapt,
Canst thou direct thy passage through the troops,
To slay them without danger?
    DIO.   Yet 'twere base,
Back to the Grecian fleet should we return,
No fresh exploit performing 'gainst the foe.
    ULY. What means this language? hast thou not performed
A great exploit? have we not slain the spy
Who to our navy went, and are not these
The spoils of Dolon? how canst thou expect
To spread a general havoc through their troops?
Comply; let us retire: may Fortune speed
Our progress homeward.

MINERVA, ULYSSES, DIOMEDE.

    MIN.   With affliction stung,
Why from the Trojan camp do ye retire?
Although the gods forbid you to destroy
Hector or Paris, heard ye not that Rhesus,
A mighty chief, with numerous troops is come
To Troy? If he outlives this night, nor Ajax,
Nor can Achilles hinder him from wasting
The camp of Greece, demolishing your walls,
And forcing a wide passage through your gates
With his victorious spear: him slay, and all
Is yours; but go not to the couch of Hector,
Nor hope to leave that chief a weltering trunk,
For he must perish by another hand.
    ULY. Dread goddess, O Minerva, I distinguished
Thy well-known voice: for midst unnumbered toils
Thou ever dost support me: but, oh say,

Where sleeps the mighty warrior thou hast named,
And in what part of the barbarian host
Have they assigned his station?
    MIN.   Near at hand,
And separate from the Phrygian troops, he lies;
Hector hath placed him just without the lines
Till morn arise; conspicuous in the gloom
Of night, and close beside their sleeping lord,
Yoked to the car his Thracian coursers stand,
White as the glossy plumage of the swan:
Them bear away when ye have slain their lord,
A glorious prize, for the whole world can boast
No car beside drawn by such beauteous steeds.
    ULY. Either do thou, O Diomede, transpierce
The Thracian soldiers, or to me consign
That task; meanwhile seize thou the steeds.
    DIO.   To slay
The foe be mine; do you the coursers guide,
For you are practised in each nicer art,
And quick of apprehension. To each man
Should that peculiar station be assigned
In which he can be useful.
    MIN.   But to us
Paris I see is coming, who hath heard
A doubtful rumour from the watch, that foes
Enter the trenches.
    DIO.   Hath he any comrade,
Or marches he alone?
    MIN.   Alone he seems
To go to Hector's chamber, to announce
That there are foes discovered in the camp.
    DIO. Is it not first ordained that he shall die?
    MIN. You can no more, the Destinies forbid:
For Hector must not perish by your hand;
But haste to him on whom ye came to wreak
Fate's dreadful purposes: myself meanwhile
Assuming Venus' form, who 'midst the toils
Of battle by her tutelary care
Protects him, will with empty words detain
Paris your foe. Thus much have I declared:
Yet he, whom you must smite, though near at hand,
Nor knows, nor hears, the words which I have uttered.
                            [*Exeunt* ULYSSES *and* DIOMEDE.

PARIS, MINERVA.

    PAR. General and brother, Hector, thee I call:
Yet sleep'st thou? doth not this important hour
Demand thy vigilance? some foes approach,
Robbers or spies.

MIN.   Be of good cheer; for Venus
Protects you: I in all your battles feel
An interest, mindful of the prize I gained
Favoured by you, and am for ever grateful:
Now to the host of Ilion I conduct
Your noble Thracian friend, who from the Muse,
Harmonious goddess, and from Strymon springs.
    PAR. To Troy and me thou ever art a friend.
In thy behalf when I that judgment gave,
I boast that for this city I obtained
The greatest treasure life affords. But hither,
Hearing an indistinct account, I come;
For 'mong the guards there hath prevailed a rumour,
That Grecian spies have entered Ilion's walls:
Though the astonished messenger who bore
These tidings, saw them not himself, nor knows
Who saw them: I on this account am going
To Hector's tent.
    MIN.   Fear nought; for in the camp
No new event hath happened. To arrange
The Thracian troops is Hector gone.
    PAR.   Thy words
Are most persuasive, and to them I yield
Implicit credence. From all fears released,
I to my former station will return.
    MIN. Go and depend upon my guardian care
To see my faithful votaries ever blest;
For you in me shall find a zealous friend.   [*Exit* PARIS.

ULYSSES, DIOMEDE, MINERVA.

    MIN. But now to you, my real friends, I speak.
Son of Laertes, O conceal your sword,
For we have slain the Thracian chief, and seized
His coursers, but our foes have ta'en th' alarm
And rush upon you, therefore fly with speed,
Fly to the naval ramparts. Why delay
To save your lives when hostile throngs approach?
            [*Exit* MINERVA.

CHORUS, ULYSSES, DIOMEDE.

    CHOR. Come on, strike, strike, destroy. Who marches
        yonder?
Look, look, 'tis him I mean! these are the robbers
Who in the dead of night alarmed our host.
Hither, my friends, haste hither; I have seized them.
What answer mak'st thou? tell me whence thou cam'st,
And who thou art.
    ULY.   No right hast thou to know;
Insult me, and this instant thou shalt die.

CHOR. Wilt thou not, ere this lance transpierce thy
  breast,
Repeat the watchword?
  ULY.   That thou soon shalt hear;
Be satisfied.
  1st SEMICHOR. Come on, my friends, strike! strike!
  2nd SEMICHOR. Hast thou slain Rhesus?
  ULY.   I have slain the man
Who would have murdered thee: forbear.
  1st SEMICHOR.   I will not.
  2nd SEMICHOR. Forbear to slay a friend.
  1st SEMICHOR.   Pronounce the watchword.
  ULY. Apollo.
  2nd SEMICHOR. Thou art right; let not a spear
Be lifted up against him.
  1st SEMICHOR.   Know'st thou whither
Those men are gone?
  2nd SEMICHOR.   We saw not.
  1st SEMICHOR.   Follow close
Their steps, or we must call aloud for aid.
  2nd SEMICHOR. Yet were it most unseemly to disturb
Our valiant comrades with our nightly fears.
            [*Exeunt* ULYSSES *and* DIOMEDE.

CHORUS.

ODE.

I.

What chief is he, who moved along;
What daring plunderer fleet and strong,
Shall boast he 'scaped my vengeful hand?
How overtake his rapid flight?
To whom compare him, who by night,
With dauntless step passed through our armed band
  And slumbering guards? doth he reside
In Thessaly, near ocean's boisterous tide
In Locris, or those islands scattered o'er
The waves? whence comes he to this fell debate?
  What power supreme doth he adore?
  1st SEMICHOR. Was this Ulysses' enterprise, or whose?
  2nd SEMICHOR. If we may form our judgment from the past,
Who but Ulysses——
  1st SEMICHOR.   Think'st thou that it was?
  2nd SEMICHOR. Why not?
  1st SEMICHOR.   He is an enterprising foe.
  2nd SEMICHOR. What bravery? whom do you applaud?
  1st SEMICHOR.   Ulysses.
  2nd SEMICHOR. Praise not the treacherous weapon of a
  robber.

Chorus.

II.

He entered Ilion once before,
With foam his eyes were covered o'er,
In tatters hung his squalid vest;
He artfully concealed his sword,
And sued for fragments from our board;
Shorn was his head, and like a beggar dressed;
He cursed with simulated hate
Th' Atrides, rulers of the Grecian state.
May just revenge his forfeit life demand:
Would he had perished as his crimes deserve,
Before he reached the Phrygian land.

1st SEMICHOR. Whether this deed was by Ulysses wrought
It matters not, I shrink with fear, for Hector
Will to us guards impute the blame.
   2nd SEMICHOR.   What charge
Can he allege?
   1st SEMICHOR. He will suspect.
   2nd SEMICHOR.   Why shrink
With terror?
   1st SEMICHOR. 'Twixt our ranks they passed.
   2nd SEMICHOR.   Who passed?
   1st SEMICHOR. They, who this night have entered Phrygia's camp.

Charioteer of Rhesus, Chorus.

CHA. Alas! intolerable stroke of fate!
1st SEMICHOR. Be silent.
   2nd SEMICHOR.   Rouse! for some one may have fallen
Into the snare.
   CHA.   O dire calamity
Of Troy's allies, the Thracians!
   1st SEMICHOR.   Who is he
That groans?
   CHA.   Ah! wretched me, and O thou king
Of Thrace, who in an evil hour beheld'st
Accursed Ilion; what an end of life
Was thine!
   CHOR.   But which of our allies art thou?
For o'er these eyes the gloom of night is spread,
And I discern thee not.
   CHA.   Where shall I find
Some of the Trojan chiefs? beneath his shield
O where doth Hector taste the charms of sleep?
To which of Ilion's leaders shall I tell
All we have suffered? and what wounds unseen

Some stranger hath on us with ruthless hand
Inflicted? but he vanished and hath heaped
Conspicuous sorrows on the Thracian realm.
 CHOR. Some terrible disaster to the troops
Of Thrace it seems hath happened, if aright
I comprehend what I from him have heard.
 CHA. Our host is utterly destroyed, our king
Hath been despatched by some foul secret stroke.
How am I tortured by a deadly wound,
Yet know not to what cause I must impute
My perishing! 'Twas by the Fates ordained,
That I, and Rhesus, who to Ilion led
Auxiliar troops, ingloriously should bleed.
 CHOR. He in no riddle hath expressed the tale
Of our misfortunes; he asserts too clearly
That our allies are slain.
 CHA.   We are most wretched,
And to our wretchedness have joined disgrace,
A twofold evil. For, to die with glory,
If glory must be purchased at the expense
Of life, is very bitterness I deem
To him who bleeds (for what can make amends
For such a loss as life); but to the living
Is he the source of pride, from him his house
Derives renown. But we, alas! like fools,
Ignobly perish. Hector in the camp
No sooner fixed our station, and pronounced
The watchword, than we slept upon the plain,
O'ercome with toil; no sentinels were stationed
To watch our troops by night, nor were our arms
Duly arranged, and to the harnessed steeds
Hung no alarm bell; for our monarch heard
That ye had proved victorious, and with ruin
Threatened the Grecian fleet. Immersed we lay
In luckless slumber; till disturbed in mind
I started up, and with a liberal hand
Measured the coursers' food, resolved betimes
To yoke them for the battle. I beheld
Two men, who, in the midnight darkness, walked
Around our camp; but when I moved, they fled,
And disappeared immediately; with threats
I bade them keep aloof: 'twas my conjecture
That robbers, some of our own countrymen,
Approached: they answered not, nor know I more.
Returning to my tent, again I slept,
And forms tremendous hovered in my dream.
For near my royal master, as I stood,
I saw two visionary wolves ascend
Those coursers' backs which I was wont to guide,

Oft lashing with their tails they forced them on,
Indignant breathing as they champed the bit,
And struggling with dismay; but in attempting
To drive away these ravenous beasts, I woke,
Roused by the terrors of the night, and heard,
Soon as I raised my head, expiring groans;
The tepid current of my master's blood,
Yet gasping in the agonies of death,
Besprinkled me. As from the couch I leaped
Unarmed, and sought for weapons, some strong warrior
Smote with his sword my ribs; the ghastly wound
Displayed his might: prostrate I sunk to earth.
Bearing the steeds away, and glittering car,
They by the swiftness of their feet escaped,
Tortured with pain, too faint to stand, I know
Too well the dire calamity these eyes
Beheld; but cannot say, or through what means,
Or by the hand of whom, my lord was slain:
Yet can I guess that by our friends we suffer.
  CHOR. O charioteer of Thracia's wretched king,
Be well assured this deed was by our foes
Committed. For lo! Hector's self, apprized
Of this calamity, draws near; he feels
Such anguish as he ought for thy disasters.

HECTOR, CHARIOTEER OF RHESUS, CHORUS.

  HEC. O ye accursed authors of this mischief,
How did those spies, who by the foe were sent
Thus, to your infamy, escape, and spread
Dire havoc through the host; both as they entered
And as they left the camp? Yet, unmolested,
Ye suffered them to pass. Who should be punished
But you? for you, I say, were stationed here
To watch the camp; but they without a wound
Are vanished, laughing at the Phrygian troops
For their unmanly cowardice, and me
Their leader. Be assured, by Jove I swear,
All-gracious father, or the scourge or death
Shall wait you for such guilt, else deem that Hector
Is but a thing of nought, a very coward.
  CHOR. Great is, alas! my danger, mighty prince,
The foe stole in while I to you conveyed
Those tidings, that the Greeks around their ships
Had kindled fires: through all the live-long night
These watchful eyes have ne'er been sealed by sleep.
By Simois' holy fountain I conjure you,
My royal lord, impute no blame to me,
For I am wholly guiltless. If you learn
That in my deeds or words I have offended,

Plunge me alive beneath earth's deepest vault;
I ask no mercy.
          CHA.   Why dost thou upbraid
These for the guilt? by plausible harangues
Wouldst thou impose on thy barbarian friends;
O thou barbarian, thou the bloody deed
Didst perpetrate; nor can our slaughtered comrades,
Nor we who linger pierced with ghastly wounds,
Admit that 'twas another. There requires
A long and subtle speech to make me think
Thou didst not basely murder thy allies,
Because the beauty of our steeds attracted
Thy admiration, and on their account
Hast thou slain those who at thy earnest prayer
Landed on Ilion's shore; they came, they died.
With greater decency than thou observ'st,
Who dost assassinate thy friends, did Paris
The rites of hospitality infringe.
Pretend not that some Grecian came unseen
And smote us. Who subdued the Phrygian host,
Who reached our quarters unobserved by Hector?
Thou with the Trojan army wert before us;
But who was wounded, who among thy troops
Expired, when through their ranks as thou pretend'st
The foe to us advanced? But I was wounded,
And they, whom a more grievous ill o'ertook,
No more behold the sun. To be explicit,
I charge no Greek: what foe could come by night
And find out Rhesus' tent, unless some god
Had told the murderers, for they sure knew nought
Of his arrival? therefore all this mischief
Must be thy sole contrivance.
          HEC.   Our allies
Have long assisted us since first the Greeks
This realm invaded; and I never heard
They to my charge imputed any crime.
Could I begin with thee? by such desire
For beauteous steeds may I be never seized,
As to induce me to destroy my friends.
Ulysses was the author of this deed.
What Greek could have accomplished or contrived
Such an exploit, but he? Him much I fear:
My soul is also troubled lest he light
On Dolon too, and slay him, for 'tis long
Since he went forth, nor doth he yet return.
     CHA. I know not that Ulysses whom thou nam'st,
Nor did a foe inflict this ghastly wound.
     HEC. Therefore retain, since thus to thee it seems,
Thy own opinion.

CHA.   O my native land,
Might I but die in thee!
  HEC.   Thou shalt not die:
For of the dead the number is sufficient.
  CHA. Reft of my lord, but whither shall I turn?
  HEC. Thou in my house shalt careful treatment find,
And healing balsams.
  CHA.   Shall the ruthless hands
Of murderers dress my wounds?
  HEC.   He will not cease
Alleging the same charge.
  CHA.   Perdition seize
The author of this bloody deed! my tongue
Has fixed no charge, as thou pretend'st, on thee;
But Justice knows.
  HEC.   Conduct him to my palace
With speed, that we may 'scape his clamorous plaints.
But you must go, and to the citizens
Proclaim, acquainting Priam, and the elders
Who sit in council, first, that I direct
The bodies of the slain shall be interred
With due respect beside the public road.
      [*Exit* CHARIOTEER, *supported by one of*
          HECTOR'S *Attendants.*
  CHOR. Why from the summit of exalted bliss
Into fresh woes hath some malignant god
Plunged Troy, why caused this sad reverse of fortune?

The MUSE *appears in the air,* HECTOR, CHORUS.

  CHOR. High o'er our heads what deity, O king,
Is hovering? in her hands a recent corse
She bears: I shudder at the dreadful sight.
  MUSE. Ye Trojans, mark me well: for I a Muse
Who by the wise am worshipped, hither come,
One of the nine famed sisters, having seen
The wretched fate of this my dearest son,
Who by the foe was slain: but he who smote
The generous youth, Ulysses, that dissembler,
At length shall suffer as his crimes deserve.

              ODE.
              I.
    Parental anguish rends my breast,
    For thee my son, my son, I grieve,
    Thy mother sinks with woes oppressed.
    Why didst thou take this road, why leave
    Thy home, and march to Ilion's gate,
    Where death did thy arrival wait?

Oft with maternal zeal I strove
Thy luckless courage to restrain,
And oft thy sire opposed in vain.
But now with ineffectual love,
My dearest son, thee now no more,
Thee, O my son, must I deplore.

CHOR. As far as bosoms, by no kindred ties
United, can partake a mother's grief,
Do I bewail thy son's untimely fate.

MUSE.

II.

On him your tenfold vengeance shed
From Oeneus who derives his birth,
Smite base Ulysses' perjured head,
Ye fiends who desolate the earth;
Through them with agonizing pain
I mourn my valiant offspring slain;
May Helen too partake their doom,
Who from her bridal mansions fled,
And sought th' adulterer's Phrygian bed;
For thou in Troy art to the tomb
By her consigned; and many a state
Bewails its bravest warriors' fate.

Much while on earth, and since thy murmuring ghost
Was plunged in Orcus' dreary mansions more,
O offspring of Philammon, didst thou wound
My soul: that arrogance which caused thy ruin,
That contest with Pieria's choir, gave birth
To this unhappy youth: for having passed
The rapid current, with incautious step
Approaching Strymon's genial bed, we mounted
Pangæum's summit, for its golden mines
Distinguished; each melodious instrument
Around us in full concert breathed; our strife
Was there decided with the Thracian minstrel;
That Thamyris who dared blaspheme our art,
We of his eyes deprived. But since I bore
Thee, O my son, through deference for my sisters,
And for my own reputed chastity,
Thee to the watery mansions of thy sire
I sent; and Strymon, to no human care,
But to the nymphs who haunt his limpid founts,
For nurture did consign thee; from those virgins
When, O my dearest son, thou hadst received
The best of educations, thou becam'st
Monarch of Thrace, the first of men. I felt

No boding apprehensions of thy death;
By thee, while marshalled on thy native ground,
Athirst for blood the dauntless squadrons moved.
But thee I cautioned, for I knew thy fate,
That thou to Troy shouldst never go; but thee
Th' ambassadors of Hector and the Senate,
By oft repeated messages, persuaded
To come to the assistance of thy friends.
Yet think not, O Minerva, thou sole cause
Of my son's fate, that thou these watchful eyes
Hast 'scaped; Ulysses and the son of Tydeus
Were not the authors of this bloody deed,
Although they gave the wound. We sister Muses
Honour thy city, in thy land we dwell.
Orpheus, the kinsman of this hapless youth
Whom thou hast slain, dark mysteries did unfold;
And by Apollo, and our sister choir,
Thy venerable citizen Musæus
Was taught to soar beyond each warbled strain
Of pristine melody: but in return
For all these favours, bearing in my arms
My son, I utter this funereal dirge;
But I no other minstrel will employ.

CHOR. Falsely the wounded Thracian charioteer
Charged us with a conspiracy to slay him.

HEC. Full well I knew, there needed not a seer
T' inform me, that he perished by the arts
Of Ithacus. But was it not my duty
When I my country saw by Grecian troops
Besieged, to send forth heralds to my friends,
Requesting them to aid us? I did send,
And Rhesus came, by gratitude constrained,
Illustrious partner of my toils. His death
Lamenting, will I raise a tomb to grace
The corse of my ally, and o'er the flame
Strew tissued vests: for with confederate arms
Dauntless he came, though piteous was his death.

MUSE. They shall not plunge him in the yawning grave,
Such vows will I address to Pluto's bride,
Daughter of fruitful Ceres, to release
His ghost from the drear shades beneath: she owes
To Orpheus' friends such honours. But henceforth,
Dead as it were to me, will he no more
Behold the sun, we ne'er must meet again,
Nor shall he see his mother, but shall lie
Concealed beneath the caverns of that land
With silver mines abounding, from a man
Exalted to a god, restored to life,
The priest of Bacchus, and of him who dwells

Beneath Pangeum's rock, a god adored
By those who haunt his orgies. But ere long
To yonder goddess of the briny waves
Shall I bear doleful tidings: for by fate
It is decreed, her offspring too shall die;
But first our sisterhood, in choral plaints,
Will sing of thee, O Rhesus, and hereafter
Achilles, son of Thetis, shall demand
Our elegiac strains, not she who slew
Thee, hapless youth, Minerva, can redeem him;
Such an inevitable shaft is stored
In Phœbus' quiver. O ye pangs that rend
A mother's breast, ye toils the lot of man;
They who behold you in your real light
Will live without a progeny, nor mourn
With hopeless anguish o'er their children's tomb.

[Exit the MUSE.

CHOR. To bury the deceased with honours due,
Will be his mother's care: but if, O Hector,
Thou mean'st to execute some great emprise,
'Tis now the time: for morn already dawns.

HEC. Go, and this instant bid our comrades arm,
Harness the steeds: but while ye in these toils
Are busied, ye the signal must await,
Th' Etrurian trumpet's clangour; for I trust
I first shall o'er the Grecian host prevail,
Shall storm their ramparts, and then burn their fleet,
And that Hyperion's orient beams will bring
A day of freedom to Troy's valiant race.

CHOR. Obey the monarch: clad in glittering mail
Let us go forth, and his behests proclaim
To our associates; for that god who fights
Our battles, haply will bestow success.

The Trojan Captives.

PERSONS OF THE DRAMA.

NEPTUNE.
MINERVA.
HECUBA.
CHORUS OF CAPTIVE
   TROJAN DAMES.

TALTHYBIUS.
CASSANDRA.
ANDROMACHE.
MENELAUS.
HELEN.

SCENE.—BEFORE THE ENTRANCE OF AGAMEMNON'S TENT
IN THE GRECIAN CAMP NEAR TROY.

NEPTUNE.

FROM the Ægean deep, in mazy dance
Where Nereus' daughters glide with agile feet,
I Neptune hither come. For round the fields
Of Ilion, since Apollo and myself
With symmetry exact reared many a tower
Hewn from the solid rock; the love I bore
The city where my Phrygian votaries dwelt,
Laid waste by Greece, where smoke e'en now ascends
The heavens, hath ne'er been rooted from this breast,
For on Parnassus bred, the Phocian chief
Epeus, by Minerva's arts inspired,
Framed with a skilful hand, and through the gates
Sent that accursed machine, the horse which teemed
With ambushed javelins. Through forsaken groves,
Through the polluted temples of the gods,
Flow tides of crimson slaughter; at the base
Of altars sacred to Hercæan Jove,
Fell hoary Priam. But huge heaps of gold
And Phrygian plunder, to the fleet of Greece
Are sent: the leaders of the host that sacked
This city, wait but for a prosperous breeze,
That after ten years absence they their wives
And children may with joy behold. Subdued
By Juno, Argive goddess, and Minerva,
Who leagued in Phrygia's overthrow, I leave

Troy the renowned, and my demolished shrines.
For when pernicious solitude extends
O'er cities her inexorable sway,
Abandoned are the temples of the gods,
None comes to worship there. Scamander's banks
Re-echo many a shriek of captive dames
Distributed by lot; th' Arcadians, some,
Some the Thessalians gain, and some the sons
Of Theseus leaders of th' Athenian troops:
But they whom chance distributes not, remain
Beneath yon roof selected by the chiefs
Of the confederate army. Justly deemed
A captive, among them is Spartan Helen:
And if the stranger wishes to behold
That wretched woman, Hecuba lies stretched
Before the gate, full many are her tears,
And her afflictions many: at the tomb
Of stern Achilles her unhappy daughter
Polyxena died wretchedly, her lord
The royal Priam, and her sons are slain,
That spotless virgin too whom from his shrine
Apollo with prophetic gifts inspired,
Cassandra, spurning every sacred rite,
Did Agamemnon violently drag
To his adulterous bed. But, O farewell,
Thou city prosperous once; ye splendid towers,
Had not Minerva's self ordained your fall,
Ye still on your firm basis might remain.

MINERVA, NEPTUNE.

MIN. May I accost the god who to my sire
In blood is nearest, mighty, through high Heaven
Revered, and lay aside our ancient hate?
 NEP. 'Tis well, thou royal maid: an interview
'Twixt those of the same house, is to the soul
An efficacious philtre.
 MIN. I applaud
Those who are temperate in their wrath, and bring
Such arguments, O monarch, as affect
Both you and me.
 NEP. From all th' assembled gods
Some new commission bear'st thou, or from Jove,
Or what celestial power?
 MIN. From none of these.
But in the cause of Troy, whose fields we tread,
I to your aid betake me, and would join
Our common strength.
 NEP. Hast thou then laid aside

Thy former hate, to pity Troy, consumed
By the relentless flames?
    MIN.   First, thither turn
Your views: to me will you unfold your counsels,
And aid the schemes I would effect?
    NEP.   With joy:
But I meanwhile would thy designs explore,
Whether thou com'st on the behalf of Greece,
Or Troy.
    MIN.   The Trojans, erst my foes, I wish
To cheer, and to embitter the return
Of the victorious Grecian host.
    NEP.   What means
This change of temper? to excess thou hat'st
And lov'st at random.
    MIN.   Know you not the insult
Which hath been shown to me, and to my temple?
    NEP. I know that Ajax violently tore
Cassandra thence.
    MIN.   Yet by the Greeks unpunished
He 'scaped, and e'en uncensured.
    NEP.   Though the Greeks
O'erthrew Troy's walls through thy auxiliar might——
    MIN. And for this very cause will I conspire
With you to punish them.
    NEP.   I am prepared
For any enterprise thou wilt. What mean'st thou?
    MIN. Their journey home I am resolved to make
Most inauspicious.
    NEP.   While they yet remain
Upon the shore, or 'midst the briny waves?
    MIN. As to their homes from Ilion's coast they sail.
For Jove will send down rain, immoderate hail,
And pitchy blasts of air: he promises
To give me too his thunderbolts to smite
The Greeks and fire their ships; but join your aid,
Cause the Ægean deep with threefold waves,
And ocean's whirlpools horribly to rage,
Fill with their courses the unfathomed caves
Beneath Eubœa's rocks, that Greece may learn
My shrines to reverence, nor provoke the gods.
    NEP. It shall be done: there need not many words
To recommend thy suit. My storms shall rouse
Th' Ægean deep; the shores of Myconè,
Scyros with Lemnos, all the Delian rocks,
And steep Caphareus with full many a corse
Will I o'erspread. But mount Olympus' height,
And from the Thunderer's hand his flaming shafts
Receiving, mark when the devoted host

Of Greece weigh anchor. Frantic is the man
Who dares to lay the peopled city waste,
Temples with tombs profaning, and bereaves
Of their inhabitants those sacred vaults
Where sleep the dead; at length shall vengeance smite
That hardened miscreant in his bold career. [*Exeunt.*

The Scene opens, and discovers HECUBA *on a couch.*

HEC. Arise, thou wretch, and from the dust uplift
Thy drooping head; though Ilion be no more,
And thou a queen no longer, yet endure
With patience Fortune's change, and as the tide
Or as capricious Fortune wills, direct
Thy sails, nor turn against the dashing wave
Life's stubborn prow, for chance must guide thy voyage.
Alas! for what but groans belongs to me
Whose country, children, husband, are no more?
Oh, mighty splendour of my sires, now pent
In a small tomb, how art thou found a thing
Of no account! What portion of my woes
Shall I suppress, or what describe, how frame
A plaintive strain? Now fixed on this hard couch,
Wretch that I am, are my unwieldy limbs.
Ah me! my head, my temples, ah, my side!
Oh, how I wish to turn, and to stretch forth
These joints! My tears shall never cease to flow,
For like the Muse's lyre, th' affecting tale
Of their calamities consoles the wretched.
Ye prows of those swift barks which to the coast
Of fated Ilion, from the Grecian ports
Adventurous launched amid the purple wave,
Accompanied by inauspicious pæans
From pipes, and the shrill flute's enlivening voice,
While from the mast devolved the twisted cordage
By Egypt first devised, ye to the bay
Of Troy did follow Menelaus' wife,
Helen, abhorred adult'ress, who disgraced
Castor her brother, and Eurotas' stream:
She murdered Priam, sire of fifty sons,
And me the wretched Hecuba hath plunged
Into this misery. Here, alas! I sit
In my loathed prison, Agamemnon's tent;
From princely mansions dragged, an aged slave,
My hoary tresses shorn, this head deformed
With baldness. But, alas! ye hapless wives
Of Ilion's dauntless warriors, blooming maids,
And brides affianced in an evil hour,
Together let us weep, for Ilion's smoke
Ascends the skies. Like the maternal bird,

Who wails her callow brood, I now commence
A strain far different from what erst was heard
When I on mighty Priam's sceptred state
Proudly relying, led the Phrygian dance
Before the hallowed temples of the gods.
            [*She rises, and comes forth from the tent.*

SEMICHORUS, HECUBA.

  SEMICHOR. O Hecuba, what mean these clamorous notes,
These shrieks of woe? for from the vaulted roof
Thy plaints re-echoing smite my distant ear,
And fresh alarms seize every Phrygian dame
Who in these tents enslaved deplores her fate.
  HEC. E'en now, my daughter, at the Grecian fleet
Th' exulting sailors ply their oars.
  SEMICHOR.   Ah me!
What mean they? will they instantly convey me
Far from my ruined country?
  HEC.   By conjecture
Alone am I acquainted with our doom.
  SEMICHOR. Soon shall we hear this sentence: "From
      these doors
Come forth ye Trojan captives, for the Greeks
Are now preparing to return."
  HEC.   O cease,
My friends, nor from her chambers hither bring
Cassandra, frantic prophetess, defiled
By Argive ruffians, for the sight of her
Would but increase my griefs.
  SEMICHOR.   Troy, wretched Troy,
Thou art no more, they to whom fate ordains
No longer on thy fostering soil to dwell
Are wretched, both the living and the slain.

CHORUS, HECUBA.

  CHOR. Trembling I come from Agamemnon's tent,
Of thee my royal mistress to inquire
Whether the Greeks have doomed me to be slain,
And whether yet along the poop arranged
The mariners prepare to ply their oars.
  HEC. Deprived of sleep through horror, O my daughter,
I hither came: but on the road I see
A Grecian herald.
  CHOR.   Tell me to what lord
Am wretched I consigned.
  HEC.   E'en now the lot
Is casting to decide your fate.
  CHOR.   What chief
To Argos, or to Phthia, me shall bear,
Or to some island, sorrowing, far from Troy?

HEC. To whom shall wretched I, and in what land
Become a slave, decrepit like the drone
Through age, mere semblance of a pallid corse,
Or flitting spectre from the realms beneath?
Shall I be stationed or to watch the door,
Or tend the children of a haughty lord,
Erst placed at Troy in rank supreme?
CHOR.   Alas!
HEC. With what loud plaints dost thou revive thy woes!
CHOR. I never more through Ida's loom shall dart
The shuttle, nor behold a blooming race
Of children, in those lighter tasks employed
Which suit the young and beauteous, to the couch
Of some illustrious Greek conveyed, the joys
Which night and fortune yields are lost to me;
Or filled with water, from Pirene's spring
Shall I be doomed to bear the ponderous urn.
HEC. O could we reach the famed and happy realm
Of Theseus, distant from Eurotas' tide,
And curst Therapne's gates, where I should meet
Perfidious Helen, and remain a slave
To Menelaus, who demolished Troy.
CHOR. By fame's loud voice I am informed, the vale
Of Peneus, at Olympus base, abounds
With wealth and plenteous fruitage.
HEC.   This I make
My second option, next the blest domain
Of Theseus.
CHOR.   I am told that Vulcan's realm
Of Ætna, opposite Phœnicia's coast
The mother of Sicilian hills, is famed
For palms obtained by valour. Through the realm
Adjacent, bordering on th' Ionian deep,
Crathis the bright, for auburn hair renowned,
The tribute of its holy current pours,
And scatters blessings o'er a martial land.
But lo, with hasty step a herald comes
Bearing some message from the Grecian host!
What is his errand? for we now are slaves
To yon proud rulers of the Doric realm.

TALTHYBIUS, HECUBA, CHORUS.

TAL. O Hecuba, full oft, you know, to Troy
I, as their herald, by the Grecian host
Have been despatched; you cannot be a stranger
To me, Talthybius, who to you, and all,
One message bring.
HEC.   This, this, my dearest friends,
Is what I long have feared.

TAL. The lots are cast
Already, if your terrors thence arose.
  HEC. Alas, to what Thessalian city saidst thou,
Or to the Phthian, or the Theban realm
Shall we be carried?
  TAL. To a separate lord
Hath each of you distinctly been assigned.
  HEC. To whom, alas, to whom am I allotted?
What Phrygian dames do happier fortunes wait?
  TAL. I know; but be distinct in your inquiries,
Nor ask at once a multitude of questions.
  HEC. Say who by lot hath gained my wretched daughter
Cassandra?
  TAL. Her the royal Agamemnon
His chosen prize hath taken.
  HEC. As a slave
To tend his Spartan wife? ah, me!
  TAL. No slave,
But concubine.
  HEC. What, Phœbus' votive maid,
To whom the god with golden tresses gave
This privilege, that she should pass her life
In celibacy?
  TAL. With the shafts of love
Hath the prophetic nymph transpierced his breast.
  HEC. My daughter, cast the sacred keys away,
And rend the garlands thou with pride didst wear.
  TAL. Is it not great for captives to ascend
The regal couch?
  HEC. But where is she whom late
Ye took away, and whither have ye borne
That daughter?
  TAL. Speak you of Polyxena,
Or for whom else would you inquire?
  HEC. On whom
Hath chance bestowed her?
  TAL. At Achilles' tomb
It is decreed that she shall minister.
  HEC. Wretch that I am! for his sepulchral rites
Have I then borne a priestess? but what law
Is this, what Grecian usage, O my friend?
  TAL. Esteem your daughter happy; for with her
All now is well.
  HEC. What saidst thou? doth she live?
  TAL. 'Tis her peculiar fate to be released
From all affliction.
  HEC. But, alas! what fortune
Attends the warlike Hector's captive wife,
How fares it with the lost Andromache?

TAL. Her to Achilles' son hath from the band
Of captives chosen.
  HEC.   As to me who need
For a third foot, the staff which in these hands
I hold, whose head is whitened o'er with age,
To whom am I a slave?
  TAL.   By lot the king
Of Ithaca Ulysses hath obtained you.
  HEC. Alas! alas! let your shorn temples feel
The frequent blow; rend your discoloured cheeks.
Ah me! I am allotted for a slave
To a detestable and treacherous man,
Sworn foe of justice, to that lawless viper,
With double tongue confounding all, 'twixt friends
Exciting bitter hate. Ye Trojan dames,
O shed the sympathizing tear: I sink
Beneath the pressure of relentless fate.
  CHOR. Thy doom, O queen, thou know'st: but to what chief,
Hellenian or Achaian, I belong
Inform me.
  TAL. Peace! Conduct Cassandra hither
With speed, ye guards, into our general's hands
When I his captive have delivered up,
That we the rest may portion out. Why gleams
That blazing torch within? would Ilion's dames
Their chambers fire? what mean they? doomed to leave
This land, and to be borne to Argive shores,
Are they resolved to perish in the flames?
The soul, inspired with an unbounded love
Of freedom, ill sustains such woes. Burst open
The doors, lest, to their honour and the shame
Of Greece, on me the censure fall.
  HEC.   They kindle
No conflagation, but, with frantic step,
My daughter, lo! Cassandra rushes hither.

   CASSANDRA, TALTHYBIUS, HECUBA, CHORUS.

  CAS. Avaunt! the sacred flame I bring
  With reverential awe profound,
  And wave the kindled torch around,
  O Hymen, thou benignant king.
  The bridegroom comes with jocund pride,
  I too am styled a happy bride,
  My name through Argos' streets shall ring,
  O Hymen, thou benignant king!
  While thou attend'st my father's bier,
  O Hecuba, with many a tear,
  While Ilion's ramparts overthrown
  From thee demand th' incessant groan,

Ere the bright sun withhold his ray,
E'en in the glaring front of day,
I bid the nuptial incense blaze
To thee, O Hymen, thee whose power
Invoking at her bridal hour
The bashful virgin comes. Yon maze
Encircling, 'mid the choral dance,
As ancient usage bids, advance,
And in thy hand a flaming pine,
O mother, brandish. God of wine,
Thy shouting votaries hither bring,
As if in Ilion thou hadst found
Old Priam still a happy king.
Range that holy group around,
O Phœbus, in thy laureate mead,
Thy temple, shall the victim bleed.
Let Hymen, Hymen, Hymen, sound.
My mother, for the dance prepare,
Vault nimbly, and our revels share.
At Hymen's shrine, my friends, prolong
Your vows, awake th' ecstatic song;
In honour of my bridal day,
Chant, Phrygian nymphs, the choral lay,
And celebrate the chief whom fate
Ordains to be Cassandra's mate.

CHOR. Wilt thou not stop the princess, lest she rush
With frantic step amid the Grecian host?

HEC. O Vulcan, wont to light the bridal torch,
Now dost thou brandish an accursed flame;
My soul foresaw not this. Alas! my daughter,
I little thought, that 'midst the din of arms,
Or while we crouch beneath the Argive spear,
Thou couldst have celebrated such espousals.
Give me the torch, for while with frantic speed
Thou rushest on, it trembles in thy hand.
Nor yet have thy afflictions, O my daughter,
Brought back thy wandering reason, thou remain'st
Disordered as before. Ye Trojan dames,
Remove yon blazing pines, and in the stead
Of these her bridal songs let tears express
The anguish of your souls.

CAS. O mother, place
A laureate wreath on my victorious brow,
Exulting lead me to the monarch's bed.
And if for thee too slowly I advance,
Drag me along by force; for I am now
No more the spouse of Phœbus; but that king
Of Greece, famed Agamemnon, shall in me
Take to his arms a bride more inauspicious

Than even Helen's self: him will I smite,
And lay his palace waste, in great revenge
For my slain sire and brothers. But I cease
These menaces, and speak not of the axe
Which shall smite me and others, or the conflict
My wedlock shall produce, whence by the hands
Of her own son a mother shall be slain,
And th' overthrow of Atreus' guilty house.
This city will I prove to have been happier
Than the victorious Greeks (for though the gods
Inspire, I curb the transports of my soul),
Who for one single woman, to regain
The beauteous Helen only, wasted lives
Unnumbered. Their wise leader, in the cause
Of those he hated, slew whom most he loved;
He to his brother yielded up his daughter,
Joy of his house, for that vile woman's sake,
Who with her own consent, and not by force,
Was borne away. But at Scamander's banks
When they arrived, they died, though not by exile
Torn from their country, or their native towers:
But them who in embattled fields were slain
Their children saw not, nor in decent shroud
Were they enwrapped by their loved consorts' hands,
But lie deserted on a foreign coast:
Their sorrows also who remained at home
Are similar; in widowhood forlorn
Some die; and others, of their own brave sons
Deprived, breed up the children of a stranger;
Nor at their slighted tombs is blood poured forth
To drench the thirsty ground. Their host deserves
Praises like these. 'Tis better not to speak
Of what is infamous, nor shall my Muse
Record the shameful tale. But, first and greatest
Of glories, in their country's cause expired
The Trojans; the remains of those who fell
In battle, by their friends borne home, obtained
Sepulchral honours in their native soil,
That duteous office kindred hands performed:
While every Phrygian who escaped the sword
Still with his wife and children did reside,
Joy to the Greeks unknown. Now hear the fate
Of Hector, him whom thou bewail'st, esteemed
The bravest of our heroes, by the Greeks
Landing on Ilion's coast the warrior fell;
In their own country had the foe remained,
His valour ne'er had been displayed: but Paris
Wedded the daughter of imperial Jove,
In her possessing an illustrious bride.

It is the wise man's duty to avoid
Perilous war. After the die is cast,
He who undaunted meets the fatal stroke,
Adds to his native city fair renown;
But the last moments of a coward shame
The land which gave him birth. Forbear to weep,
My mother, for thy ruined country's fate;
Weep not because thou seest thy daughter borne
To Agamemnon's bed, for by these spousals
Our most inveterate foes shall I destroy.

CHOR. How sweetly 'midst the sorrows of thy house
Thou smil'st! ere long perchance wilt thou afford
A melancholy instance that thy strains
Are void of truth.

TAL. Had not Apollo fired
E'en to distraction thy perverted soul,
Thou on my honoured leader, ere he quit
The shores of Ilion, shouldst not unavenged
Pour forth these omens. But, alas! the great,
And they who in th' opinion of mankind
Are wise, in no respect excel the vulgar.
For the dread chieftain of the Grecian host,
The son of Atreus, loves with boundless passion
This damsel frantic as the Mænades.
Myself am poor, yet would not I accept
A wife like her. Since thou hast lost thy reason,
I to the winds consign thy bitter taunts
'Gainst Argos, with the praises thou bestow'st
On Troy. Thou bride of Agamemnon, come,
Follow me to the fleet. But when Ulysses
Would bear you hence, O Hecuba, obey
The summons, you are destined to attend
A queen called virtuous by all those who come
To Ilion.

CAS. Arrogant, detested slave!
All heralds are like thee, the public scorn,
Crouching with abject deference to some king
Or city. Say'st thou, "To Ulysses' house
My mother shall be borne?" Of what account
Were then the oracles Apollo gave
Uttered by me his priestess, which declare,
"She here shall die?" I spare the shameful tale.
He knows not, the unhappy Ithacus,
What evils yet await him, in the tears
Of me and every captive Phrygian maid,
While he exults, and deems our misery gain.
Ten more long years elapsed beyond the term
Spent in besieging Ilion, he alone
Shall reach his country; witness thou who dwell'st

'Midst ocean's straits tempestuous, dire Charybdis,
Ye mountains where on human victims feast
The Cyclops, with Ligurian Circe's isle,
Whose wand transforms to swine, the billowy deep,
Covered with shipwrecks, the bewitching Lotus,
The sacred Oxen of the Sun, whose flesh
Destined to utter a tremendous voice
The banquet shall embitter: he at length,
In a few words his history to comprise,
Alive must travel to the shades beneath,
And hardly 'scaping from a watery grave
In his own house find evils numberless.
But why do I recount Ulysses' toils?
Lead on, that I the sooner in the realms
Of Pluto, with that bridegroom may consummate
My nuptials. Ruthless miscreant as thou art,
Thou in the tomb ignobly shalt be plunged
At midnight; nor shall the auspicious beams
Of day illumine thy funereal rites,
O leader of the Grecian host, who deem'st
That thou a mighty conquest hast achieved.
Near to my lord's remains, and in that vale,
Where down a precipice the torrent foams,
My corse shall to the hungry wolves be thrown,
The corse of Phœbus' priestess. O ye wreaths
Of him whom best of all the gods I loved,
Adieu, ye symbols of my holy office,
I leave those feasts the scenes of past delight,
Torn from my brows avaunt, for I retain
My chastity unsullied still; the winds
To thee shall waft them, O prophetic king.
Where is your general's bark, which I am doomed
T' ascend? the rising breezes shall unfurl
Your sails this instant; for in me ye bear
One of the three Eumenides from Troy.
Farewell, my mother, weep not for my fate,
O my dear country, my heroic brothers,
And aged father, in the realms beneath,
Ere long shall ye receive me: but victorious
Will I descend among the mighty dead,
When I have laid th' accursed mansions waste
Of our destroyers, Atreus' impious sons.
            [*Exeunt* CASSANDRA *and* TALTHYBIUS.

CHOR. Attendants of the aged Hecuba,
Behold ye not your mistress, how she falls
Upon the pavement speechless? Why neglect
To prop her sinking frame! Ye slothful nymphs,
Raise up this woman, whom a weight of years
Bows to the dust.

HEC.   Away, and on this spot
Allow me, courteous damsels, to remain:
No longer welcome as in happier days
Are your kind offices; this humble posture,
This fall best suits my present lowly state,
Best suits what I already have endured
And still am doomed to suffer. O ye gods,
In you I call upon no firm allies,
Yet sure 'tis decent to invoke the gods
When we by adverse fortune are opprest.
First, therefore, all the blessings I enjoyed
Would I recount, hence shall my woes demand
The greater pity. Born to regal state,
And with a mighty king in wedlock joined,
A race of valiant sons did I produce;
I speak not of their numbers, but the noblest
Among the Phrygian youths, such as no Trojan,
Nor Grecian, nor barbarian dame could boast:
Them saw I fall beneath the hostile spear,
And at their tomb these tresses cut: their sire,
The venerable Priam, I bewailed not,
From being told of his calamitous fate
By others, but these eyes beheld him slain,
E'en at the altar of Hercæan Jove,
And Ilion taken. I those blooming maids
Have also lost, whom with maternal love
I nurtured for some noble husband's bed;
They from these arms are torn: nor can I hope
Or to be seen by them, or e'er to see
My children more. But last of all, to crown
My woes, an aged slave, shall I be borne
To Greece; and in such tasks will they employ me
As are most grievous in the wane of life;
Me, who am Hector's mother, at the door
Stationed to keep the keys, or knead the bread,
And on the pavement stretch my withered limbs,
Which erst reposed upon a regal couch,
And in such tattered vestments, as belie
My former rank, enwrap my wasted frame.
Wretch that I am, who, through one woman's nuptials,
Have borne, and am hereafter doomed to bear,
Such dreadful ills. O my unhappy daughter,
Cassandra, whom the gods have rendered frantic,
With what sad omens hath thy virgin zone
Been loosed! and where, Polyxena, art thou,
O virgin most unfortunate? but none
Of all my numerous progeny, or male
Or female, comes to aid their wretched mother.
Why, therefore, would ye lift me up? what room

Is there for hope? me who with tender foot
Paced through the streets of Troy, but now a slave,
Drag from the palace to the rushy mat
And stony pillow, that where'er I fall
There may I die, through many, many tears
Exhausted.   Of the prosperous and the great
Pronounce none happy till the hour of death.

CHORUS.
ODE.

I.

Prepare, O Muse, prepare a song
Expressive of the fall of Troy;
The sympathetic dirge prolong
And banish every note of joy.
I with loud voice of Ilion's fate will speak,
  Sing how the foe our ramparts stormed
  Through the machine their treachery formed,
The vehicle of many a daring Greek,
Who burst like thunder from that wooden steed,
With gorgeous trappings graced, in mimic state,
Concealing armed bands, which passed the Scæan gate,
  They whom such semblance could mislead,
    The unsuspecting crowd,
  As on Troy's citadel they stood,
    Exclaimed; "Henceforth our toils shall cease,
  Come on, and to Minerva's fane convey
    This holy image, pledge of peace."
What veteran paused? what youth but led the way?
Enlivening songs breathed round in notes so sweet,
That gladly they received the pestilential cheat.

II.

Then did all Phrygia's race combine
  Through their devoted gates to bear,
  Enclosed in the stupendous pine
The fraud of Greece, that latent snare,
To glut Minerva with Dardanian blood,
  To pacify th' immortal maid,
  They the huge mass with ropes conveyed;
Thus the tall bark, into the briny flood
Too ponderous to be borne, is rolled along:
  Till they had lodged it in th' ill-omened fane
Of her to whom we owe our ruined country's bane.
  After their toil and festive song,
    The cloud-wrapped evening spread
    Her veil o'er each devoted head,
  Shrill Phrygian voices did resound,

And Libya's flutes accompanied the choir,
  While nymphs high vaulting from the ground,
  Mixed their applauses with the chorded lyre,
  And from each hearth the flames with radiance bright,
While heedless warriors slept, dispelled the shades of night.

III.

Then o'er the genial board, to her who reigns
In woodland heights, Diana, child of Jove,
  I waked the choral strains.
  But soon there flew a dismal sound
  Pergamus' wide streets around:
  The shrieking infant fondly strove
To grasp the border of a mother's vest,
And with uplifted hands its little fears expressed:
  Mars from his ambush by Minerva's aid
Conspicuous issued and the fray began,
  Thick gore adown our altars ran,
And many a slaughtered youth was laid
  A headless trunk on the disfigured bed,
That Greece might shine with laureate wreaths arrayed,
  By Troy while fruitless tears are shed.

Andromache, Hecuba, Chorus.

Chor. Seest thou, Andromache, O queen, this way
Advancing, wafted in a foreign car?
Eager to cling to the maternal breast
Close follows her beloved Astyanax,
The son of Hector.
  Hec.   Whither art thou borne,
O wretched woman, on a chariot placed
'Midst Hector's brazen armour, and those spoils
From captive Phrygian chiefs in combat torn,
With which Achilles' son from Ilion's siege
Triumphant, will the Phthian temples grace?
  And. Our Grecian masters drag me hence.
  Hec.   Alas!
  And. Why with your groans my anguish strive t' assuage?
  Hec. Oh!
  And.   I by griefs am compassed——
  Hec.   Mighty Jove!
  And. And dread vicissitudes of fate.
  Hec.   My children.
  And. We once were blest.
  Hec.   Now are those prosperous days
No more; and Ilion is no more.
  And.   Most wretched!
  Hec. My noble sons.
  And.   Alas!

HEC. Alas my——
AND. Woes.
HEC. O piteous fortune——
AND. Of the city——
HEC. Wrapt
In smoke.
AND. Return, my husband, O return,
HEC. In clamorous accents thou invok'st my son,
Whom Pluto's realms detain, unhappy woman.
AND. Thy consort's tutelary power.
HEC. And thou,
Whose courage long withstood the Grecian host,
Thou aged father of our numerous race,
Lead me, O Priam, to the shades beneath.
AND. Presumptuous are such wishes.
HEC. We endure
These grievous woes.
CHOR. While ruin overwhelms
Our city, for on sorrows have been heaped
Fresh sorrows, through the will of angry Heaven,
Since in an evil hour thy son was snatched
From Pluto, who, determined to avenge
Those execrable nuptials, with the ground
Hath levelled Pergamus' beleaguered towers.
Near Pallas' shrine the corses of the slain
Weltering in gore to vultures lie exposed,
And Ilion droops beneath the servile yoke.
Thee, O my wretched country, I with tears
Forsake: e'en now thou view'st the piteous end
Of all thy woes, and my loved native house.
HEC. My children! O my desolated city!
Your mother is bereft of every joy.
CHOR. What shrieks, what plaints resound! what floods of tears
Stream in our houses! but the dead forget
Their sorrows, and for ever cease to weep.
HEC. To those who suffer, what a sweet relief
Do tears afford! the sympathetic Muse
Inspires their plaints.
AND. O mother of that chief,
Whose forceful javelin thinned the ranks of Greece,
Illustrious Hector, seest thou this?
HEC. I see
The gods delight in raising up the low,
And ruining the great.
AND. Hence with my son,
A captive am I hurried; noble birth
Subject to these vicissitudes now sinks
Into degrading slavery.

THE TROJAN CAPTIVES.

HEC.   Uncontrolled
The power of fate: Cassandra from these arms
But now with brutal violence was torn!
    AND. A second Ajax to thy daughter seems
To have appeared. Yet hast thou other griefs.
    HEC. All bounds, all numbers they exceed; with ills
Fresh ills as for pre-eminence contend.
    AND. Polyxena, thy daughter, at the tomb
Of Peleus' son hath breathed her last, a gift
To the deceased.
    HEC.   Wretch that I am, alas!
Too clearly now I understand the riddle
Which in obscurer terms Talthybius uttered.
    AND. I saw her bleed, and lighting from this car
Covered her with the decent shroud and wailed
O'er her remains.
    HEC.   Alas! alas! my child
To bloody altars dragged by impious hands,
Alas! alas! how basely wert thou slain!
    AND. Most dreadfully she perished; yet her lot
Who perished is more enviable than mine.
    HEC. Far different, O my daughter, is the state
Of them who live, from them who breathe no more:
For the deceased are nothing: but fair hope,
While life remains, can never be extinct.
    AND. Thou whom, although I sprung not from thy womb,
I deem a mother, to my cheering words
With patience listen, they will yield delight
To thy afflicted soul. 'Tis the same thing
Ne'er to be born, or die; but better far
To die, than to live wretched: for no sorrow
Affects th' unconscious tenant of the grave.
But he who once was happy, he who falls
From fortune's summit down the vale of woe,
With an afflicted spirit wanders o'er
The scenes of past delight. In the cold grave,
Like one who never saw the blessed sun,
Polyxena remembers not her woes.
But I who aimed the dextrous shaft, and gained
An ample portion of renown, have missed
The mark of happiness. In Hector's house
I acted as behoves each virtuous dame.
First, whether sland'rous tongues assail or spare
The matron's chastity, an evil name,
Her who remains not at her home, pursues:
Such vain desires I therefore quelled, I stayed
In my own chamber, a domestic life
Preferring, and forbore to introduce
Vain sentimental language, such as gains

Too oft the ear of woman: 'twas enough
For me to yield obedience to the voice
Of virtue, that best monitor. My lord
With placid aspect and a silent tongue
I still received, for I that province knew
In which I ought to rule, and when to yield
Submission to a husband's will. The fame
This conduct gained me, reached the Grecian camp,
And proved my ruin: for when I became
A captive, Neoptolemus resolved
To take me to his bed, and in the house
Of murderers I to slavery am consigned.
If shaking off my Hector's loved remembrance
To this new husband I my soul incline,
I shall appear perfidious to the dead ;
Or, if I hate Achilles' son, become
Obnoxious to my lords ; though some assert
That one short night can reconcile th' aversion
Of any woman to the nuptial couch ;
I scorn that widow, reft of her first lord,
Who listens to the voice of love, and weds
Another. From her comrade torn, the mare
Sustains the yoke reluctant, though a brute
Dumb and irrational, by nature formed
Subordinate to man : but I in thee
Possessed a husband, O my dearest Hector,
In wisdom, fortune, and illustrious birth,
For me sufficient, great in martial deeds :
A spotless virgin-bride, me from the house
Of my great father, didst thou first receive ;
But thou art slain, and I to Greece must sail
A captive, and endure the servile yoke!
Is not the death of that Polyxena,
Whom thou, O Hecuba, bewail'st, an ill
More tolerable than those which I endure ?
For hope, who visits every wretch beside,
To me ne'er comes ; to me no promised joys
Afford a flattering prospect to deceive
This anxious bosom ; for 'tis sweet to think
E'en of ideal bliss.

CHOR.   Thou art involved
In the same sufferings, and in plaintive notes
Bewailing thy calamity, inform'st me
What treatment to expect.

HEC.   I ne'er did mount
A ship, yet I from pictures and report
These matters know : amidst a moderate storm,
Such as they hope to weather out, the sailors
To save themselves, exert a cheerful toil :

This to the rudder, to the shattered sails
That goes, a third laborious at the pump
Draws off the rising waters; but if vanquished
By the tempestuous ocean's rage, they yield
To fortune, and consigning to the waves
Their vessel, are at random driven along.
Thus I am mute beneath unnumbered woes,
Nor can this tongue expatiate, for the gods
Such torrents pour as drown my feeble voice!
But, O my daughter, cease to name the fate
Of slaughtered Hector, whom no tears can save.
Pay due attention to thy present lord,
With amorous glances and a fond compliance
Receiving him; act thus, and thou wilt cheer
Our friends, and this my grandson educate
A bulwark to fallen Ilion, that his race
The city may rebuild, and dwell in Troy.
But a fresh topic of discourse ensues.
What servant of the Greeks do I behold
Again draw near, t' announce some new design?

TALTHYBIUS, ANDROMACHE, HECUBA, CHORUS.

TAL. O thou who erst wert Hector's wife, that bravest
Of Phrygians, hate me not; for with reluctance
Will I the general sentence of the Greeks
And Pelops' progeny, announce.
 AND.   What means
This evil prelude.
 TAL.   'Tis decreed thy son—
How shall I speak it?
 AND.   To a separate lord
Shall be consigned?
 TAL.   None of the Grecian chiefs
Shall ever o'er Astyanax bear rule.
 AND. Must I leave here, him who alone remains
Of all that erst was dear to me in Troy?
 TAL. Alas! I know not in what terms t' express
The miseries that await thee?
 AND.   I commend
Such modesty, provided thou canst speak
Aught to afford me comfort.
 TAL.   They resolve
To slay thy son; thou hear'st my dismal errand.
 AND. Ah me! thou hast unfolded to these ears
An evil, greater than my menaced spousals.
 TAL. By his harangues to the assembled Greeks,
Ulysses hath prevailed.
 AND.   Alas! alas!
Immoderate are the sorrows I endure.

TAL. Saying they ought not to train up the son
Of that heroic sire.
    AND.   May he obtain
O'er his own children triumphs great as these!
    TAL. He from the towers of Ilion must be thrown:
But I entreat thee, and thou hence shall seem
More prudent, strive not to withhold thy son,
But bear thy woes with firmness; nor, though weak,
Deem thyself strong; for thou hast no support,
And therefore must consider that thy city
Is overthrown, thy husband is no more,
Thou art reduced to servitude; and we
Are strong enough to combat with one woman:
O therefore brave not this unequal strife,
Stoop not to aught that's base, nor yet revile,
Nor idly scatter curses on thy foes;
For if thou utter aught that may provoke
The anger of the host, thy son will bleed
Unburied and unwept: but if thou bear
With silence and composure thy misfortunes,
Funereal honours shall adorn his grave,
And Greece to thee her lenity extend.
    AND. Thee, O my dearest son, thy foes will slay;
Soon art thou doomed to leave thy wretched mother.
What saves the lives of others, the renown
Of an illustrious sire, to thee will prove
The cause of death: by this paternal fame
Art thou attended in an evil hour.
To me how luckless proved the genial bed,
And those espousals, that to Hector's house
First brought me, when I trusted I should bear
A son, no victim to the ruthless Greeks,
But an illustrious Asiatic king.
Weep'st thou, my son? dost thou perceive thy woes?
Why cling to me with timid hands? Why seize
My garment? thus beneath its mother's wings
The callow bird is sheltered. From the tomb,
No Hector brandishing his massive spear
Rushes to saves thee; no intrepid kinsman
Of thy departed father, nor the might
Of Phrygian hosts is here: but from aloof
Borne headlong by a miserable leap,
Shalt thou pour forth thy latest gasp of life
Unpitied. Tender burden in the arms
Of thy fond mother! what ambrosial odours
Breathed from thy lips? I swathed thee to my breast
In vain, I toiled in vain, and wore away
My strength with fruitless labours. Yet embrace
Thy mother once again; around my neck
Entwine thine arms, and give one parting kiss.

Ye Greeks, who studiously invent new modes
Of unexampled cruelty, why slay
This guiltless infant? Helen, O thou daughter
Of Tyndarus, never didst thou spring from Jove,
But I pronounce thee born of many sires,
An evil Genius, Envy, Slaughter, Death,
And every evil that from Earth receives
Its nourishment; nor dare I to assert
That Jove himself begot a pest like thee,
Fatal to Greece and each barbarian chief.
Perdition overtake thee! for those eyes
By their seducing glances have o'erthrown
The Phrygian empire. Bear this child away,
And cast him from the turrets if ye list,
Then banquet on his quivering flesh: the gods
Ordain that I shall perish: nor from him
Can I repel the stroke of death. Conceal
This wretched form from public view, and plunge me
In the ship's hold; for I have lost my son,
Such the blest prelude to my nuptial rite.

CHOR. Thy myriads, hapless Ilion, did expire
In combat for one woman, to maintain
Paris' accursed espousals.

AND. Cease, my child,
Fondly to lisp thy wretched mother's name,
Ascend the height of thy paternal towers,
Whence 'tis by Greece decreed thy parting breath
Shall issue. Take him hence. Aloud proclaim
This deed ye merciless: that wretch alone
Who never knew the blush of virtuous shame,
Your sentence can applaud.

[*Exeunt* ANDROMACHE *and* TALTHYBIUS.

HEC. O child, thou son
Of my unhappy Hector, from thy mother
And me thou unexpectedly art torn.
What can I do, what help afford? for thee
I smite this head, this miserable breast;
Thus far my power extends. Alas! thou city,
And, O my grandson! is there yet a curse
Beyond what we have felt? remains there aught
To save us from the yawning gulf of ruin?

CHORUS.

ODE.

I. I.

In Salamis' profound retreat
Famed for the luscious treasures of the bee,
High raised above th' encircling sea
Thou, Telamon, didst fix thy regal seat;

Near to those sacred hills, where spread
The olive first its fragrant sprays,
To form a garland for Minerva's head,
And the Athenian splendor raise:
With the famed archer, with Alcmena's son
Thou cam'st exulting with vindictive joy;
By your confederate arms was Ilion won,
When from thy Greece thou cam'st our city to destroy.

I. 2.

Repining for the promised steeds,
From Greece Alcides led a chosen band,
With hostile prows th' indented strand
He reached, and anchored near fair Simois' meads;
Selected from each ship, he led
Those who with dextrous hand could wing
Th' unerring shaft, till slaughter reached thy head,
Laomedon, thou perjured king:
Those battlements which Phœbus' self did rear
The victor wasted with devouring flame;
Twice o'er Troy's walls hath waved the hostile spear,
Twice have insulting shouts announced Dardania's shame.

II. I.

Thou bear'st the sparkling wine in vain
With step effeminate, O Phrygian boy,
Erewhile didst thou approach with joy
To fill the goblet of imperial Jove;
For now thy Troy lies levelled with the plain,
And its thick smoke ascends the realms above.
On th' echoing coast our plaints we vent,
As feathered songsters o'er their young bewail,
A child or husband these lament,
And those behold their captive mothers sail:
The founts where thou didst bathe, th' athletic sports,
Are now no more. Each blooming grace
Sheds charms unheeded o'er thy placid face,
And thou frequent'st Heaven's splendid courts.
Triumphant Greece hath levelled in the dust
The throne where Priam ruled the virtuous and the just.

II. 2.

With happier auspices, O love,
Erst didst thou hover o'er this fruitful plain,
Hence caught the gods thy thrilling pain;
By thee embellished, Troy's resplendent towers
Reared their proud summits blest by thundering Jove,
For our allies were the celestial powers,
But I no longer will betray

Heaven's ruler to reproach and biting shame.
    The white-winged morn, blest source of day,
Who cheers the nations with her kindling flame,
Beheld these walls demolished, and th' abode
    Of that dear prince who shared her bed
In fragments o'er the wasted champaign spread:
    While swift along the starry road,
Her golden car his country's guardian bore:
False was each amorous god, and Ilion is no more.

MENELAUS, HECUBA, CHORUS.

MEN. Hail, O ye solar beams, who on this day,
When I my consort Helen shall regain
Your radiance shed. For I am he who long
Endured the toils of battle, Menelaus,
Attended by the Grecian host. To Troy,
Not in a woman's cause, as many deem,
I came, but came to punish him who broke
The laws of hospitality, and ravished
My consort from my palace. He hath suffered
As he deserved, such was the will of Heaven,
He and his country by the spear of Greece
Have been destroyed. But I am come to bear
That Spartan dame away, whom with regret
I term my consort, though she once was mine.
But she beneath these tents is with the rest
Of Phrygia's captives numbered: for the troops
Whose arms redeemed her, have to me consigned
That I might either take away, or spare
Her life, and waft her to the Argive coast.
I am resolved that Helen shall not bleed
In Troy, but o'er the foaming waves to Greece
Will I convey her, and to them whose friends
Before yon walls were slain, surrender up
To perish by their vengeance. But with speed
Enter the tent, thence by that hair defiled
With murder, O my followers, drag her forth,
And hither bring: for when a prosperous breeze
Arises, her will I to Greece convey.

HEC. O thou who mov'st the world, and in this earth
Hast fixed thy station, whosoe'er thou art,
Impervious to our reason, whether thou,
O Jove, art dread necessity which rules
All nature, or that soul which animates
The breasts of mortals, thee do I adore,
For in a silent path thou tread'st and guid'st
With justice the affairs of man.

MEN.   What means

This innovation in the solemn prayer
You to the gods address?
  HEC.   I shall applaud
The stroke, O Menelaus, if thou slay
Thy wife; but soon as thou behold'st her, fly,
Lest she with love ensnare thee. For the eyes
Of men she captivates, o'erturns whole cities,
And fires the roofs of lofty palaces,
She is possessed of such resistless charms;
Both I and thou and thousands to their cost,
Alas! are sensible how great her power.

  HELEN, MENELAUS, HECUBA, CHORUS.

  HEL. O Menelaus, this is sure a prelude
To greater horrors. For with brutal hands
I by your servants from these tents am dragged?
Too well I know you hate me, yet would learn,
How you and Greece have of my life disposed.
  MEN. Thou by the utmost rigour of the laws
Hast not been sentenced; but the host, to me
Whom thou hast wronged, consign thee to be slain.
  HEL. May not I answer to these harsh resolves,
That if I bleed, unjustly shall I bleed?
  MEN. I came not hither to debate, but slay thee?
  HEC. Hear her, nor let her die, O Menelaus,
Without this privilege. Me too allow
To make reply to her defence; for nought
Of the foul deeds, which she in Troy committed
Yet know'st thou: if united, the whole tale
Must force thee to destroy her, and preclude
All means of her escaping.
  MEN.   An indulgence
Like this supposes leisure to attend;
However, if she have a wish to speak,
She may: but be assured, that my compliance
To your request is owing, for such favour
To her I would not grant.
  HEL.   Perhaps with me
Whom you account a foe, you will not deign,
Whether I seem to utter truth or falsehood,
To parley. But to each malignant charge
With which, O Hecuba, I know thou com'st
Prepared against me, will I make reply,
And to o'erbalance all that thou canst urge
Produce recriminations. First, she bore
Paris, the author of these mischiefs, next
Did aged Priam ruin Troy and me,
When erst that infant he forbore to slay,
That baleful semblance of a flaming torch!

Hear what ensued; by Paris were the claims
Of the three rival goddesses decided.
The gift Minerva proffered; that commanding
The Phrygians, he should conquer Greece; while Juno
Promised, that he his empire should extend
From Asia to remotest Europe's bounds,
If he to her adjudged the golden prize;
But Venus, who in rapturous terms extolled
My charms, engaged that as the great reward
She would on him bestow me; to her beauty
If o'er each goddess he the preference gave.
Observe the sequel: Venus, o'er Minerva
And Juno, gained the triumph; and my nuptials
Thus far have been a benefit to Greece;
Ye are not subject to barbarian lords,
Crushed by invasion, or tyrannic power.
But I my ruin owe to what my country
Hath found thus advantageous, for my charms
To Paris sold, and branded with disgrace,
E'en for such deeds as merited a wreath
To crown these brows. But you may urge, that all
I have alleged is of no real weight,
Because by stealth I from your palace fled.
Accompanied by no mean goddess, came
That evil genius, sprung from Hecuba,
Distinguish him by either name you list,
Paris or Alexander, in your house,
Whom, O delirious, you behind you left,
And sailed from Sparta to the Cretan isle.
Well, be it so. Of my own heart, not you
I in regard to all that hence ensued
Will ask the question. What could have induced me,
Following that stranger, to forsake my home,
False to my native land? impute the guilt
To Venus, and assume a power, beyond
E'en that of Jove, who rules th' inferior gods
But yields to her behests. My crime was venial;
Yet hence you may allege a specious charge
Against me; since to earth's dark vaults the corse
Of Paris was consigned, no longer bound
Through Heaven's supreme decree in nuptial chains,
I to the Grecian fleet should have escaped
From Ilion's palace; such was my design:
This can the guards of Troy's beleaguered towers,
And sentinels who on the walls were stationed,
Attest, that oft they caught me, as with ropes
By stealth I strove to light upon the ground;
But a new husband, fierce Deiphobus,
Obtained me for a wife by brutal force,

Though every Phrygian disapproved. What law
Can sentence me, whom 'gainst my will he wedded,
By you, my lord, with justice to be slain?
But for the benefits through me derived
To Greece, I in the stead of laureate wreaths
With slavery am requited. If you wish
To overcome the gods' supreme behests,
That very wish were folly.
  CHOR.   O my Queen,
Assert thy children's and thy country's cause,
'Gainst her persuasive language, for she speaks
With eloquence, though guilty: curst imposture!
  HEC. I those three goddesses will first defend,
And prove that she has uttered vile untruths:
For of such madness ne'er can I suspect
Juno and Pallas that immortal maid,
As that the first should to barbarian tribes
Propose to sell her Argos, or Minerva
To make her Athens subject to the Phrygians:
Seeking in sportive strife the palm of beauty
They came to Ida's mount. For through what motive
Could Juno with such eagerness have wished
Her charms might triumph? to obtain a husband
Greater than Jove? could Pallas, who besought
Her sire she ever might remain a virgin,
Propose to wed some deity? Forbear
To represesent these goddesses as foolish,
That thy transgressions may by their example
Be justified: thou never canst persuade
The wise. Thou hast presumed t' assert (but this
Was a ridiculous pretence) that Venus
Came with my son to Menelaus' house.
Could she not calmly have abode in Heaven,
Yet wafted thee and all Amycla's city
To Ilion? but the beauty of my son
Was great, and thy own heart, when thou beheld'st him
Became thy Venus: for whatever folly
Prevails, is th' Aphrodite of mankind:
That of Love's goddess, justly doth commence
With the same letters as an idiot's name.
Him didst thou see in a barbaric vest
With gold refulgent, and thy wanton heart
Was thence inflamed with love, for thou wert poor
While yet thou didst reside in Greece; but leaving
The Spartan regions, thou didst hope, the city
Of Troy, with gold o'erflowing, could support
Thy prodigality; for the revenues
Of Menelaus far too scanty proved
For thy luxuriant appetites: but sayst thou

That Paris bore thee thence by force? what Spartan
Saw this? or, with what cries didst thou invoke
Castor or Pollux, thy immortal brothers,
Who yet on earth remained, nor had ascended
The starry height? But since thou cam'st to Troy,
And hither the confederate troops of Greece
Tracing thy steps, began the bloody strife,
Whene'er thou heard'st that Menelaus prospered
Him didst thou praise, and make my son to grieve
That such a mighty rival shared thy love:
But if the Trojan army proved victorious,
He shrunk into a thing of nought. On Fortune
Still didst thou look, still deaf to Virtue's call
Follow her banners: yet dost thou assert
That thou by cords hast from the lofty towers
In secrecy attempted to descend,
As if thou here hadst been constrained to stay?
Where then wert thou surprised, or sharpened sword,
Or ropes preparing, as each generous dame
Who sought her former husband would have done?
Oft have I counselled thee in many words:
"Depart, O daughter, that my sons may take
Brides less obnoxious:- thee aboard the ships
Of Greece, assisting in thy secret flight,
Will I convey. O end the war 'twixt Greece
And Ilion." But to thee was such advice
Unwelcome; for with pride thou in the house
Of Paris didst behave thyself, and claim
The adoration of barbaric tribes,
For this was thy great object. But e'en now
Thy charms displaying, clad in gorgeous vest
Dost thou go forth, still daring to behold
That canopy of Heaven which o'erhangs
Thy injured husband; thou detested woman!
Whom it had suited, if in tattered vest
Shivering, with tresses shorn, in Scythian guise
Thou hadst appeared, and for transgressions past
Deep smitten with remorse, assumed the blush
Of virtuous matrons, not that frontless air.
O Menelaus! I will now conclude;
By slaying her, prepare for Greece the wreaths
It merits, and extend to the whole sex
This law, that every woman who betrays
Her lord shall die.

  CHOR.   As that illustrious stem
Whence thou deriv'st thy birth, and as thy rank
Demand, on thy adulterous wife inflict
Just punishment, and purge this foul reproach,
This instance of a woman's lust, from Greece:

So shall thy very enemies perceive
Thou art magnanimous.
  MEN.   Your thoughts concur
With mine, that she a willing fugitive
My palace left and sought a foreign bed;
But speaks of Venus merely to disguise
Her infamy!—Away! thou shalt be stoned,
And in one instant for the tedious woes
Of Greece make full atonement; I will teach thee
That thou didst shame me in an evil hour.
  HEL. I by those knees entreat you, O forbear
To slay me, that distraction sent by Heaven
To me imputing: but forgive me.
  HEC.   Wrong not
Thy partners in the war, whom she hath slain;
In theirs, and in my children's cause, I sue.
  MEN. Desist, thou hoary matron: her entreaties
Move not this steadfast bosom. O my followers
Attend her, I command you, to the ships
Which shall convey her hence.
  HEC.   Let her not enter
Thy ship.
  MEN. Is she grown heavier than before?
  HEC. He never loved who doth not always love,
Howe'er the inclinations of the dame
He loves may fluctuate.
  MEN.   All shall be performed
According to thy wish; she shall not enter
My bark: for thou hast uttered wholesome counsels:
But soon as she in Argos' lands, with shame,
As she deserves, shall she be slain, and warn
All women to be chaste. No easy task:
Yet shall her ruin startle every child
Of folly, though more vicious still than Helen.

CHORUS.

ODE.

I. 1.

E'en thus by too severe a doom,
 To Greece, O Jove, hast thou betrayed
Our shrines, our altars, dropping rich perfume,
The lambent flame that round the victims played,
 Myrrh's odorous smoke that mounts the skies,
Yon holy citadel, with Ida's grove
Around whose oaks the clasping ivy plies,
 Where rivulets meandering rove

Cold and translucent from the drifted snows;
   On that high ridge with orient blaze
The sun first scatters his enlivening rays,
And with celestial flame th' ecstatic priestess glows.

I. 2.

   Each sacrifice, each pious rite,
     Hence vanished, with th' harmonious choirs
Whose accents soothed the languid ear of night,
While to the gods we waked our sounding lyres;
     Their golden images no more
Twelve times each year, on that revolving eve
When shines the full-orbed moon, do we adore.
     Harassed by anxious fears, I grieve,
Oft thinking whether thou, O Jove, wilt deign
     To listen to our piteous moan,
High as thou sitt'st on thy celestial throne;
For Troy, by fire consumed, lies level with the plain.

II. 1.

Thou, O my husband, roam'st a flitting shade,
To thee are all funereal rites denied,
     To thee no lustral drops supplied:
But I by the swift bark shall be conveyed
     Where Argos' cloud-capped fortress stands,
Erected by the Cyclops' skilful hands.
Before our doors assembling children groan,
     And oft repeat with clamorous moan
A mother's name. Alone shall I be borne
Far from thy sight, by the victorious host
     Of Greece, and leaving Ilion's coast,
O'er ocean's azure billows sail forlorn,
Either to Salamis, that sacred land,
Or where the Isthmian summit o'er two seas
A wide extended prospect doth command,
Seated in Pelops' straits where Greece the prize decrees.

II. 2.

Its arduous voyage more than half complete,
In the Ægean deep, and near the land,
     May the red lightning by Jove's hand
Winged from the skies with tenfold ruin, meet
     The bark that wafts me o'er the wave
From Troy to Greece a miserable slave.
Before the golden mirror wont to braid
     Her tresses, like a sportive maid,
May Helen never reach the Spartan shore,
Those household gods to whom she proved untrue,
     Nor her paternal mansions view,

Enter the streets of Pitane no more,
Nor Pallas' temple with its brazen gate;
Because her nuptials teemed with foul disgrace
To mighty Greece through each confederate state;
And hence on Simois' banks were slain Troy's guiltless race

But ha! on this devoted realm are hurled
Successive woes. Ye hapless Phrygian dames,
Behold the slain Astyanax, whom Greece
With rage inhuman from yon towers hath thrown.

TALTHYBIUS, HECUBA, CHORUS.

The Body of ASTYANAX *borne in upon a Shield.*

TAL. O Hecuba, one ship is left behind
To carry the remainder of the spoils
Which to Achilles' son have been adjudged,
To Phthia's coast. For Neoptolemus,
Hearing that recent evils hath befall'n
His grandsire Peleus, and that Pelias' son
Acastus hath expelled him from his realm,
Already hath departed with such speed
As would admit of no delay: with him
Andromache is gone, for whom I shed
A stream of tears, when from the land she went
Wailing her country, and to Hector's tomb
Her plaints addressing: the victorious chief
Hath she entreated, to allow the corse
Of your unhappy Hector's son, who perished
From Ilion's ramparts thrown, to be interred,
Nor bear this shield, the terror of the Greeks,
With brass refulgent, which his father placed
Before his flank in battle, to the house
Of Peleus; nor to that ill-omened chamber
Where spousals dire on her arrival wait
The mother of the slain; for such an object
Must grieve her to behold: but in the stead
Of cedar and the monumental stone,
Bury the child in this: for she the corse
Hath to your arms consigned, that you may grace it
With many a fragrant garland, and with vests
Such as your present fortunes will afford.
For she has sailed, and through his haste her lord
Prevented her from lodging in the grave
Her son. While thus you his remains adorn
We will mark out the spot, and with our spears
Dig up the ground. Without delay perform
These duties: I one task to you most irksome
Have rendered needless: for I laved the body,

And cleansed the wounds as o'er Scamander's stream
I passed. But to prepare for the deceased
A tomb, I go, that with united toil
When this we have accomplished, they may steer
Our vessel homeward.   [*Exit* TALTHYBIUS.
   HEC.   Place that orbed shield
Of Hector on the ground, a spectacle
Most piteous, and unwelcome to these eyes.
How, O ye Greeks, whose abject souls belie
Your brave achievements, trembling at a child,
Could ye commit this unexampled murder,
Lest at some future time he should rebuild
The walls of Ilion? Ye inhuman cowards!
Our ruin from that fatal hour we date
When Hector with unnumbered heroes fell.
But having sacked our city, and destroyed
Each Phrygian warrior, feared ye such an infant
The dastard I abhor who meanly shrinks
Through groundless panic. O for ever loved,
By what a piteous fate didst thou expire!
Hadst thou, the champion of thy country, died,
In riper years, when married, and endued
With power scarce second to th' immortal gods,
Thou hadst been blest, if aught on earth deserves
The name of bliss: But thou, my son, beheld'st
And hadst a distant knowledge of these joys,
Which thou didst ne'er experience: for to thee
The treasures which the palaces of Troy
Contained, proved useless. O unhappy youth,
How wert thou hurled from thy paternal walls
Reared by Apollo's hand; and through those ringlets,
Which oft thy mother smoothed and kissed, the gore
Bursts from thy fractured skull: but let me waive
So horrid a description. O ye hands,
How in your fingers do ye still retain
A pleasing sad remembrance of your sire,
Or why do ye lie motionless before me?
Dear mouth, full many a babbling accent wont
To utter, art thou closed by death? Thy voice
Deceived me erst, when clinging to these garments,
"O mother," oft didst thou exclaim, "the hair
Shorn from my brows to thee I will devote,
Lead round thy tomb my comrades, and address
Thy hovering ghost in many a plaintive strain."
Now not to me, alas! dost thou perform
These duteous offices, but I, bowed down
With age, an exile, of my children reft,
Must bury the disfigured corse of thee
A tender infant. These unnumbered kisses,

My cares in nurturing thee, and broken sleep,
Proved fruitless. What inscription can the bard
Place o'er thy sepulchre? "The Greeks who feared
This infant, slew him!" Such an epitaph
Would shame them. As for thee who hast obtained
Nought of thy wealth paternal, yet this shield
In which thou shalt be buried will be thine.
O brazen orb, which erst wert wont to guard
The nervous arm of Hector, thou hast lost
Thy best possessor: in thy concave circle
How is that hero's shape impressed; it bears
Marks of that sweat which dropped from Hector's brow,
Wearied with toil, when 'gainst thy edge he leaned
His cheek. Hence carry, to adorn the corse,
Whate'er our present station will afford,
For such the fortunes which Jove grants us now
As splendour suits not: yet accept these gifts
Out of the little I possess. An idiot
Is he, who thinking himself blest, exults
As if his joys were stable: like a man
Smitten with frenzy, changeful fortune bounds
Inconstant in her course, now here, now there,
Nor is there any one who leads a life
Of bliss uninterrupted.
  CHOR.   All is ready:
For from the spoils yon Phrygian matrons bear
Trappings to grace the dead.
  HEC.   On thee, my son,
Not as a victor who with rapid steeds
Didst ever reach the goal, or wing the shaft
With surer aim, an exercise revered
By each unwearied Phrygian youth, thy grandame
Places these ornaments which erst were thine:
But now hath Helen, by the gods abhorred,
Stripped thee of all thou didst possess, and caused
Thy murder, and the ruin of our house.
  CHOR. Alas! thou hast transpierced my inmost soul,
O thou, whom I expected to have seen
Troy's mighty ruler.
  HEC.   But I now enwrap
Thy body with the vest thou shouldst have worn
At Hymen's festive rites, in wedlock joined
With Asia's noblest princess. But, O source
Of triumphs numberless, dear shield of Hector,
Accept these laureate wreaths: for though by death
Thou canst not be affected, thou shalt lie
Joined with this corse in death; since thou deserv'st
More honourable treatment, than the arms
Of crafty and malignant Ithacus.

CHOR. Thee, much lamented youth, shall earth receive.
Now groan, thou wretched mother.
    HEC.   Oh!
    CHOR.   Commence
Those wailings which are uttered o'er the dead.
    HEC. Ah me!
    CHOR.   Alas! too grievous are thy woes
To be endured.
    HEC.   These fillets o'er thy wounds
I bind, and exercise the healing art
In name and semblance only, but, alas!
Not in reality. Whate'er remains
Unfinished, 'mid the shades beneath, to thee
With tender care thy father will supply.
    CHOR. Smite with thy hand thy miserable head
Till it resound. Alas!
    HEC.   My dearest comrades.
    CHOR. Speak to thy friends; O Hecuba, what plaints
Hast thou to utter?
    HEC.   Nought but woe for me
Was by the gods reserved; beyond all cities
To them hath Troy been odious. We in vain
Have offered sacrifice. But had not Jove
O'erthrown and plunged us in the shades beneath,
We had remained obscure, we by the Muse
Had ne'er been sung, nor ever furnished themes
To future bards. But for this hapless youth
Go and prepare a grave; for the deceased
Is with funereal wreaths already crowned:
Although these pomps, I deem, are to the dead
Of little consequence; an empty pride
They in the living serve but to display.
    CHOR. Thy wretched mother on thy vital thread
Had stretched forth mighty hopes: though styled most happy
From thy illustrious birth, thou by a death
Most horrid didst expire.
    HEC.   Ha! who are these
Whom I behold, in their victorious hands
Waving those torches o'er the roofs of Troy?
E'en now o'er Ilion some fresh woes impend.

            TALTHYBIUS, HECUBA, CHORUS.

    TAL. To you I speak, O leaders of the troops
Who are ordained to burn this town of Priam.
No longer in your hands without effect
Reserve those blazing torches: but hurl flames
On this devoted city, for when Troy
Is utterly demolished, we shall leave

Its hated shores, exulting. But to you,
O Phrygians, I the same behests address;
When the shrill trumpet of our chief resounds,
Ye to the Grecian navy must repair
And from these regions sail. But as for thee,
Thou aged and most miserable dame,
Follow their steps who from Ulysses come,
To whom thy fate consigns thee for a slave
Far from thy country in a foreign land.

HEC. Ah, wretched me! this surely is the last,
The dire completion this, of all my woes.
I leave my country: Ilion's bulwarks flame.
Yet, O decrepit feet, with painful haste
Bear me along, that I may bid adieu
To my unhappy city. Thou, O Troy,
Distinguished erst among barbarian tribes
By thy superior prowess, soon shalt lose
The most illustrious name thou didst acquire:
Thee will the flames consume, and us our foes
Drag from our home to slavery. O ye gods!
Upon the gods yet wherefore should I call?
For when we erst invoked them oft, they heard not.
Come on, and let us rush amid the flames:
For in the ruins of my blazing country
'Twill be to me most glorious to expire.

TAL. Thy griefs, O wretched woman, make thee frantic.
But lead her hence, neglect not. For Ulysses
Obtained this prize, and she to him must go.

HEC. O dread Saturnian king, from whom the Phrygians
Derive their origin, dost thou behold
Our sufferings, most unworthy of the race
Of Dardanus?

CHOR. He surely doth behold:
But this great city, city now no more,
Is ruined: nought remains of Troy.

HEC. The blaze
Of Ilion glares, the fire hath caught the roofs,
The streets of Pergamus, and crashing towers.

CHOR. As the light smoke on rapid wing ascends
To heaven, how swiftly vanishes fallen Troy!
Torrents of flame have laid the palace waste,
And o'er its summit waves the hostile spear.

HEC. O fostering soil, that gave my children birth.

CHOR. Alas! alas!

HEC. Yet hear me, O my sons,
Your mother's voice distinguish.

CHOR. With loud plaints
Thou call'st upon the dead, those aged limbs
Stretched on the ground, and scraping up the dust

With either hand. I follow thy example
Kneeling on earth's cold bosom, and invoke
My wretched husband in the shades beneath.
  HEC. We forcibly are borne——
  CHOR.   Most doleful sound!
  HEC. To servile roofs.
  CHOR.   From my dear native land.
  HEC. Slain, uninterred, abandoned by thy friends,
Thou sure, O Priam, know'st not what I suffer.
For sable death hath closed thine eyes for ever;
Though pious, thou by impious hands wert murdered.
O ye polluted temples of the gods,
And thou my dearest city.
  CHOR.   Ye, alas!
Are by the deadly flame and pointed spear
Now occupied, on this beloved soil
Soon shall you lie a heap of nameless ruins:
For dust, which mixed with smoke, to Heaven ascends,
No longer will permit me to discern
Where erst my habitation stood: the land
Loses its very name, and each memorial
Of pristine grandeur; wretched Troy's no more.
  HEC. Ye know the fatal truth, ye heard the crash
Of falling towers. Our city to its basis
Is shaken. O ye trembling, trembling limbs,
Support my steps!
  TAL.   Depart to end thy days
In servitude. Alas! thou wretched city!
Yet to the navy of the Greeks proceed.

The Cyclops.

PERSONS OF THE DRAMA.

SILENUS. | ULYSSES.
CHORUS OF SATYRS. | POLYPHEME THE CYCLOPS.

SCENE.—THE MOUNTAIN OF ÆTNA IN SICILY.

SILENUS.

O BACCHUS, for thy sake have I endured
Unnumbered toils, both at the present hour,
And when these nerves by vigorous youth were strung:
By Juno first with wild distraction fired,
Thou didst forsake the mountain nymphs whose care
Nurtured thy infancy. Next in that war
With the gigantic progeny of earth,
Stationed beside thee to sustain thy shield,
Piercing the buckler of Enceladus,
I slew him with my lance. Is this a dream?
By Jove it is not: for I showed his spoils
To Bacchus, and the labours I endure
At present, are so great that they exceed
E'en those. For since 'gainst thee Saturnia roused,
To bear thee far away, Etruria's race
Of impious pirates, I soon caught th' alarm,
And sailed in quest of thee with all my children:
Myself the stern ascended, to direct
The rudder, and each satyr plied an oar
Till ocean's azure surface with white foam
Was covered; thee, O mighty King, they sought.
Near Malea's harbour as the vessel rode,
An eastern blast arose, and to this rock
Of Ætna, drove us, where the sons of Neptune,
The one-eyed Cyclops, drenched with human gore,
Inhabit desert caves; by one of these
Were we made captives, and beneath his roof
To slavery are reduced. Our master's name

Is Polypheme; instead of Bacchus' orgies
We tend the flocks of an accursed Cyclops.
My blooming sons, on yonder distant cliffs,
Feed the young lambs; while I at home am stationed
The goblet to replenish, and to scrape
The rugged floor; to this unholy lord,
A minister of impious festivals:
And now must I perform the task assigned
Of cleansing with this rake the filthy ground,
So shall the cave be fit for his reception,
When with his flocks my absent lord returns.
But I already see my sons approach,
Their fleecy charge conducting. Ha! what means
This uproar? would ye now renew the dance
Of the Sicinnides, as when ye formed
The train of amorous Bacchus, and assembled,
Charmed by the lute, before Althæa's gate?

CHORUS, SILENUS.

CHORUS.

ODE.

I.

Sprung from an untainted race,
Hardy father of the fold,
Why, bounding o'er that craggy space,
Roam'st thou desperately bold,
Far from the refreshing gale,
The verdant herbage of the mead,
And sloping channel wont to feed
Thy trough with springs that never fail?
Yon caves with bleating lambkins ring,
Come, depasture with the flock;
Leave, O leave the dewy rock,
Ere this ponderous stone I fling.
Thee with speeding horns I call
To the Cyclops' lofty stall.

II.

Thou too those swollen udders yield,
That thy young ones may be fed,
Who, while thou browsest o'er the field,
Lie neglected in the shed;
Slumbering all the livelong day
At length with clamorous plaints they wake,
Thou t' appease them wilt forsake
Ætna's valleys ever gay.

Young Bromius and his jocund rout
Here their orgies ne'er repeat,
No thyrsus waves, no drums they beat ;
Where the gurgling currents spout,
Here no vineyards yield delight,
Nor sport the nymphs on Nyssa's height.

III.

Yet here I chaunt the strains which Bacchus taught,
    To that Venus whom I sought
    When with the Mænades I ranged.
   Where, gentle Evan, dost thou tread
Alone, and from thy comrades far estranged,
Those auburn ringlets floating from thy head?
Thy votary once, but now a slave
To yonder one-eyed Cyclops, I abide
    In this detested cave :
    Covered with a goat's vile hide,
    Thy friend, alas! exposed to scorn
    Wanders helpless and forlorn.

  SIL. My sons, be silent : bid your followers drive
Their flocks into the stony cave.
  CHOR.   Proceed.
But wherefore, O my father, in this haste?
  SIL. A Grecian vessel, stranded on the coast,
I see, and to this cave the mariners
Attend their leader, on their heads they bear
Those empty vessels which express they want
Provisions, with fresh water too their urns
Would they replenish. O unhappy strangers!
Who are they? unapprised what lord here rules,
Dread Polypheme, they in an evil hour
Are entering this inhospitable threshold,
And rushing headlong e'en into the jaws
Of this fierce Cyclops, gorged with human flesh.
But interrupt me not ; I will inquire
Whence to Sicilian Ætna's mount they came.

ULYSSES, SILENUS, CHORUS.

  ULY. Can ye direct me, strangers, where to find
Fresh springs to slake our thirst ; or who will sell
Food to the hungry sailor? But what means
That group of satyrs, whom before yon cave
I see assembled? we at Bacchus' city
Seem to have landed. Thee, the elder-born,
Thee first I hail.

SIL. Hail! foreigner; acquaint us
Both who you are, and from what realm you came.
　ULY. Ulysses, king of Ithaca, and th' isle
Of Cephalenè.
　SIL. That loquacious man,
The crafty brood of Sisyphus, full well
I know.
　ULY. Reproach me not, for I am he.
　SIL. Whence sailed you to Sicilia?
　ULY. From the shores
Of blazing Ilion, from the war of Troy.
　SIL. What, knew you not the way to your own country?
　ULY. The tempests violently drove me hither.
　SIL. By Heaven, your fortunes are the same with mine.
　ULY. What cam'st thou hither too against thy will?,
　SIL. Yes, in pursuit of those accursed pirates
Who seized on Bromius.
　ULY. But what land is this,
And by what men inhabited?
　SIL. This mountain,
Called Ætna, overlooks Sicilia's plains.
　ULY. Where are the fortresses and lofty towers
Which guard its peopled cities?
　SIL. They exist not.
No men, O stranger, on these summits dwell.
　ULY. But who possess the land, a savage race
Of beasts?
　SIL. The Cyclops occupy these caves,
They have no houses.
　ULY. Governed by what chief?
Is this a mere democracy?
　SIL. They lead
The life of shepherds, and in no respect
Yield to each other.
　ULY. Do they sow the grain
Of Ceres, or on what do they subsist?
　SIL. On milk, on cheese, and on their sheep, they feed.
　ULY. Affords the vine, nectareous juice, the drink
Bacchus invented?
　SIL. No such thing: they dwell
In an ungrateful soil.
　ULY. But do they practise
The rites of hospitality, and hold
The stranger sacred?
　SIL. They aver the flesh
Of strangers is a most delicious food.
　ULY. What saidst thou, banquet they on human flesh?
　SIL. Here no man lands who is not doomed to bleed.
　ULY. Where is this Cyclops, in the cave?

SIL.   He went
To Ætna's summit, with his hounds to trace
The savage beasts.
    ULY.   But know'st thou by what means
We from this region may escape?
    SIL.   I know not.
But, O Ulysses, I'll do everything
To serve you.
    ULY.   Sell us bread, supply our want.
    SIL. I told you we have nothing here but flesh.
    ULY. By this, sharp hunger, which makes all things sweet,
May be assuaged.
    SIL.   Cheese from the press, and milk
Of heifers too.
    ULY.   Produce them: while the day
Yet lasts, should we conclude our merchandise.
    SIL. With how much gold will you repay me? Speak.
    ULY. No gold I bring, but Bacchus' cheering juice.
    SIL. My dearest friend, you mention what we long
Have stood in need of.
    ULY.   This enchanting liquor
Did Maron, offspring of the courteous god,
On us bestow.
    SIL.   Whom erst, while yet a boy
I in these arms sustained.
    ULY.   The son of Bacchus,
T' inform thee more minutely who he is.
    SIL. Aboard the ship, or have you hither brought it?
    ULY. Here is the cask, old man, which thou perceiv'st
Contains the wine.
    SIL.   It hardly is a sup.
    ULY. But we have twice as much as this will yield.
    SIL. A most delicious spring is that you named.
    ULY. Shall I first treat thee with some wine unmixed,
That thou may'st taste?
    SIL.   Well judged: this specimen
Soon will induce me to conclude the purchase.
    ULY. A cup too I have brought as well as cask.
    SIL. Pour forth, that I may drink, and recollect
The grateful taste of wine.
    ULY.   Look there!
    SIL.   Ye gods!
How beauteous is its odour!
    ULY.   Hast thou seen it?
    SIL. By Jove I have not, but I smell its charms.
    ULY. Taste, nor to words alone confine thy praise.
    SIL. Ha! ha! now Bacchus to the choral dance
Invites me.
    ULY.   Hath it moistened well thy palate?

SIL. So well as e'en to reach my fingers' ends.
ULY. Beside all this, shall money too be thine.
SIL. Empty the vessel, and reserve your gold.
ULY. Bring forth the cheese and lambs.
SIL. That will I do,
Regardless of my lord, because I wish
To drain one goblet of this wine, and give
The flocks of all the Cyclops in its stead.
I'd from Leucadè, when completely drunk,
Into the ocean take a lover's leap,
Shutting my eyes. For he who, when he quaffs
The mantling bowl, exults not, is a madman.
Through wine new joys our wanton bosoms fire,
With eager arms we clasp the yielding fair,
And in the giddy dance forget each ill
That heretofore assailed us. So I kiss
The rich potation; let the stupid Cyclops
Weep with that central eye which in his front
Glares horribly. *[Exit* SILENUS.

CHOR. Attend: for we must hold
A long confabulation, O Ulysses.
ULY. We meet each other like old friends.
CHOR. Was Troy
By you subdued? was Helen taken captive?
ULY. And the whole house of Priam we laid waste.
CHOR. When ye had seized on that transcendent fair,
Did ye then all enjoy her in your turn,
Because she loves variety of husbands?
False to her vows, when she the painted greaves
Around the legs of Paris, on his neck
The golden chain, beheld, with love deep smitten
From Menelaus, best of men, she fled.
Ah! would to Heaven no women had been born
But such as were reserved for my embraces.

SILENUS *returning*, ULYSSES, CHORUS.

SIL. Here, King Ulysses, is the shepherd's food:
Banquet on bleating lambs, and bear away
As many curdled cheeses as you can;
But from these caverns with your utmost speed
Depart, when ye have given me in return
The clustering vine's rich juice which Bacchus loves.
ULY. The Cyclops comes. What shall we do? Old man,
We are undone. Ah, whither can we fly?
SIL. Ye may conceal yourselves beneath that rock.
ULY. Most dangerous is the scheme thou hast proposed,
To rush into the toils.
SIL. No danger truly;
For in this rock is many a hiding-place.
ULY. Not thus: indignant Troy might groan indeed

If from a single arm we basely fled.
Oft with my shield against a countless band
Of Phrygians have I fought. If we must die,
Let us die nobly : or with life maintain
The fame we erst in dubious fields acquired.

POLPYHEME, SILENUS, CHORUS, ULYSSES.

POL. What mean these transports, this insensate uproar,
These Bacchanalian orgies? Nyssa's god,
The brazen timbrel, and the rattling drum,
Are distant from these regions. In the cave
How fare the new-yeaned lambkins? do they suck,
Or follow they the ewes? have ye prepared
In wicker vats the cheeses? No reply?
This club shall make ye weep forthwith. Look up,
Not on the ground.
  CHOR.   We lift our dazzled eyes
To Jove himself; I view the twinkling stars
And bright Orion.
  POL.   Is my dinner ready?
  CHOR. It is. Prepare your jaws for mastication.
  POL. Are the bowls filled with milk?
  CHOR.   They overflow,
And you may drink whole hogsheads if you will.
  POL. Of sheep, or cows, or mixed?
  CHOR.   Whate'er you please;
But swallow not me too.
  POL.   No certainly;
For ye would foot it in my tortured paunch,
And kill me with those antics. But what crowd
Behold I in the stalls? Some thieves or pirates
Are landed: at the mouth of yonder cave
The lambs are bound with osiers, on the floor
The cheese-press scattered lies, and the bald head
Of this old man is swoll'n with many bruises.
  SIL. Ah me! into a fever I am beaten.
  POL. By whom, old man, who smote thy hoary head?
  SIL. O Cyclops, by these ruffians whom I hindered
From carrying off their plunder.
  POL.   Know they not
I am a god sprung from the blest immortals?
  SIL. All this I told them, yet they seized your goods,
Eat up your cheese without my leave, dragged forth
The lambs, declared they would exhibit you
In a huge collar of three cubits long,
Closely imprisoned, and before that eye,
Which in the centre of your forehead glares,
Bore out your entrails, soundly scourge your hide,
Then throw you into their swift vessel's hold
Tied hand and foot, and sell you, with a lever

To heave up ponderous stones, or to the ground
Level some door.
  POL.   Indeed I go whet the knives
Without delay, collect a mighty pile
Of wood, and light it up with flaming brands,
They shall be slain immediately, and broiled
To satisfy my appetite with viands
Hot from the coals. The rest shall be well sodden;
For I am sated with unsavoury beasts,
Enough on lions have I banqueted
And stags that haunt this mountain : but 'tis long
Since human flesh I tasted.
  SIL.   My dread lord,
Variety is sweet : no other strangers
Have reached of late these solitary caves.
  ULY. O Cyclops, hear the strangers also speak,
In their defence. We, wanting to buy food,
Came to your caverns from our anchored bark.
These lambs to us he bartered for our wine,
And of his own accord, when he had drank,
Yielded them up; no violence was used :
But the account he gives is utter falsehood,
Since he was caught without your privity
Vending your goods.
  SIL.   I? curses on your head !
  ULY. If I have uttered an untruth.
  SIL.   By Neptune
Your sire, O Cyclops, by great Triton, Nereus,
Calypso, Nereus' daughters, by the waves,
And all the race of fishes, I protest,
Most beauteous Cyclops, my dear little lord,
I sold not to the foreigners your goods ;
May swift perdition, if I did, o'ertake
These sinners here, my children, whom I love
Beyond expression.
  CHOR.   Curb thy tongue: I saw thee
Vending thy lord's possessions to the strangers:
If I speak falsehood, may our father perish !
But injure not these foreigners.
  POL.   Ye lie;
For I in him much rather would confide
Than Rhadamanthus, and pronounce that he
Is a more upright judge. But I to them
Some questions would propose. Whence sailed, strangers ?
Where is your country and your native town ?
  ULY. We in the realms of Ithaca were born;
But after we had laid Troy's bulwarks waste,
O Cyclops, by those howling winds which raise
The ocean's boisterous surges, to your coast
Our vessel was impelled.

POL.   Are ye the men
Who worthless Helen's ravisher pursued
To Ilion's turrets on Scamander's bank?
　　ULY. The same: most dreadful toils have we endured.
　　POL. Dishonourable warfare; in the cause
Of one vile woman ye to Phrygia sailed.
　　ULY. Such was the will of Jove; on no man charge
The fault. But we to you, O generous son
Of ocean's god, our earnest prayers address,
Nor fear with honest freedom to remonstrate
That we your hapless friends, who to these caves
For refuge fly, deserve not to be slain
To satiate with accursed human food
Your appetite: for to your sire, great king,
Full many a temple on the shores of Greece
Have we erected; Tænarus' sacred haven
To him remains inviolate, the cliff
Of Malea, Sunium for its silver mines
Renowned, on whose steep promontory stands
Minerva's fane, and the Gerastian bay.
But those intolerable wrongs which Greece
From Troy had suffered, could we not forgive.
Our triumph interests you, who in a land
With Greece connected, dwell, beneath the rock
Of flaming Ætna. Let those public laws
Which all mankind obey, on you prevail
To change your ruthless purpose, and admit
Your suppliants to a conference, who have long
Endured the perils of the billowy deep;
With hospitable gifts, and change of raiment
Assist us, nor affix our quivering limbs
On spits, to sate your gluttony. Enough
Hath Priam's land depopulated Greece,
Whole myriads have in fighting fields been slain;
The widowed bride, the aged childless matron,
And hoary sire, hath Troy made ever wretched.
But if you burn, and at your hateful feasts
Devour the scattered relics of our host,
Whither shall any Grecian turn? but listen
To my persuasion, Cyclops, and control
Your gluttony. What piety enjoins,
Prefer to this defiance of the gods:
For ruin oft attends unrighteous gain.
　　SIL. Leave not the smallest morsel of his flesh;
Take my advice, and if you eat his tongue,
You certainly, O Cyclops, will become
A most accomplished orator.
　　POL.   Vile caitiff,
Wealth is the deity the wise adore,
But all things else are unsubstantial boasts,

And specious words alone. I nought regard
Those promontories sacred to my sire.
Why dost thou talk of them? I tremble not,
O stranger, at the thunderbolts of Jove,
Him I account not a more powerful god
Than I am, nor henceforth will heed him : hear
My reasons; when he from the skies sends down
The rain, secure from its inclemency
Beneath this rock I dwell, and make a feast
On roasted calves, or on the savage prey,
Stretched at my length supine, then drain a pitcher
Of milk, and emulate the thunder's sound.
When Thracian Boreas pours his flaky showers,
In hides of beasts my body I enwrap,
Approach the fire, nor heed the pelting snows.
Compelled by strong necessity, the ground
Produces grass, and nourishes my herds,
Whom, to no other god except myself,
And to this belly, greatest of the gods,
I sacrifice. Because each day to eat,
To drink, and feel no grief, is bliss supreme,
The Heaven, the object of the wise man's worship.
I leave those gloomy lawgivers to weep,
Who by their harsh impertinent restrictions
Have chequered human life ; but will indulge
My genius, and devour thee. That my conduct
May be exempt from blame, thou shalt receive
As pledges of our hospitality
The fire, and that hereditary cauldron
Well heated, which shall boil thy flesh : walk in,
Ye shall adorn my table, and produce
Delicious meals to cheer my gloomy cave,
Such as a god can relish.

ULY.   I have 'scaped,
Alas! each danger at the siege of Troy,
'Scaped the tempestuous ocean; but in vain
Attempt to soften the unpitying heart
Of him who spurns all laws. Now, sacred queen,
Daughter of Jove, now aid me, O Minerva,
For I such perils as far, far exceed
My Phrygian toils, encounter: and, O Jove,
Dread guardian of each hospitable rite,
Who sitt'st enthroned above the radiant stars,
Look down : for if thou view not this, though deemed
Omnipotent, thou art a thing of nought.

Exeunt POLYPHEME, ULYSSES, *and* SILENUS.

1st SEMICHOR. That insatiate throat expand,
  Boiled and roast are now at hand
  For thee, O Cyclops, to devour ;
  From the coals in evil hour

    Yet reeking, shall thy teeth divide
    The limbs of each unhapppy guest,
    To thy table served when dressed
    In dishes formed of shaggy hide.
    O betray me not, my friend,
    For I on you alone depend:
    Now approach the shades of night,
    Launch the bark, and aid our flight.
2nd SEMICHOR. Thou cave, and ye unholy rites,
    Adieu, the Cyclops' cursed delights,
    Who on his prisoners wont to feed,
    Hath banished pity from his breast.
    Inhuman execrable deed !
    On his own hearth, the suppliant guest,
    Regardless of the Lares' guardian powers,
    Now he slays, and now devours:
    Hot from the coals, with odious jaws,
    Human flesh the miscreant gnaws.

    ULYSSES, CHORUS.

  ULY. How, mighty Jove ! 'shall I express myself?
The dreadful scenes I in the cave have viewed
Are so astonishing, they more resemble
Some fable than the actions of a man.
  CHOR. What now, Ulysses, on your loved companions
Feasts this most impious Cyclops?
  ULY.   Two, the fattest,
Having well viewed and poised them in his hands——
  CHOR. How did you bear, O miserable man,
These cruel outrages?
  ULY.   Soon as we entered
The rocky cave, he lighted first the fire,
On the wide blaze heaped trunks of lofty oaks,
A load sufficient for three wains to bear ;
Then near the flaming hearth, upon the ground,
Arranged his couch of pine leaves, filled a bowl,
Holding about ten firkins, with the milk
Of heifers, and beside it placed a jug
Adorned with ivy, the circumference seemed
Three spacious ells, the depth no less than four:
Then made his cauldron bubble, and reached down
Spits burnt at the extremities, and polished
Not with a knife, but hatchets ; Ætna furnished
Such instruments for sacrifice, the stems
Of thorn. No sooner had the hellish cook
Finished his preparations, than he seized
Two of my valiant comrades, whom he slew
With calm deliberation ; one he cast
Into the hollow cauldron ; from the ground
Then lifting up his fellow by the foot

Dashed out his brains against the pointed rock;
Severing his flesh with an enormous knife,
Part at the fire he roasted, and to boil,
His other joints into the cauldron threw.
But I, though from these eyes full many a tear
Burst forth, approached the Cyclops, and on him
Attended, while my friends, like timorous birds
Lurked in the distant crannies of the rock,
And all the blood forsook their pallid frame.
When sated with his feast the monster lay
Supine, and snored, a thought by Heaven inspired
Entered this bosom; having filled a cup
With Maron's juice unmingled, I to him
Bore it, that he might drink; and cried, "Behold,
O Cyclops, son of Neptune, how divine
The beverage which our Grecian vineyards yield
The stream of Bacchus." But already g'utted
With his abominable food, he seized
And emptied the whole bumper at one draught,
Then lifting up, in token of applause,
His hand: "O dearest stranger," he exclaimed,
"To a delicious banquet thou hast added
Delicious wine." Perceiving he grew merry
I plied him with a second cup, well knowing
That wine will stagger him: he soon shall feel
Such punishment as he deserves. He sung;
I poured forth more and more, to warm his bowels
With strong potations: 'midst my weeping crew
He makes the cave with unharmonious strains
Re-echo. But I silently came forth,
And, if ye give consent, design to save
You, and myself. Say, therefore, will ye fly
From this unsocial monster, and reside
With Grecian maids beneath the roofs of Bacchus?
Your sire within approves of these proposals:
But now grown feeble and o'ercharged with wine,
Attracted by the goblet, as if birdlime
Had smeared his wings, he wavers. But with me
Do thou preserve thyself, for thou art young:
And I to Bacchus, to thy ancient friend
Far different from this Cyclops, will restore thee.

CHOR. My dearest friend, O could we see that day,
And 'scape yon impious monster! for we long
Have been deprived of the enlivening bowl,
Nor entertain a single hope of freedom.

ULY. Now hear the means by which I can requite
This odious savage, and thou too mayst 'scape
From servitude.

CHOR. Speak, for we should not hear

The sound of Asia's harp with more delight,
Than the glad tidings of the Cyclops' death.
    ULY. By wine enlivened, he resolves to go
And revel with his brethren.
    CHOR.   I perceive
You mean to seize and kill him when alone,
By some enchantment, or to dash him headlong
From the steep rock.
    ULY.   I have no such design
As these: on craft alone my plan depends.
    CHOR. How then will you proceed? For we long since
Have heard that you for wisdom are renowned.
    ULY. I will deter him from the feast, and say
He must not portion out among the Cyclops
This liquor, but reserve it for himself
And lead a joyous life: when overcome
By Bacchus' gifts he sleeps, this sword shall point
An olive pole, which to my purpose suited
Lies in the cave: I in the fire will heat,
And, when it flames, direct the hissing brand
Full on the Cyclops' forehead, to extinguish
The orb of sight. As when some artist frames
A nautic structure, he by thongs directs
The ponderous auger: thus will I whirl round
Within the Cyclops' eye the kindled staff,
And scorch his visual nerve.
    CHOR.   Ho! I rejoice;
This blest invention almost makes me frantic.
    ULY. Thee, and thy friends, and thy decrepit sire,
This done, aboard my vessel will I place,
And from this region with a double tier
Of oars convey.
    CHOR.   But is it possible
That I, as if dread Jove were my confederate,
Shall guide the well-poised brand, and of his eyesight
Deprive the monster? For I wish to share
In such assassination.
    ULY.   I expect
Your aid: the brand is weighty, and requires
Our social efforts.
    CHOR.   I'd sustain a load
Equal to what a hundred teams convey,
Could I dash out the cursed Cyclops' eye
E'en as a swarm of wasps.
    ULY.   Be silent now;
(Ye know my stratagem) and at my bidding
To those who o'er th' adventurous scheme preside
Yield prompt obedience: for I scorn to leave
My friends within, and save this single life.

True, 'scape I might, already having passed
The cavern's deep recess : but it were mean
If I should extricate myself alone,
False to the faithful partners of my voyage.
                                                [*Exit* ULYSSES.

CHOR. Who first, who next, with steadfast hand
Ordained to guide the flaming brand,
The Cyclops' radiant eye shall pierce?
   1st SEMICHOR. Silence! for from within a song
Bursts on my ear in tuneless verse,
Insensate minstrel, doomed ere long
This luxurious meal to rue,
He staggers from yon rocky cave.
Him let us teach who never knew
How at the banquet to behave,
Outrageous and unmannered hind,
Soon shall he totally be blind.
   2nd SEMICHOR. Thrice blest is he, in careless play
'Midst Bacchus' orgies ever gay,
Streched near the social board whence glides
The vine's rich juice in purple tides,
Who fondly clasps with eager arms
The consenting virgin's charms;
Rich perfumes conspire to shed
Sweetest odours on his head,
While enamoured of the fair
He wantons with her auburn hair.
But hark! for surely 'tis our mate
Exclaiming, "Who will ope the gate?"

POLYPHEME, ULYSSES, SILENUS, CHORUS.

  POL. Ha! ha! I am replete with wine, the banquet
Hath cheered my soul: like a well-freighted ship
My stomach's with abundant viands stowed
Up to my very chin. This smiling turf
Invites me to partake a vernal feast
With my Cyclopean brothers. Stranger, bring
That vessel from the cave.   [*Exit* ULYSSES.
  CHOR.   With bright-eyed grace
Our master issues from his spacious hall;
(Some god approves—the kindled torch—) that form
Equals the lustre of a blooming nymph
Fresh from the dripping caverns of the main.
Soon shall the variegated wreath adorn
Your temples.
  ULY. [*returning.*] Hear me, Cyclops; well I know
Th' effect of this potation, Bacchus' gift,
Which I to you dispensed.

POL.   Yet say what sort
Of god is Bacchus by his votaries deemed?
   ULY. The greatest source of pleasure to mankind.
   POL. I therefore to my palate find it sweet.
   ULY. A god like this to no man will do wrong.
   POL. But in a bottle how can any god
Delight to dwell?
   ULY.   In whatsoever place
We lodge him, the benignant power resides.
   POL. The skins of goats are an unseemly lodging
For deities.
   ULY.   If you admire the wine,
Why quarrel with its case?
   POL.   Those filthy hides
I utterly detest, but love the liquor.
   ULY. Stay here; drink, drink, O Cyclops, and be gay.
   POL. This luscious beverage, must I not impart
To cheer my brothers?
   ULY.   Keep it to yourself
And you shall seem more honourable.
   POL.   More useful,
If I distribute largely to my friends.
   ULY. Broils, taunts, and discord from the banquet rise.
   POL. Though I am fuddled, no man dares to touch me.
   ULY. He who hath drunk too freely, O my friend,
Ought to remain at home.
   POL.   Devoid of reason
Is he who when he drinks pays no regard
To mirth and to good-fellowship.
   ULY.   More wise,
O'ercharged with wine, who ventures not abroad.
   POL. Shall we stay here? What think'st thou, O
      Silenus?
   SIL. With all my heart. What need, for our carousals,
Of a more numerous company?
   POL.   The ground
Beneath our feet, a flowery turf adorns.
   SIL. O how delightful 'tis to drink, and bask
Here in the sunshine: on this grassy couch
Beside me take your seat.
   POL.   Why dost thou place
The cup behind my elbow?
   SIL.   Lest some stranger
Should come and snatch the precious boon away.
   POL. Thou mean'st to tope clandestinely: between us
Here let it stand. O stranger, by what name
Say shall I call thee?
   ULY.   Noman is my name.
But for what favour shall I praise your kindness?

POL. The last of all the crew will I devour.
ULY. A wondrous privilege is this, O Cyclops,
Which on the stranger you bestow.
POL.   What mean'st thou?
Ha! art thou drinking up the wine by stealth?
SIL. Only the gentle Bacchus gave that kiss,
Because I look so blooming.
POL.   Thou shalt weep,
Because thy lips were to the wine applied,
Nor did it seek thy mouth.
SIL.   Not thus, by Jove;
I drank because the generous god of wine
Declared that he admired me for my beauty.
POL. Pour forth; give me a bumper.
SIL.   I must taste
To see what mixture it requires.
POL.   Damnation!
Give it me pure.
SIL.   Not so, the heavens forbid!
Till you the wreath bind on your ample front,
And I again have tasted.
POL.   What a knave
Is this my cupbearer!
SIL.   Accuse me not;
The wine is sweet: you ought to wipe your mouth
Before you drink.
POL.   My lips and beard are clean.
SIL. Loll thus upon your elbow with a grace,
Drink as you see me drink, and imitate
My every gesture.
POL.   What art thou about?
SIL. I swallowed then a most delicious bumper.
POL. Take thou the cask, O stranger, and perform
The office of my cupbearer.
ULY.   These hands
Have been accustomed to the pleasing office.
POL. Now pour it forth.
ULY.   Be silent: I obey.
POL. Thou hast proposed a difficult restraint
To him who largely drinks.
ULY.   Now drain the bowl;
Leave nought behind: the toper must not prate
Before his liquor's ended.
POL.   In the vine
There's wisdom.
ULY.   When to plenteous food you add
An equal share of liquor, and well drench
The throat beyond what thirst demands, you sink
Into sweet sleep: but if you leave behind

Aught of th' unfinished beverage in your cup,
Bacchus will scorch your entrails.
    POL.   'Tis a mercy
How I swam out ; the very heavens whirl round
Mingled with earth. I view Jove's throne sublime,
And the whole synod of encircling gods.
Were all the Graces to solicit me,
I would not kiss them : Ganymede himself
Appears in matchless beauty.
    SIL.   I, O Cyclops,
Am Jove's own Ganymede.
    POL.   By Heaven thou art !
Whom from the realms of Dardanus I bore.
                            [*Exit* POLYPHEME.

    SIL. Ruin awaits me.
    CHOR.   Dost thou loathe him now
    SIL. Ah me ! I from this sleep shall soon behold
The most accursed effects.   [*Exit* SILENUS.
    ULY.   Come on, ye sons
Of Bacchus, generous youths ; for soon dissolved
In slumber shall the monster from those jaws
Vomit forth flesh, within the hall now smokes
The brand, and nought remains but to burn out
The Cyclops' eye : act only like a man.
    CHOR. The firmness of my soul shall equal rocks
And adamant. But go into the cave
With speed, before tumultuous sounds assail
Our aged father's ears ; for to effect
Your purpose, all is ready.
    ULY.   Vulcan, king
Of Ætna, from this impious pest, who haunts
Thy sacred mountain, free thyself at once,
By burning out his glaring eye ; and thou
Nurtured by sable night, O sleep, invade
With thy resistless force this beast abhorred
By Heaven ; nor after all the glorious deeds
Achieved at Ilion, with his faithful sailors,
Destroy Ulysses' self, by him who heeds
Nor god nor mortal. Else must we hold fortune
A goddess, and all other deities
Inferior to resistless fortune's power.   [*Exit* ULYSSES.
    CHOR. The neck of him who slays his guest,
            With burning pincers shall be prest,
            And fire bereaving him of sight
            Soon shall destroy that orb of light.
            Within the embers near at hand
            Lies concealed a smoking brand,
            Torn from its parental tree.
            Maron, we depend on thee ;

May th' exasperated foe
With success direct the blow!
May the Cyclops lose his eye,
And curse his ill-timed jollity!
Thee, Bromius, how I long to meet
Thy front adorned with ivy twine;
Leaving this abhorred retreat.
Ah, when shall such delight be mine?

ULYSSES, CHORUS.

ULY. Be silent, O ye savages, restrain
Those clamorous tongues: by Heaven ye shall not breathe,
Nor wink your eyes, nor cough, lest ye awaken
This pest, the Cyclops, ere he of his eyesight
Is by the fire bereft.
    CHOR.   We will be silent,
And in our jaws confine the very air.
    ULY. The ponderous weapon seize with dauntless hands,
Entering the cavern; for 'tis fully heated.
    CHOR. Will you not give directions who shall first
Manage the glowing lever, and burn out
The Cyclops' eye, that in one common fortune
We all may share.
    1st SEMICHOR.   We who before the portals
Are stationed, are not tall enough to drive
Full on its destined mark the hissing brand.
    2nd SEMICHOR. But I am with a sudden lameness seized.
    1st SEMICHOR. The same calamity which you experience
To me hath also happened; for my feet
Are by convulsions tortured, though the cause
I know not.
    ULY.   If ye feel such dreadful spasms,
How can ye stand?
    CHOR.   Our eyes are also filled
With dust or ashes.
    ULY.   These allies of mine
Are worthless cowards.
    CHOR.   We forsooth want courage
Because we feel compassion for our shoulders,
Nor would be beaten till our teeth drop out.
But I a magic incantation know,
Devised by Orpheus, which hath such effect,
That of its own accord the brand shall pierce
The skull of him, the one-eyed son of earth.
    ULY. Long have I known ye are by nature such;
But more than ever do I know you now.
On my own friends I therefore must rely.
Yet if thou hast no vigour in that arm,
Exhort my drooping friends to act with valour
And let thy counsels aid the bold emprise. [*Exit* ULYSSES.

CHOR. Such be my province: we this Carian's life
Will hazard. But my counsels shall induce them
To burn the Cyclops. Ho! with courage whirl
The brand, delay not to scorch out the eye
Of him who banquets on the stranger's flesh.
With fire assail the savage, pierce the front
Of Ætna's shepherd, lest, with anguish stung,
On you he perpetrate some deed of horror.
   POL. [*within.*] Ah me! by burning coals I am deprived
Of eyesight.
   CHOR.   That was a melodious pæan:
To me, O Cyclops, sing th' enchanting strain.

POLYPHEME, CHORUS.

POL. Ah, how am I insulted and destroyed!
Yet shall ye never from this hollow rock
Escape triumphant, O ye things of nought:
For in my station rooted, where this cleft
Opens a door, will I spread forth my hands
And stop your passage!
   CHOR.   Ha! what means these outcries,
O Cyclops?
   POL.   I am ruined.
   CHOR.   You appear
To have much been abused.
   POL.   Deplorably.
   CHOR. When fuddled, did you fall 'mid burning coals?
   POL. Noman hath ruined me.
   CHOR.   To you then no one
Hath offered any wrong.
   POL.   These lids hath Noman
Deprived of sight.
   CHOR.   You therefore are not blind.
   POL. Would thou couldst see as little.
   CHOR.   How can no man
Put out your eye?
   POL.   Thou art disposed to jest.
But where is Noman?
   CHOR.   He is nowhere, Cyclops.
   POL. That execrable stranger, mark me well,
Is author of my ruin, who produced
The fraudful draught, and burned my visual nerves.
   CHOR. Wine is invincible.
   POL.   By all the gods,
Answer me I conjure you; did they fly,
Or are they here within?
   CHOR.   They on the top
Of yonder rock which screens them from your reach,
In silence take their stand.
   POL.   But on which side?

CHOR. Your right.
POL. Where, where?
CHOR. Upon that very rock.
Have you yet caught them?
POL. To mischance succeeds
Mischance; I have fallen down and cracked my skull.
CHOR. They 'scape you now.
POL. Ye misinformed me sure;
They are not here.
CHOR. I say not that they are.
POL. Where then?
CHOR. They wheel around you on your left.
POL. Ah me! I am derided, ye but mock
At my affliction.
CHOR. They are there no longer:
But Noman stands before you.
POL. O thou villain,
Where art thou?

ULYSSES, POLYPHEME, CHORUS.

ULY. Keeping cautiously aloof,
Thus I, Ulysses, guard my threatened life.
POL. What saidst thou? Wherefore hast thou changed thy name
T' assume a new one?
ULY. Me my father named
Ulysses. It was destined you should suffer
A just requital for your impious feast;
For I in vain had with consuming flames
Laid Ilion waste, had I forborne t' avenge
On you the murder of my valiant friends.
POL. Now is that ancient oracle, alas!
Accomplished, which foretold, that I by thee,
On thy return from Troy, should be deprived
Of sight: but that thou also for a deed
So cruel, shalt be punished, and full long
Endure the beating of tempestuous waves.
ULY. Go weep, my actions justify these words.
But to the shore I haste; and to my country
Will steer the vessel o'er Sicilia's waves.
POL. Thou shalt not; with this fragment of the rock
Hurled at thy head, thee and thy perjured crew
Will I demolish: for I yet, though blind,
Can mount the cliff which overhangs the port,
And in its wonted crannies fix my steps.
CHOR. But we, blest partners in Ulysses' voyage,
Henceforth the laws of Bacchus will obey.

HELEN.

PERSONS OF THE DRAMA.

HELEN.	FEMALE SERVANT.
TEUCER.	MESSENGER.
CHORUS OF GRECIAN DAMES	THEOCLYMENUS.
(HELEN'S ATTENDANTS).	THEONOE.
MENELAUS.	CASTOR AND POLLUX.

SCENE.—PROTEUS' TOMB, AT THE ENTRANCE OF THEOCLYMENUS' PALACE IN PHAROS, AN ISLAND AT THE MOUTH OF THE NILE.

HELEN.

BRIGHT are these virgin currents of the Nile
Which water Egypt's soil, and are supplied,
Instead of drops from heaven, by molten snow.
But Proteus, while he lived, of these domains
Was lord, he in the isle of Pharos dwelt,
King of all Ægypt; for his wife he gained
One of the nymphs who haunt the briny deep,
Fair Psamathe, after she left the bed
Of Æacus; she in the palace bore
To him two children, one of them a son
Called Theoclymenus, because his life
Is passed in duteous homage to the gods;
A daughter also of majestic mien,
Her mother's darling, in her infant years
(Eidothea called by her enraptured sire):
But when the blooming maid became mature
For nuptial joys, Theonoe was the name
They gave her; all the counsels of the gods,
The present and the future, well she knew,
Such privilege she from her grandsire Nereus
Inherited. But not to fame unknown
Are Sparta's realm, whence I derive my birth,
And my sire, Tyndarus. There prevails a rumour
That to my mother Leda Jove was borne
On rapid wings, the figure of a swan

Assuming, and by treachery gained admission
To her embraces, flying from an eagle,
If we may credit such report. My name
Is Helen; but I also will recount
What woes I have endured; three goddesses,
For beauty's prize contending, in the cave
Of Ida, came to Paris; Juno, Venus,
And Pallas, virgin progeny of Jove,
Requesting him to end their strife, and judge
Whose charms outshone her rivals. But proposing
For a reward, my beauty (if the name
Of beauty suit this inauspicious form)
And promising in marriage to bestow me
On Paris, Venus conquered: for the swain
Of Ida, leaving all his herds behind,
Expecting to receive me for his bride,
To Sparta came. But Juno, whose defeat
Fired with resentment her indignant soul,
Our nuptials frustrated; for to the arms
Of royal Priam's son, she gave not me,
But in my semblance formed a living image
Composed of ether. Paris falsely deemed
That he possessed me; from that time these ills
Have been increased by the decrees of Jove,
For he with war hath visited the realms
Of Greece, and Phrygia's miserable sons,
That he might lighten from th' unrighteous swarms
Of its inhabitants the groaning earth,
And on the bravest of the Grecian chiefs
Confer renown. While in the Phrygian war,
As the reward of their victorious arms,
I to the host of Greece have been displayed,
Though absent, save in likeness and in name.
But Mercury, receiving me in folds
Of air, and covering with a cloud (for Jove
Was not unmindful of me), in this house
Of royal Proteus, who of all mankind
Was in his judgment the most virtuous, placed me,
That undefiled I might preserve the bed
Of Menelaus. I indeed am here;
But with collected troops my hapless lord
Pursues the ravisher to Ilion's towers.
Beside Scamander's stream hath many a chief
Died in my cause; but I, who have endured
All these afflictions, am a public curse;
For 'tis supposed, that treacherous to my lord,
I have through Greece blown up the flames of war.
Why then do I prolong my life? these words
I heard from Mercury: "That I again

In Sparta, with my husband shall reside,
When he discovers that I never went
To Troy:" he therefore counselled me to keep
A spotless chastity. While Proteus viewed
The solar beams, I from the nuptial yoke
Still lived exempt; but since the darksome grave
Hath covered his remains, the royal son
Of the deceased solicits me to wed him:
But honouring my first husband, at this tomb
Of Proteus, I a suppliant kneel, to him,
To him I sue, to guard my nuptial couch,
That if through Greece I bear a name assailed
By foul aspersions, no unseemly deed
May cover me with real infamy.

TEUCER, HELEN.

TEU. Who rules this fortress? such a splendid dome
With royal porticos and blazoned roofs
Seems worthy of a Plutus for its lord.
But, O ye gods, what vision! I behold
That hateful woman who hath ruined me,
And all the Greeks. Heaven's vengeance on thy head!
Such a resemblance bear'st thou to that Helen,
That if I were not in a foreign land,
I with this stone would smite thee: thou shouldst bleed
For being like Jove's daughter.
  HEL.   Wretched man,
Whoe'er you are, why do you hate me thus
Because of her misfortunes?
  TEU.   I have erred
In giving way to such unseemly rage.
All Greece abhors Jove's daughter. But forgive me,
O woman, for the words which I have uttered.
  HEL. Say who you are, and from what land you come?
  TEU. One of that miserable race the Greeks.
  HEL. No wonder is it then, if you detest
The Spartan Helen. But to me declare,
Who are you, whence, and from what father sprung?
  TEU. My name is Teucer, Telamon my sire;
The land which nurtured me is Salamis.
  HEL. But wherefore do you wander o'er these meads
Laved by the Nile?
  TEU.   I from my native land
Am banished.
  HEL.   You, alas! must needs be wretched.
Who drove you thence?
  TEU.   My father Telamon.
What friend canst thou hold dearer?
  HEL.   For what cause

Were you to exile doomed? your situation
Is most calamitous.
    TEU.   My brother Ajax,
Who died at Troy, was author of my ruin.
    HEL. How? by your sword deprived of life?
    TEU.   He fell,
On his own blade, and perished.
    HEL.   Was he mad?
Who could act thus whose intellects are sound?
    TEU. Know'st thou Achilles, Peleus' son?
    HEL.   He erst,
I heard, to Helen as a suitor came.
    TEU. He, at his death, his comrades left to strive
Which should obtain his arms.
    HEL.   But why was this
Hurtful to Ajax?
    TEU.   When another won
Those arms, he gave up life.
    HEL.   Do your afflictions
Rise from his fate?
    TEU.   Because I died not with him.
    HEL. O stranger, went you then to Troy's famed city?
    TEU. And having shared in laying waste its bulwarks,
I also perished.
    HEL.   Have the flames consumed,
And utterly destroyed them?
    TEU.   Not a trace
Of those proud walls is now to be discerned.
    HEL. Through thee, O Helen, do the Phrygians perish.
    TEU. The Greeks too: for most grievous are the mischiefs
Which have been wrought.
    HEL.   What length of time's elapsed
Since Troy was sacked?
    TEU.   Seven times the fruitful year
Hath almost turned around her lingering wheel.
    HEL. But how much longer did your host remain
Before those bulwarks?
    TEU.   Many a tedious moon;
There full ten years were spent.
    HEL.   And have ye taken
That Spartan dame?
    TEU.   By her dishevelled hair,
Th' adult'ress, Menelaus dragged away.
    HEL. Did you behold that object of distress,
Or speak you from report?
    TEU.   These eyes as clearly
Witnessed the whole, as I now view thy face.
    HEL. Be cautious, lest for her ye should mistake
Some well-formed semblance which the gods have sent.

TEU. Talk if thou wilt on any other subject;
No more of her.
  HEL.   Believe you this opinion
To be well-grounded?
  TEU.   With these eyes I saw her,
And she e'en now is present to my soul.
  HEL. Have Menelaus and his consort reached
Their home.
  TEU.   They are not in the Argive land,
Nor on Eurotas' banks.
  HEL.   Alas! alas!
The tale you have recounted, is to her
Who hears you, an event most inauspicious.
  TEU. He and his consort, both they say are dead.
  HEL. Did not the Greeks in one large squadron sail?
  TEU. Yes; but a storm dispersed their shattered fleet.
  HEL. Where were they, in what seas?
  TEU.   They at that time
Through the mid waves of the Ægean deep
Were passing.
  HEL. Can none tell if Menelaus
Escaped this tempest?
  TEU.   No man; but through Greece
'Tis rumoured he is dead.
  HEL.   I am undone.
Is Thestius' daughter living?
  TEU.   Mean'st thou Leda?
She with the dead is numbered.
  HEL.   Did the shame
Of Helen cause her wretched mother's death?
  TEU. Around her neck, 'tis said the noble dame
Entwined the gliding noose.
  HEL.   But live the sons
Of Tyndarus, or are they too now no more?
  TEU. They are, and are not, dead; for two accounts
Are propagated.
  HEL.   Which is best confirmed?
O wretched me!
  TEU.   Some say that they are gods
Under the semblance of two radiant stars.
  HEL. Well have you spoken. But what else is rumoured?
  TEU. That on account of their lost sister's guilt
They died by their own swords. But of these themes
Enough: I wish not to renew my sorrows.
But O assist me in the great affairs
On which I to these royal mansions came,
Wishing to see the prophetess Theonoe,
And learn, from Heaven's oracular response,
How I may steer my vessel with success

To Cyprus' isle, where Phœbus hath foretold
That I shall dwell, and on the walls I rear
Bestow the name of Salamis, yet mindful
Of that dear country I have left behind.
 HEL. This will your voyage of itself explain:
But fly from these inhospitable shores,
Ere Proteus' son, the ruler of this land,
Behold you: fly, for he is absent now
Pursuing with his hounds the savage prey.
He slays each Grecian stranger who becomes
His captive: ask not why, for I am silent;
And what could it avail you to be told?
 TEU. O woman, most discreetly hast thou spoken;
Thy kindness may the righteous gods repay!
For though thy person so resemble Helen,
Thou hast a soul unlike that worthless dame.
Perdition seize her; never may she reach
The current of Eurotas: but mayst thou,
Most generous woman, be for ever blest. [*Exit* TEUCER.
 HEL. Plunged as I am 'midst great and piteous woes,
How shall I frame the plaintive strain, what Muse
With tears, or doleful elegies, invoke?

ODE.

I. I.

Ye syrens, winged daughters of the earth,
Come and attune the sympathetic string,
 Expressive now no more of mirth,
To soothe my griefs, the flute of Libya bring;
Record the tortures which this bosom rend,
And echo back my elegiac strains:
Proserpine next will I invoke, to send
Numbers adapted to her votary's pains;
So shall her dark abode, while many a tear I shed,
 Waft the full dirge to soothe th' illustrious dead.

CHORUS, HELEN.

CHORUS.

I. 2.

Near the cerulean margin of our streams
I stood, and on the tufted herbage spread
 My purple vestments in those beams
Which from his noontide orb Hyperion shed,
When on a sudden from the waving reeds
I heard a plaintive and unwelcome sound
Of bitter lamentation; o'er the meads
Groans inarticulate were poured around:
Beneath the rocky cave, dear scene of past delight,
 Some Naiad thus bewails Pan's hasty flight.

HELEN.

II. I.

Ye Grecian nymphs, whom those barbarians caught,
And from your native land reluctant bore,
    The tidings which yon sailor brought
Call forth these tears; for Ilion is no more,
By him of Ida, that predicted flame
Destroyed; through me, alas! have myriads bled,
If not through me, through my destested name.
By th' ignominious noose is Leda dead
Who my imaginary guilt deplored;
And doomed by the relentless Fates in vain
To tedious wanderings, my unhappy lord
At length hath perished 'midst the billowy main:
The twin protectors of their native land,
Castor and Pollux, from all human eyes
Are vanished, they have left Eurotas' strand,
And fields, in playful strife where each young wrestler vies.

CHORUS.

II. 2.

My royal mistress, your disastrous fate
With many a groan and fruitless tear I mourn.
    I from that hour your sorrows date
When amorous Jove on snowy pinions borne,
In form a swan, by Leda was carest.
Is there an evil you have not endured?
Your mother is no more, through you unblest
Are Jove's twin sons. Nor have your vows procured
Of your dear country the enchanting sight.
A rumour too through various realms hath spread,
Caught by the envious vulgar with delight,
Assigning you to the barbarian's bed.
Amid the waves, far from the wished-for shore,
Your husband hath been buried in the main.
You shall behold your native walls no more
Nor under burnished roofs your wonted state maintain.

HELEN.

III.

What Phrygian artist on the top of Ide,
    Or vagrant of a Grecian line,
    Felled that inauspicious pine,
To frame the bark which Paris o'er the tide
    Dared with barbaric oars to guide,

When to my palace, in an evil hour
 Caught by beauty's magic power,
 He came to seize me for his bride?
But crafty Venus, authoress of these broils,
Marched thither, leagued with death, t' annoy
 Triumphant Greece and vanquished Troy,
(Wretch that I am, consumed with endless toils!)
And Juno seated on her golden throne,
 Consort of thundering Jove,
 Sent Hermes from the realms above,
Who found me, when I carelessly had strewn
 Leaves plucked from roses in my vest,
 As Minerva's votary drest;
 He bore me through the paths of air
 To this loathed, this dreary land,
Called Greece, and Priam's friends the strife to share,
And roused to bloody deeds each rival band;
 Where Simois' current glides, my name
 Hence is marked with groundless shame.

CHOR. Your woes I know are grievous: but to bear
With tranquil mind the necessary ills
Of life, is most expedient.

HEL. To what ills
Have I been subject, O my dear companions!
Did not my mother, as a prodigy
Which wondering mortals gaze at, bring me forth?
For neither Grecian nor barbaric dame
Till then produced an egg, in which her children
Enveloped lay, as they report, from Jove
Leda engendered. My whole life and all
That hath befallen me, but conspires to form
One series of miraculous events;
To Juno some, and to my beauty some,
Are owing. Would to Heaven, that, like a tablet
Whose picture is effaced, I could exchange
This form for one less comely, since the Greeks
Forgetting those abundant gifts showered down
By prosperous Fortune which I now possess,
Think but of what redounds not to my honour,
And still remember my ideal shame.
Whoever therefore, with one single species
Of misery is afflicted by the gods,
Although the weight of Heaven's chastising hand
Be grievous, may with fortitude endure
Such visitation: but by many woes
Am I oppressed, and first of all exposed
To slanderous tongues, although I ne'er have erred.
It were a lesser evil e'en to sin
Then be suspected falsely. Then the gods,

'Midst men of barbarous manners, placed me far
From my loved country: torn from every friend,
I languish here, to servitude consigned
Although of free born race: for 'midst barbarians
Are all enslaved but one, their haughty lord.
My fortunes had this single anchor left,
Perchance my husband might at length arrive
To snatch me from my woes; but he, alas!
Is now no more, my mother too is dead,
And I am deemed her murd'ress, though unjustly,
Yet am I branded with this foul reproach;
And she who was the glory of our house,
My daughter in the virgin state grown grey,
Still droops unwedded: my illustrious brothers,
Castor and Pollux, called the sons of Jove,
Are now no more. But I impute my death,
Crushed as I am by all these various woes,
Not to my own misdeeds, but to the power
Of adverse fortune only: this one danger
There yet remains, if at my native land
I should again arrive, they will confine me
In a close dungeon, thinking me that Helen
Who dwelt in Ilion, till she thence was borne
By Menelaus. Were my husband living,
We might have known each other, by producing
Those tokens to which none beside are privy:
But this will never be, nor can he e'er
Return in safety. To what purpose then
Do I still lengthen out this wretched being?
To what new fortunes am I still reserved?
Shall I select a husband, but to vary
My present ills, to dwell beneath the roof
Of a barbarian, at luxurious boards
With wealth abounding, seated? for the dame
Whom wedlock couples with the man she hates
Death is the best expedient. But with glory
How shall I die? the fatal noose appears
To be so base, that e'en in slaves 'tis held
Unseemly thus to perish; in the poniard
There's somewhat great and generous. But to me
Delays are useless: welcome instant death:
Into such depth of misery am I plunged.
For beauty renders other women blest,
But hath to me the source of ruin proved.

  CHOR. O Helen, whosoe'er the stranger be
Who hither came, believe not that the whole
Of what he said, is truth.

  HEL.   But in plain terms
Hath he announced my dearest husband's death.

CHOR. The false assertions which prevail, are many.
HEL. Clear is the language in which honest Truth
Loves to express herself.
CHOR.   You are inclined
Rather to credit inauspicious tidings
Than those which are more favourable.
HEL.   By fears
Encompassed, am I hurried to despair.
CHOR. What hospitable treatment have you found
Beneath these roofs?
HEL.   All here, except the man
Who seeks to wed me, are my friends.
CHOR.   You know
How then to act: leave this sepulchral gloom.
HEL. What are the counsels, or the cheering words
You wish to introduce?
CHOR.   Go in, and question
The daughter of the Nereid, her who knows
All hidden truths, Theonoe, if your lord
Yet live, or view the solar beams no more:
And when you have learnt this, as suit your fortunes
Indulge your joys, or pour forth all your tears:
But ere you know aught fully, what avail
Your sorrows? therefore listen to my words;
Leaving this tomb, attend the maid: from her
Shall you know all. But why should you look farther
When truth is in these mansions to be found?
With you the doors I'll enter; we together
The royal virgin's oracles will hear.
For 'tis a woman's duty to exert
Her utmost efforts in a woman's cause.
HEL. My friends, your wholesome counsels I approve:
But enter ye these doors, that ye, within
The palace, my calamities may hear
CHOR. You summon her who your commands obeys
Without reluctance.
HEL.   Woeful day! ah me,
What lamentable tidings shall I hear?
CHOR. Forbear these plaintive strains, my dearest queen,
Nor with presaging soul anticipate
Evils to come.
HEL.   What hath my wretched lord
Endured? Doth he yet view the light, the sun
Borne in his radiant chariot, and the paths
Of all the starry train? Or hath he shared
The common lot of mortals, is he plunged
Among the dead, beneath th' insatiate grave?
CHOR. O construe what time yet may bring to pass
In the most favourable terms.

HEL.   On thee
I call to testify, and thee adjure,
Eurotas, on whose verdant margin grow
The waving reeds : O tell me, if my lord
Be dead, as fame avers.
    CHOR.   Why do you utter
These incoherent ditties?
    HEL.   Round my neck
The deadly noose will I entwine, or drive
With my own hand a poinard throught my breast;
For I was erst the cause of bloody strife;
But now am I a victim, to appease
The wrath of those three goddesses who strove
On Ida's mount, when 'midst the stalls where fed
His lowing herds, the son of Priam waked
The sylvan reed, to celebrate my beauty.
    CHOR. Cause these averted ills, ye gods, to light
On other heads; but, O my royal mistress,
May you be happy.
    HEL.   Thou, O wretched Troy,
To crimes which thou hast ne'er committed, ow'st
Thy ruin, and those horrible disasters
Thou hast endured. For as my nuptial gifts,
Hath Venus caused an intermingled stream
Of blood and tears to flow, she, griefs to griefs
And tears to tears hath added; all these sufferings
Have been the miserable Ilion's lot.
Of their brave sons the mothers were bereft
The virgin sisters of the mighty dead
Strewed their shorn tresses on Scamander's banks,
While, by repeated shrieks, victorious Greece
Her woes expressing, smote her laurelled head,
And with her nails deep furrowing tore her cheeks.
Happy Calisto, thou Arcadian nymph
Who didst ascend the couch of Jove, transformed
To a four-footed savage, far more blest
Art thou than she to whom I owe my birth:
For thou beneath the semblance of a beast,
Thy tender limbs with shaggy hide o'erspread,
And glaring with stern visage, by that change
Didst end thy griefs. She too whom Dian drove
Indignant from her choir, that hind whose horns
Were tipped with gold, the bright Titanian maid,
Daughter of Merops, to her beauty owed
That transformation : but my charms have ruined
Both Troy and the unhappy Grecian host.
            [*Exeunt* HELEN *and* CHORUS.

MENELAUS.

O Pelops, in the strife on Pisa's field,
Who didst outstrip the fiery steeds that whirled
The chariot of Oenomaus, would to Heaven
That when thy severed limbs before the gods
Were at the banquet placed, thou then thy life
Amidst the blest immortal powers hadst closed,
Ere thou my father Atreus didst beget,
Whose issue by his consort Ærope
Were Agamemnon and myself, two chiefs
Of high renown. No ostentatious words
Are these ; but such a numerous host, I deem,
As that which we to Ilion's shore conveyed,
Ne'er stemmed the tide before ; these troops their king
Led not by force to combat, but bore rule
O'er Grecian youths his voluntary subjects,
And among these, some heroes, now no more,
May we enumerate ; others from the sea
Who 'scaped with joy, and to their homes returned,
E'en after fame had classed them with the dead.
But I, most wretched, o'er the briny waves
Of ocean wander, since I have o'erthrown
The battlements of Troy, and though I wish
Again to reach my country ; by the gods
Am I esteemed unworthy of such bliss.
E'en to the Libyan deserts have I sailed,
And traversed each inhospitable scene
Of brutal outrage ; still as I approach
My country, the tempestuous winds repel me,
Nor hath a prosperous breeze from Heaven yet filled
My sails, to waft me to the Spartan coast :
And now a shipwrecked, miserable man,
Reft of my friends, I on these shores am cast,
My vessel hath been shivered 'gainst the rocks
Into a thousand fragments : on the keel,
The only part which yet remains entire
Of all that fabric, scarce could I and Helen,
Whom I from Troy have borne, escape with life
Through fortunes unforeseen : but of this land
And its inhabitants, the name I know not :
For with the crowd I blushed to intermingle
Lest they my squalid garments should observe,
Through shame my wants concealing. For the man
Of an exalted station, when assailed
By adverse fortune, having never learned
How to endure calamity, is plunged
Into a state far worse than he whose woes
Have been of ancient date. But pinching need

Torments me: for I have not either food
Or raiment to protect my shivering frame,
Which may be guessed from these vile rags I wear
Cast up from my wrecked vessel: for the sea
Hath swallowed up my robes, my tissued vests,
And every ensign of my former state.
Within the dark recesses of a cave
Having concealed my wife, that guilty cause
Of all my woes, and my surviving friends
Enjoined to guard her, hither am I come.
Alone, in quest of necessary aid
For my brave comrades whom I there have left,
If by my search I haply can obtain it,
I roam; but when I viewed this house adorned
With gilded pinnacles, and gates that speak
The riches of their owner, I advanced:
For I have hopes that from this wealthy mansion
I, somewhat for my sailors, shall obtain.
But they who want the necessary comforts
Of life, although they are disposed to aid us,
Yet have not wherewithal. Ho! who comes forth
From yonder gate, my doleful tale to bear
Into the house?

FEMALE SERVANT, MENELAUS.

FEMALE SER. Who at the threshold stands?
Wilt thou not hence depart, lest thy appearance
Before these doors give umbrage to our lords?
Else shalt thou surely die, because thou cam'st
From Greece, whose sons shall never hence return.
  MEN. Well hast thou spoken, O thou aged dame.
Wilt thou permit me? For to thy behests
Must I submit: but suffer me to speak.
  FEMALE SER. Depart: for 'tis my duty to permit
No Greek to enter this imperial dome.
  MEN. Lift not thy hand against me, nor attempt
To drive me hence by force.
  FEMALE SER.   Thou wilt not yield
To my advice, thou therefore art to blame.
  MEN. Carry my message to thy lords within.
  FEMALE SER. I fear lest somewhat dreadful might ensue,
Should I repeat your words.
  MEN.   I hither come
A shipwrecked man, a stranger, one of those
Whom all hold sacred.
  FEMALE SER.   To some other house,
Instead of this, repair.
  MEN.   I am determined
To enter: but comply with my request.

FEMALE SER. Be well assured thou art unwelcome here,
And shalt ere long by force be driven away.
MEN. Alas! alas! where are my valiant troops?
FEMALE SER. Elsewhere, perhaps, thou wert a mighty man;
But here art thou no longer such.
MEN.   O Fortune,
How am I galled with undeserved reproach!
FEMALE SER. Why are those eyelids moist with tears, why
  griev'st thou?
MEN. Because I once was happy.
FEMALE SER.   Then depart,
And mingle social tears with those thou lov'st.
MEN. But what domain is this, to whom belong
These royal mansions?
FEMALE SER.   Proteus here resides;
This land is Egypt.
MEN.   Egypt? wretched me!
Ah, whither have I sailed!
FEMALE SER.   But for what cause
Scorn'st thou the race of Nile?
MEN.   I scorn them not:
My own disastrous fortunes I bewail.
FEMALE SER. Many are wretched, thou in this respect
Art nothing singular.
MEN.   Is he, the king
Thou speak'st of, here within?
FEMALE SER.   To him belongs
This tomb; his son is ruler of this land.
MEN. But where is he: abroad, or in the palace?
FEMALE SER. He's not within: but to the Greeks he bears
The greatest enmity.
MEN.   Whence rose this hate,
Productive of such bitter fruits to me?
FEMALE SER. Beneath these roofs Jove's daughter Helen
  dwells.
MEN. What mean'st thou? Ha! what words with wonder
  fraught
Are these which thou hast uttered? O repeat them.
FEMALE SER. The child of Tyndarus, she who in the realm
Of Sparta erst abode.
MEN.   Whence came she hither?
How can this be?
FEMALE SER.   From Lacedæmon's realm.
MEN. When? Hath my wife been torn from yonder cave?
FEMALE SER. Before the Greeks, O stranger, went to Troy
Retreat then from these mansions, for within
Hath happened a calamitous event,
By which the palace is disturbed. Thou com'st
Unseasonably, and if the king surprise thee,

Instead of hospitable treatment, death
Must be thy portion. To befriend the Greeks
Though well inclined, yet thee have I received
With these harsh words, because I fear the monarch.
      [*Exit* FEMALE SERVANT.
 MEN. What shall I say? For I, alas! am told
Of present sorrows added to the past.
Come I not hither, after having borne
From vanquished Troy my consort, whom I left
Within yon cave well guarded? Yet here dwells
Another Helen, whom that woman called
Jove's daughter. Lives there on the banks of Nile
A man who bears the sacred name of Jove?
For in the heavens there's only one. What country,
But that where glides Eurotas' stream beset
With waving reeds, is Sparta? Tyndarus' name
Suits him alone. But is there any land
Synonymous with Lacedæmon's realm,
And that of Troy? I know not how to solve
This doubt; for there are many, it appears,
In various regions of the world, who bear
Like appellations; city corresponds
With city; woman borrows that of woman;
Nor must we therefore wonder. Yet again
Here will I stay, though danger be announced
By yonder aged servant at the door:
For there is no man so devoid of pity
As not to give me food, when he the name
Of Menelaus hears. That dreadful fire
By which the Phrygian bulwarks were consumed
Is memorable, and I who kindled it
Am known in every land. I'll therefore wait
Until the master of this house return.
But I have two expedients, and will practise
That which my safety shall require; of soul
Obdurate, if he prove, in my wrecked bark
Can I conceal myself, but if the semblance
Which he puts on, be mild, I for relief
From these my present miseries, will apply.
But this of all the woes that I endure
Is the most grievous, that from other kings
I, though a king myself, should be reduced
To beg my food: but thus hath Fate ordained.
Nor is it my assertion, but a maxim
Among the wise established, that there's nought
More powerful than the dread behests of Fate.

HELEN, CHORUS, MENELAUS.

CHOR. I heard what yon prophetic maid foretold,
  Who in the palace did unfold
The oracles; that to the shades profound
  Of Erebus, beneath the ground
Interred, not yet hath Menelaus ta'en
  His passage: on the stormy main
Still tossed, he cannot yet approach the strand,
  The haven of the Spartan land:
The chief, who now his vagrant life bewails,
  Without a friend, unfurls his sails,
From Ilion's realm to every distant shore
  Borne o'er the deep with luckless oar.
HEL. I to this hallowed tomb again repair,
Now I have heard the grateful tidings uttered
By sage Theonoe, who distinctly knows
All that hath happened? for she says my lord
Is living, and yet views the solar beams:
But after passing o'er unnumbered straits
Of ocean, to a vagrant's wretched life
Full long inured, on these Ægyptian coasts,
When he his toils hath finished, shall arrive.
Yet there is one thing more, which she hath left
Unmentioned, whether he shall come with safety.
This question I neglected to propose,
O'erjoyed when she informed me he yet lives;
She also adds, that he is near the land,
From his wrecked ship, with his few friends, cast forth,
O mayst thou come at length; for ever dear
To me wilt thou arrive. Ha! who is that?
Am not I caught, through some deceitful scheme
Of Proteus' impious son, in hidden snares?
Like a swift courser, or the madding priestess
Of Bacchus, shall I not with hasty step
Enter the tomb, because his looks are fierce
Who rushes on, and strives to overtake me?
MEN. On thee I call, who to the yawning trench
Around that tomb, and blazing altars hiest
Precipitate. Stay: wherefore dost thou fly?
With what amazement doth thy presence strike
And almost leave me speechless!
HEL.   O my friends,
I suffer violence; for from the tomb
I by this man am dragged, who to the king
Will give me, from whose nuptial couch I fled.
  MEN. We are no pirates, nor the ministers
Of lustful villany.

Hel.　　　　　　Yet is the vest
You wear unseemly.
　　Men.　　　　　Stay thy rapid flight,
Dismiss thy fears.
　　Hel.　　　　　I stop, now I have reached
This hallowed spot.
　　Men.　　　　　Say, woman, who thou art;
What face do I behold?
　　Hel.　　　　　But who are you?
For I by the same reasons am induced
To ask this question.
　　Men.　　　　　Never did I see
A greater likeness.
　　Hel.　　　　　O ye righteous gods!
For 'tis a privilege the gods alone
Confer, to recognize our long-lost friends,
　　Men. Art thou a Grecian or a foreign dame?
　　Hel. Of Greece: but earnestly I wish to know
Whence you derive your origin.
　　Men.　　　　　In thee
A wonderful resemblance I discern
Of Helen.
　　Hel.　　Menelaus' very features
These eyes in you behold, still at a loss
Am I for words t' express my thoughts.
　　Men.　　　　　Full clearly
Hast thou discovered a most wretched man.
　　Hel. O to thy consort's arms at length restored!
　　Men. To what a consort? O forbear to touch
My garment!
　　Hel.　　　E'en the same, whom to your arms,
A noble bride, my father Tyndarus gave.
　　Men. Send forth, O Hecate, thou orb of light,
Some more benignant spectre.
　　Hel.　　　　　You in me
Behold not one of those who minister
At Hecate's abhorred nocturnal rites.
　　Men. Nor am I sure the husband of two wives.
　　Hel. Say, to whom else in wedlock are you joined?
　　Men. To her who lies concealed in yonder cave,
The prize I hither bring from vanquished Troy.
　　Hel. You have no wife but me.
　　Men.　　　　　If I retain
My reason yet, these eyes are sure deceived.
　　Hel. Seem you not then, while me you thus behold,
To view your real consort?
　　Men.　　　　　Though your person
Resemble hers, no positive decision
Can I presume to form.

HEL.   Observe me well,
And mark wherein we differ. Who can judge
With greater certainty than you?
MEN.   Thou bear'st
Her semblance, I confess.
HEL.   Who can inform you
Better than your own eyes?
MEN.   What makes me doubt
Is this; because I have another wife.
HEL. To the domains of Troy I never went:
It was my image only.
MEN.   Who can fashion
Such bodies, with the power of sight endued?
HEL. Composed of ether, you a consort have,
Heaven's workmanship.
MEN.   Wrought by what plastic god?
For the events thou speak'st of are most wondrous.
HEL. Lest Paris should obtain me, this exchange
Was made by Juno.
MEN.   How couldst thou be here,
At the same time, and in the Phrygian realm?
HEL. The name, but not the body, can be present
At once in many places.
MEN.   O release me;
For I came hither in an evil hour.
HEL. Will you then leave me here, and bear away
That shadow of a wife?
MEN.   Yet, O farewell,
Because thou art like Helen.
HEL.   I'm undone:
For though my husband I again have found,
Yet shall not I possess him.
MEN.   My conviction,
From all those grievous toils I have endured
At Ilion, I derive, and not from thee.
HEL. Ah, who is there more miserable than I am?
My dearest friends desert me: I, to Greece,
To my dear native land, shall ne'er return.

MESSENGER, MENELAUS, HELEN, CHORUS.

MES. After a tedious search, O Menelaus,
At length have I with difficulty found you,
But not till over all the wide extent
Of this barbaric region I had wandered;
Sent by the comrades whom you left behind.
MEN. Have ye been plundered then by the barbarians?
MES. A most miraculous event hath happened,
Yet less astonishing by far in name
Than in reality.

MEN. Speak, for thou bring'st
Important tidings by this breathless haste.
  MES. My words are these: in vain have you endured
Unnumbered toils.
  MEN. Those thou bewail'st are ills
Of ancient date. But what hast thou to tell me?
  MES. Borne to the skies your consort from our sight
Hath vanished, in the heavens is she concealed,
Leaving the cave in which we guarded her,
When she these words had uttered: "O ye sons
Of hapless Phrygia, and of Greece: for me
Beside Scamander's conscious stream ye died,
Through Juno's arts, because ye falsely deemed
Helen by Phrygian Paris was possest:
But after having here remained on earth
My stated time, observing the decrees
Of Fate, I to my sire the liquid ether
Return: but Tyndarus' miserable daughter,
Though guiltless, hath unjustly been accused."
Daughter of Leda hail! wert thou then here?
While I as if thou to the starry paths
Hadst mounted, through my ignorance proclaimed
Thou from this world on rapid wings wert borne.
But I no longer will allow thee thus
To sport with the afflictions of thy friends;
For in thy cause thy lord and his brave troops
On Ilion's coast already have endured
Abundant toils.
  MEN. These are the very words
She uttered; and by what ye both aver
The truth is ascertained. O happy day
Which gives thee to my arms!
  HEL. My dearest lord,
O Menelaus, it is long indeed
Since I have seen you: but joy comes at last.
My friends, transported I receive my lord
Whom I once more with these fond arms enfold,
After the radiant chariot of the sun
Hath oft the world illumined.
  MEN. I embrace
Thee too: but having now so much to say
I know not with what subject to begin.
  HEL. Joy raises my exulting crest, these tears
Are tears of ecstasy, around your neck
My arms I fling with transport, O my husband,
O sight most wished for!
  MEN. I acquit the Fates,
Since Jove's and Leda's daughter I possess,
On whom her brothers borne on milk-white steeds

Erst showered abundant blessings, when the torch
Was kindled at our jocund nuptial rite;
Though from my palace her the gods conveyed.
But evil now converted into good
To me thy husband hath at length restored
My long-lost consort: grant, O bounteous Heaven,
That I these gifts of fortune may enjoy.
   HEL. May you enjoy them, for my vows concur
With yours; nor, of us two, can one be wretched
Without the other. O my friends, I groan
No longer, I no longer shed the tear
For my past woes: my husband I possess
Whom I from Troy expected to return
Full many, many years.
   MEN.   I still am thine,
And thee with these fond arms again enfold.
But oft the chariot of the sun revolved
Through his diurnal orbit, ere the frauds
Of Juno I discerned. Yet more from joy
Than from affliction rise the tears I shed.
   HEL. What shall I say? what mortal could presume
E'er to have hoped for such a blest event?
An unexpected visitant once more
I clasp you to my bosom.
   MEN.   And I thee
Who didst appear to sail for Ida's town,
And Ilion's wretched turrets. By the gods,
Inform me, I conjure thee, by what means
Thou from my palace hither wert conveyed.
   HEL. Alas! you to the source of all my woes
Ascend, and search into most bitter tidings.
   MEN. Speak: for whate'er hath been ordained by Heaven
Ought to be published.
   HEL.   I abhor the topic
On which I now am entering.
   MEN.   Yet relate
All that thou know'st; for pleasing 'tis to hear
Of labours that are past.
   HEL.   I never went
To that barbarian youth's adulterous couch
By the swift oar impelled: but winged love
Those hapless spousals formed.
   MEN.   What god, what fate
Hath torn thee from thy country?
   HEL.   O my lord,
The son of Jove hath placed me on the banks
Of Nile.
   MEN. With what amazement do I hear
This wondrous tale of thy celestial guide!

HEL. Oft have I wept, and still the tear bedews
These eyes: to Juno, wife of Jove, I owe
My ruin.
MEN. Wherefore wished she to have heaped
Mischiefs on thee?
HEL. Ye sources of whate'er
To me hath been most dreadful, O ye baths
And fountains, where those goddesses adorned
Their rival beauties, from whose influence rose
That judgment!
MEN. Were those curses on thy head
By Juno showered, that judgment to requite?
HEL. To rescue me from Venus.
MEN. What thou mean'st
Inform me.
HEL. Who to Paris had engaged——
MEN. O wretched woman!
HEL. Wretched, wretched me!
Thus did she waft me to th' Egyptian coast.
MEN. Then in thy stead to him that image gave,
As thou inform'st me.
HEL. But alas! what woes
Thence visited our wretched house! ah mother!
Ah me!
MEN. What sayst thou?
HEL. Leda is no more.
Around her neck she fixed the deadly noose
On my account, through my unhappy nuptials
O'erwhelmed with foul disgrace.
MEN. Alas! But lives
Hermione our daughter?
HEL. Yet unwedded,
Yet childless, O my husband, she bewails
My miserable 'spousals, my disgrace.
MEN. O Paris, who hast utterly o'erthrown
All my devoted house, these curst events,
Both thee, and myriads of the Grecian troops
With brazen arms refulgent, have destroyed.
HEL. But from my country in an evil hour,
From my loved native city, and from you,
Me hath the goddess driven, a wretch accursed
In that I left our home, and bridal bed,
Which yet I left not, for those base espousals.
CHOR. If ye hereafter meet with happier fortune,
This may atone for all ye have endured
Already.
MES. To me too, O Menelaus,
Communicate a portion of that joy
Which I perceive, but know not whence it springs.

MEN. Thou too, old man, shalt in our conference share.
MES. Was not she then the cause of all the woes
Endured at Troy?
MEN.   Not she: we were deceived
By those immortal Powers, whose plastic hand
Moulded a cloud into that baleful image.
MES. What words are these you utter? have we toiled
In vain, and only for an empty cloud?
MEN. These deeds were wrought by Juno, and the strife
'Twixt the three goddesses.
MES.   But is this woman
Indeed your wife?
MEN.   E'en she: and thou for this
On my assertion safely mayst depend.
MES. My daughter, O how variable is Jove,
And how inscrutable! for he with ease
Whirls us around, now here, now there; one suffers
Full many toils; another, who ne'er knew
What sorrow was, is swallowed up at once
In swift perdition, nor in Fortune's gifts
A firm and lasting tenure doth enjoy.
Thou and thy husband have endured a war,
Of slander thou, but he of pointed spears:
For by the tedious labours he endured
He nothing could obtain, but now obtains
The greatest and the happiest of all boons,
Which comes to him unsought. Thou hast not shamed
Thy aged father, and the sons of Jove,
Nor acted as malignant rumour speaks.
I now renew thy hymeneal rite,
And still am mindful of the torch I bore,
Running before the steeds, when in a car
Thou with this favoured bridegroom wert conveyed
From thy paternal mansion's happy gates.
For worthless is that servant who neglects
His master's interests, nor partakes their joys,
Nor feels for their afflictions. I was born
Indeed a slave, yet I with generous slaves
Would still be numbered, for although the name
I bear is abject, yet my soul is free.
Far better this, than if I had at once
Suffered two evils, a corrupted heart,
And vile subjection to another's will.
MEN. Courage, old man: for thou hast borne my shield,
And in my cause endured unnumbered toils,
Sharing my dangers: now partake my joys;
Go tell the friends I left, what thou hast seen,
And our auspicious fortunes: on the shore

Bid them remain, till our expected conflict
Is finished; and observe how we may sail
From this loathed coast; that, with our better fortune
Conspiring, we, if possible, may 'scape
From these barbarians.
    MES.   Your commands, O king,
Shall be obeyed. But I perceive how vain
And how replete with falsehood is the voice
Of prophets: no dependence can be placed
Upon the flames that from the altar rise,
Or on the voices of the feathered choir.
It is the height of folly to suppose
That birds are able to instruct mankind.
For Calchas, to the host, nor by his words
Nor signs, declared, "I for a cloud behold
My friends in battle slain." The seer was mute,
And Troy in vain was taken. But perhaps
You will rejoin, "'Twas not the will of Heaven
That he should speak." Why then do we consult
These prophets? We by sacrifice should ask
For blessings from the gods, and lay aside
All auguries. This vain delusive bait
Was but invented to beguile mankind.
No sluggard e'er grew rich by divination,
The best of seers are Prudence and Discernment.
                            [*Exit* MESSENGER.
    CHOR. My sentiments on prophets well accord
With those of this old man. He whom the gods
Th' immortal gods befriend, in his own house
Hath a response that never can mislead.
    HEL. So be it. All thus far is well. But how
You came with safety, O unhappy man,
From Troy, 'twill nought avail for me to know;
Yet with the sorrows of their friends, have friends
A wish to be acquainted.
    MEN.   Thou hast asked
A multitude of questions in one short
And blended sentence. Why should I recount
To thee our sufferings on the Ægean deep,
Those treacherous beacons, by the vengeful hand
Of Nauplius kindled on Eubœa's rocks,
The towns of Crete, or in the Libyan realm,
Which I have visited, and the famed heights
Of Perseus? never could my words assuage
Thy curiosity, and, by repeating
My woes to thee, I should but grieve the more,
And yet a second time those sufferings feel.
    HEL. You in your answer have been more discreet
Than I who such a question did propose.

But pass o'er all beside, and only tell me
How long you wandered o'er the briny main.
　　MEN. Year after year, besides the ten at Troy,
Seven tedious revolutions of the sun.
　　HEL. The time you speak of, O unhappy man,
Is long indeed: but from those dangers saved
You hither come to bleed.
　　MEN.　　　　　　　What words are these?
What dost thou mean? O, how hast thou undone me!
　　HEL. Fly from these regions with your utmost speed:
Or he to whom this house belongs will slay you.
　　MEN. What have I done that merits such a fate?
　　HEL. You hither come an unexpected guest,
And are a hindrance to my bridal rite.
　　MEN. Is there a man then who presumes to wed
My consort?
　　HEL.　　　And with arrogance to treat me,
Which I, alas! have hitherto endured.
　　MEN. Of private rank, in his own strength alone
Doth he confide, or rules he o'er the land?
　　HEL. Lord of this region, royal Proteus' son.
　　MEN. This is the very riddle which I heard
From yonder female servant.
　　HEL.　　　　　　　　At which gate
Of this barbarian palace did you stand?
　　MEN. Here, whence I like a beggar was repelled.
　　HEL. What, did you beg for food! ah wretched me!
　　MEN. The fact was thus: though I that abject name
Assumed not.
　　HEL.　　　You then know, it seems, the whole
About my nuptials.
　　MEN.　　　　　This I know: but whether
Thou has escaped th' embraces of the king
I still am uninformed.
　　HEL.　　　　　　　That I have kept
Your bed still spotless, may you rest assured.
　　MEN. How canst thou prove the fact? if thou speak
　　　truth
To me, it will give pleasure.
　　HEL.　　　　　　　　Do you see,
Close to the tomb, my miserable seat?
　　MEN. I on the ground behold a couch: but what
Hast thou to do with that, O wretched woman?
　　HEL. Here I a suppliant bowed, that I might 'scape
From those espousals.
　　MEN.　　　　Couldst thou find no altar,
Or dost thou follow the barbarian mode?
　　HEL. Equally with the temples of the gods
Will this protect me.

MEN. Is not then my bark
Allowed to waft thee to the Spartan shore?
  HEL. Rather the sword than Helen's bridal bed
Awaits you.
  MEN. Thus should I of all mankind
Be the most wretched.
  HEL. Let not shame prevent
Your 'scaping from this land.
  MEN. And leaving thee,
For whom I laid the walls of Ilion waste?
  HEL. 'Twere better than to perish in the cause
Of me your consort.
  MEN. Such unmanly deeds
As these thou speak'st of would disgrace the chief
Who conquered Troy.
  HEL. You cannot slay the king,
Which is perhaps the project you have formed.
  MEN. Hath he then such a body as no steel
Can penetrate?
  HEL. My reasons you shall know.
But it becomes not a wise man t' attempt
What cannot be performed.
  MEN. Shall I submit
My hands in silence to the galling chain?
  HEL. You know not how to act in these dire straits
To which we are reduced: but of some plot
Must we avail ourselves.
  MEN. 'Twere best to die
In some brave action than without a conflict.
  HEL. One only hope of safety yet remains.
  MEN. By gold can it be purchased, or depends it
On dauntless courage, or persuasive words?
  HEL. Of your arrival if the monarch hear not.
  MEN. Who can inform him? he will never sure
Know who I am.
  HEL. He hath a sure associate,
Within his palace, equal to the gods.
  MEN. Some voice which from its inmost chambers
    sounds?
  HEL. No: 'tis his sister, her they call Theonoe
  MEN. She bears indeed a most prophetic name;
But say, what mighty deeds can she perform?
  HEL. All things she knows, and will inform her brother
That you are here.
  MEN. We both, alas! must die,
Nor can I possibly conceal myself.
  HEL. Could our united supplications move her?
  MEN. To do what action? Into what vain hope
Wouldst thou mislead me?

H

HEL.   Not to tell her brother
That you are in the land.
    MEN.   If we prevail
Thus far, can we escape from these domains?
    HEL. With ease, if she concur in our design,
But not without her knowledge.
    MEN.   This depends
On thee: for woman best prevails with woman.
    HEL. Around her knees these suppliant hands I'll twine.
    MEN. Go then; but what if she reject our prayer?
    HEL. You certainly must die; and I by force
Shall to the king be wedded.
    MEN.   Thou betray'st me;
That force thou talk'st of is but mere pretence.
    HEL. But by your head that sacred oath I swear.
    MEN. What sayst thou, wilt thou die, and never change
Thy husband?
    HEL.   By the self-same sword: my corse
Shall lie beside you.
    MEN.   To confirm the words
Which thou hast spoken, take my hand.
    HEL.   I take
Your hand, and swear that after you are dead
I will not live.
    MEN.   And I will put an end
To my existence, if deprived of thee.
    HEL. But how shall we die so as to procure
Immortal glory?
    MEN.   Soon as on the tomb
Thee I have slain, myself will I destroy.
But first a mighty conflict shall decide
Our claims who to thy bridal bed aspire.
Let him who dares, draw near: for the renown
I won at Troy, I never will belie,
Nor yet returning to the Grecian shore
Suffer unnumbered taunts for having reft
Thetis of her Achilles, and beheld
Ajax the Telamonian hero slain,
With Neleus' grandson, though I dare not bleed
To save my consort. Yet on thy behalf
Without regret, will I surrender up
This fleeting life: for if the gods are wise
They lightly scatter dust upon the tomb
Of the brave man who by his foes is slain,
But pile whole mountains on the coward's breast.
    CHOR. O may the race of Tantalus, ye gods,
At length be prosperous, may their sorrows cease!
    HEL. Wretch that I am! for such is my hard fate:
O Menelaus, we are lost for ever.

The prophetess Theonoe, from the palace
Comes forth: I hear the sounding gates unbarred.
Fly from this spot. But whither can you fly?
For your arrival here, full well she knows,
Absent, or present. How, O wretched me,
Am I undone! in safety you return
From Troy, from a barbarian land, to rush
Again upon the swords of fresh barbarians.

THEONOE, MENELAUS, HELEN, CHORUS.

THEON. [*to one of her Attendants.*]
Lead thou the way, sustaining in thy hand
The kindled torch, and fan the ambient air,
Observing every due and solemn rite,
That we may breathe the purest gales of Heaven.
Meanwhile do thou, if any impious foot
Have marked the path, with lustral flames efface
The taint, and wave the pitchy brand around,
That I may pass; and when we have performed
Our duteous homage to th' immortal powers,
Into the palace let the flame be borne,
Restore it to the Lares. What opinion
Have you, O Helen, of th' events foretold
By my prophetic voice? Your husband comes,
Your Menelaus in this land appears,
Reft of his ships, and of your image reft.
'Scaped from what dangers, O unhappy man,
Art thou arrived, although thou know'st not yet
Whether thou e'er shalt to thy home return,
Or here remain. For there is strife in Heaven;
And Jove on thy account this day will hold
A council; Juno who was erst thy foe,
Now grown benignant, with thy consort safe
To Sparta would convey thee, that all Greece
May understand that the fictitious nuptials
Of Paris, were the baleful gift of Venus.
But Venus wants to frustrate thy return,
Lest she should be convicted, or appear
At least the palm of beauty to have purchased
By vending Helen for a wife to Paris.
But this important question to decide,
On me depends; I either can destroy thee,
Which is the wish of Venus, by informing
My brother thou art here; or save thy life
By taking Juno's side, and thy arrival
Concealing from my brother, who enjoined me
To inform him whensoe'er thou on these shores
Shouldst land. Who bears the tidings to my brother,

That Menelaus' self is here, to save me
From his resentment?
  HEL.   At thy knees I fall,
O virgin, as a suppliant, and here take
My miserable seat, both for myself,
And him whom, scarce restored to me, I see
Now on the verge of death. Forbear t' inform
Thy brother, that to these fond arms my lord
Again is come. O save him, I implore thee;
Nor gratify thy brother, by betraying
The feelings of humanity, to purchase
A wicked and unjust applause: for Jove
Detests all violence, he bids us use
What we possess, but not increase our stores
By rapine. It is better to be poor,
Than gain unrighteous wealth. For all mankind
Enjoy these common blessings, Air and Earth;
Nor ought we our own house with gold to fill,
By keeping fraudfully another's right,
Or seizing it by violence. For Hermes,
Commissioned by the blest immortal powers,
Hath, at my cost, consigned me to thy sire,
To keep me for this husband, who is here
And claims me back again: but by what means
Can he receive me after he is dead?
Or how can the Ægyptian king restore me
A living consort to my breathless lord?
Consider therefore, both the will of Heaven
And that of thy great father. Would the god,
Would the deceased, surrender up or keep
Another's right? I deem they would restore it.
Hence to thy foolish brother shouldst not thou
Pay more respect than to thy virtuous sire.
And sure if thou, a prophetess, who utter'st
Th' oracular responses of the gods,
Break'st through thy father's justice, to comply
With an unrighteous brother: it were base
In thee to understand each mystic truth
Revealed by the immortal powers, the things
That are, and those that are not; yet o'erlook
The rules of justice. But O stoop to save
Me, miserable me, from all those ills
In which I am involved; this great exertion
Of thy benignant aid, my fortunes claim.
For there is no man who abhors not Helen;
'Tis rumoured through all Greece that I betrayed
My husband, and abode beneath the roofs
Of wealthy Phrygia. But to Greece once more
Should I return, and to the Spartan realm;

When they are told, and see, how to the arts
Of these contending goddesses they owe
Their ruin; but that I have to my friends
Been ever true, they to the rank I held
'Midst chaste and virtuous matrons, will restore me:
My daughter too, whom no man dares to wed,
From me her bridal portion shall receive;
And I, no longer doomed to lead the life
Of an unhappy vagrant, shall enjoy
The treasures that our palaces contain.
Had Menelaus died, and been consumed
In the funereal pyre, I should have wept
For him far distant in a foreign realm;
But now shall I for ever be bereft
Of him who lives, and seem to have escaped
From every danger. Virgin, act not thus;
To thee I kneel a suppliant; O confer
On me this boon, and emulate the justice
Of your great sire. For fair renown attends
The children, from a virtuous father sprung,
Who equal their hereditary worth.
  THEON. Most piteous are the words which you have
      spoken;
You also claim my pity: but I wish
To hear what Menelaus yet can plead
To save his life.
  MEN.   I cannot at your knees
Fall prostrate, or with tears these eyelids stain:
For I should cover all the great exploits
Which I achieved at Ilion with disgrace,
If I became a dastard; though some hold
'Tis not unworthy of the brave to weep
When wretched. But this honourable part
(If such a part can e'er be honourable)
I will not act, because the prosperous fortunes
Which erst were mine, are present to my soul.
If then you haply are disposed to save
A foreigner who justly claims his wife,
Restore her, and protect us: if you spurn
Our suit, I am not now for the first time,
But have been often wretched, and your name
Shall be recorded as an impious woman.
These thoughts, which I hold worthy of myself,
And just, and such as greatly must affect
Your inmost heart, I at your father's tomb
With energy will utter. Good old man,
Beneath this marble sepulchre who dwell'st,
To thee I sue, restore my wife, whom Jove
Sent hither to thy realm, that thou for me

Might'st guard her. Thou, I know, since thou art dead,
Canst ne'er have power to give her back again:
But she, this holy priestess, will not suffer
Reproach to fall on her illustrious sire,
Whom I invoke amid the shades beneath:
For this depends on her. Thee too I call,
O Pluto, to my aid, who hast received
Full many a corse, which fell in Helen's cause
Beneath my sword, and still retain'st the prize:
Eith'er restore them now to life, or force
Her who seems mightier than her pious father,
To give me back my wife. But of my consort
If ye resolve to rob me, I will urge
Those arguments which Helen hath omitted.
Know then, O virgin, first I by an oath
Have bound myself, your brother to encounter,
And he, or I, must perish; the plain truth
Is this. But foot to foot in equal combat,
If he refuse to meet me, and attempt
To drive us suppliants from the tomb by famine,
My consort will I slay, and with the sword
Here on this sepulchre my bosom pierce,
That the warm current of our blood may stream
Into the grave. Thus shall our corses lie
Close to each other on this polished marble:
To you eternal sorrow shall they cause,
And foul reproach to your great father's name.
For neither shall your brother wed my Helen,
Nor any man beside: for I with me
Will bear her; if I cannot bear her home,
Yet will I bear her to the shades beneath.
But why complain? If I shed tears, and act
The woman's part, I rather shall become
An object of compassion, than deserve
To be esteemed a warrior. If you list,
Slay me, for I can never fall inglorious.
But rather yield due credence to my words,
So will you act with justice, and my wife
Shall I recover.
 CHOR.   To decide the cause
On which we speak, belongs to thee, O virgin:
But so decide as to please all.
 THEON.   By nature
And inclination am I formed to act
With piety, myself too I revere:
Nor will I e'er pollute my sire's renown,
Or gratify my brother by such means
As might make me seem base. For from my birth,
Hath justice in this bosom fixed her shrine:

And since from Nereus I inherited
This temper, Menelaus will I strive
To save. But now since Juno is disposed
To be your friend, with her will I accord:
May Venus be propitious, though her rites
I never have partaken, and will strive
For ever to remain a spotless maid.
But I concur with thee, O Menelaus,
In all thou to my father at his tomb
Hast said: for with injustice should I act
If I restored not Helen: had he lived,
My sire on thee again would have bestowed
Thy consort, and her former lord on Helen.
For vengeance, in the shades of Hell beneath,
And among all that breathe the vital air,
Attends on those who break their plighted trust.
The soul of the deceased, although it live
Indeed no longer, yet doth still retain
A consciousness which lasts for ever, lodged
In the eternal scene of its abode,
The liquid ether. To express myself
Concisely, all that you requested me
Will I conceal, nor with my counsels aid
My brother's folly; I to him shall show
A real friendship, though without the semblance,
If I his vicious manners can reform
And make him more religious. Therefore find
Means to escape yourselves; for I will hence
Depart in silence. First implore the gods;
To Venus sue, that she your safe return
Would suffer; and to Juno, not to change
The scheme which she hath formed, both to preserve
Your lord and you. O my departed sire,
For thee will I exert my utmost might,
That on thy honoured name no foul reproach
May ever rest. [*Exit* THEONOE.
 CHOR. No impious man e'er prospered:
But fairest hopes attend an honest cause.
 HEL. O Menelaus, as to what depends
Upon the royal maid, are we secure:
But next doth it become you to propose
Some means our safety to effect.
 MEN. Now listen
To me; thou in this palace long hast dwelt,
An inmate with the servants of the king.
 HEL. Why speak you thus? for you raise hopes, as though
You could do somewhat for our common good.
 MEN. Canst thou prevail on any one of those

Who guide the harnessed steeds, to furnish us
With a swift car?

HEL. Perhaps I might succeed
In that attempt. But how shall we escape
Who to these fields and this barbarian land
Are strangers? An impracticable thing
Is this you speak of.

MEN. Well, but in the palace
Concealed, if with this sword the king I slay.

HEL. His sister will not suffer this in silence
If you attempt aught 'gainst her brother's life.

MEN. We have no ship in which we can escape;
For that which we brought hither, by the waves
Is swallowed up.

HEL. Now hear what I propose;
From woman's lips if wisdom ever flow.
Will you permit a rumour of your death
To be dispersed?

MEN. This were an evil omen:
But I, if any benefit arise
From such report, consent to be called dead
While I yet live.

HEL. That impious tyrant's pity
Our female choir shall move, with tresses shorn,
And chaunt funereal strains.

MEN. What tendency
Can such a project have to our deliverance?

HEL. I will allege that 'tis an ancient custom;
And of the monarch his permission crave,
That I on you, as if you in the sea
Had perished, may bestow a vacant tomb.

MEN. If he consent, how can this feigned interment
Enable us to fly without a ship?

HEL. I will command a bark to be prepared,
From whence into the bosom of the deep
Funereal trappings I may cast.

MEN. How well
And wisely hast thou spoken! but the tomb
If he direct thee on the strand to raise,
Nought can this scheme avail.

HEL. But I will say
'Tis not the usage, in a Grecian realm,
With earth to cover the remains of those
Who perished in the waves.

MEN. Thou hast again
Removed this obstacle: I then with thee
Will sail, and the funereal trappings place
In the same vessel.

HEL. 'Tis of great importance

That you, and all those mariners who 'scaped
The shipwreck, should be present.
  MEN.   If we find
A bark at anchor, with our falchions armed
In one collected band will we assail
And board it.
  HEL. To direct all this, belongs
To you; but may the prosperous breezes fill
Our sails, and guide us o'er the billowy deep.
  MEN. These vows shall be accomplished; for the gods
At length will cause my toils to cease: but whence
Wilt thou pretend thou heard'st that I was dead?
  HEL. Yourself shall be the messenger; relate
How you alone escaped his piteous doom,
A partner of the voyage with the son
Of Atreus, and the witness of his death.
  MEN. This tattered vest will testify my shipwreck.
  HEL. How seasonable was that which seemed at first
To be a grievous loss! but the misfortune
May end perhaps in bliss.
  MEN.   Must I with thee
Enter the palace, or before this tomb
Sit motionless?
  HEL.   Here stay: for if the king
By force should strive to tear you hence, this tomb
And your drawn sword will save you. But I'll go
To my apartment, shear my flowing hair,
For sable weeds this snowy vest exchange,
And rend with bloody nails these livid cheeks:
For 'tis a mighty conflict, and I see
These two alternatives: if in my plots
Detected, I must die; or to my country
I shall return, and save your life. O Juno,
Thou sacred queen, who shar'st the couch of Jove,
Relieve two wretches from their toils; to thee
Our suppliant arms uplifting high t'wards Heaven
With glittering stars adorned, thy blest abode,
We sue: and thou, O Venus, who didst gain
The palm of beauty through my promised 'spousals,
Spare me, thou daughter of Dione, spare;
For thou enough hast injured me already;
Exposing not my person, but my name,
To those barbarians; suffer me to die,
If thou wilt slay me, in my native land.
Why art thou still insatiably malignant?
Why dost thou harass me by love, by fraud,
By the invention of these new deceits,
And by thy magic philtres plunge in blood
Our miserable house? If thou hadst ruled

With mildness, thou to man hadst been most grateful
Of all the gods. I speak not this at random.
[HELEN *and* MENELAUS *retire behind the tomb*.

CHORUS.

ODE.

I. I.

On thee who build'st thy tuneful seat
Protected by the leafy groves, I call,
O nightingale, thy accents ever sweet
Their murmuring melancholy fall
Prolong! O come, and with thy plaintive strain
   Aid me to utter my distress,
Thy woes, O Helen, let the song express,
And those of Troy now levelled with the plain
By Grecian might. From hospitable shores,
   Relying on barbaric oars,
      The spoiler Paris fled,
And o'er the deep to Priam's realm with pride
   Bore his imaginary bride,
Fancying that thou hadst graced his bed,
To nuptials fraught with shame by wanton Venus led.

I. 2.

Unnumbered Greeks, transpierced with spears,
Or crushed beneath the falling ramparts, bled:
Hence with her tresses shorn, immersed in tears
   The matron wails her lonely bed,
But Nauplius, kindling near th' Eubœan deep
   Those torches, o'er our host prevailed;
Though with a single bark the traitor sailed,
He wrecked whole fleets against Caphareus' steep,
And the Ægean coasts, the beacon seemed
   A star, and through Heaven's conclave gleamed,
      Placed on the craggy height.
While flushed with conquest, from the Phrygian strand
   They hastened to their native land,
   Portentous source of bloody fight,
The cloud by Juno formed, beguiled their dazzled sight.

II. I.

Whether the image was divine,
Drew from terrestrial particles its birth,
Or from the middle region, how define
   By curious search, ye sons of earth?

Far from unravelling Heaven's abstruse intents,
    We view the world tost to and fro,
Mark strange vicissitudes of joy and woe,
Discordant and miraculous events.
Thou, Helen, art indeed the child of Jove.
      The swan, thy sire, inflamed by love,
        To Leda's bosom flew :
Yet with imputed crimes malignant fame
      Through Greece arraigns thy slandered name.
Of men I know not whom to trust,
But what the gods pronounce have I found ever just.

II. 2.

    Frantic are ye who seek renown
Amid the horrors of th' embattled field,
Who masking guilt beneath a laurel crown
    With nervous arm the falchion wield,
Not slaughtered thousands can your fury sate.
    If still success the judgment guide,
If bloody battle right and wrong decide,
Incessant strife must vex each rival state :
Hence from her home departs each Phrygian wife,
    O Helen, when the cruel strife
      Which from thy charms arose,
One conference might have closed : now myriads dwell
    With Pluto in the shades of Hell,
    And flames, as when Jove's vengeance throws
The bolt, have caught her towers and finished Ilion's woes.

THEOCLYMENUS, CHORUS (HELEN *and* MENELAUS *behind the tomb*).

THEOC. Hail, O thou tomb of my illustrious sire !
For thee have I interred before my gate,
That with thy shade I might hold frequent conference,
O Proteus ; Theoclymenus thy son
Thee, O my father, oft as he goes forth,
Oft as he enters these abodes, accosts.
But to the palace now convey those hounds
And nets, my servants. I full many a time
Have blamed myself, because I never punished
With death such miscreants ; now I am informed
That publicly some Greek to these domains
Is come unnoticed by my guards, a spy,
Or one who means to carry Helen off
By stealth : but if I seize him, he shall die.
Methinks I find all over : for the daughter
Of Tyndarus sits no longer at the tomb,
But from these shores hath fled, and now is crossing

The billowy deep. Unbar the gates, bring forth
My coursers from the stalls, and brazen cars;
Lest through my want of vigilance the dame
Whom I would make my consort, should escape me,
Borne from this land. Yet stay; for I behold
Those we pursue still here beneath this roof,
Nor are they fled. Ho! why in sable vest
Hast thou arrayed thyself, why cast aside
Thy robes of white, and from thy graceful head
With ruthless steel thy glowing ringlets shorn,
And wherefore bathed thy cheek with recent tears?
Groan'st thou, by visions of the night apprized
Of some calamity, or hast thou heard
Within, a rumour that afflicts thy soul?

HEL. My lord (for I already by that name
Accost you), I am utterly undone,
My former bliss is vanished, and I now
Am nothing.

THEOC. Art thou plunged into distress
So irretrievable? what cruel fate
Hath overtaken thee?

HEL. My Menelaus,
(Ah, how shall I express myself?) is dead.

THEOC. Although I must not triumph in th' event
Thou speak'st of, yet to me 'tis most auspicious.
How know'st thou? Did Theonoe tell thee this?

HEL. She and this mariner, who when he perished
Was present, both concur in the same tale.

THEOC. Is there a man arrived, who for the truth
Of that account can vouch?

HEL. He is arrived:
And would to Heaven that such auspicious fortune
As I could wish attended him.

THEOC. Who is he?
Where is he? I would know the real fact.

HEL. 'Tis he who stupefied with sorrow sits
Upon the tomb.

THEOC. In what unseemly garb
Is he arrayed, O Phœbus!

HEL. In that dress,
Ah me! methinks my husband I behold.

THEOC. But in what country was the stranger born,
And whence did he come hither?

HEL. He's a Greek,
One of those Greeks who with my husband sailed.

THEOC. How doth he say that Menelaus died?

HEL. Most wretchedly, engulfed amid the waves.

THEOC. Where? as he passed o'er the barbarian
 seas?

Hel. Dashed on the rocks of Libya, which affords
No haven.
Theoc. But whence happened it, that he
This partner of his voyage did not perish?
Hel. The worthless are more prosperous than the brave.
Theoc. Where left he the wrecked fragments of his ship
When he came hither?
Hel. There, where would to Heaven
Perdition had o'ertaken him, and spared
The life of Menelaus.
Theoc. He, it seems,
Is then no more: but in what bark arrived
This messenger?
Hel. Some sailors, as he says,
By chance passed by, and snatched him from the waves.
Theoc. But where's that hateful pest which in thy stead
Was sent to Ilion?
Hel. Speak you of a cloud,
Resembling me? it mounted to the skies.
Theoc. O Priam, for how frivolous a cause
Thou with thy Troy didst perish!
Hel. In their woes
I too have been involved.
Theoc. But did he leave
Thy husband's corse unburied, or strew dust
O'er his remains?
Hel. He left them uninterred,
Ah, wretched me!
Theoc. And didst thou for this cause
Sever the ringlets of thy auburn hair?
Hel. Still is he dear, lodged in this faithful breast.
Theoc. Hast thou sufficient reason then to weep
For this calamity?
Hel. Could you bear lightly
Your sister's death?
Theoc. No surely. But what means
Thy still residing at this marble tomb?
Hel. Why do you harass me with taunting words,
And why disturb the dead?
Theoc. Because, still constant
To thy first husband, from my love thou fliest.
Hel. But I will fly no longer: haste, begin
The nuptial rite.
Theoc. 'Twas long ere thou didst come
To this: but I such conduct must applaud.
Hel. Know you then how to act? let us forget
All that has passed.
Theoc. Upon what terms? with kindness
Should kindness be repaid.

HEL.   Let us conclude
The peace, and O be reconciled.
  THEOC.   All strife
With thee I to the winds of heaven consign.
  HEL. Now, since you are my friend, I by those knees
Conjure you.
  THEOC.   With what object in thy view,
To me an earnest suppliant dost thou bend?
  HEL. I my departed husband would inter.
  THEOC. What tomb can be bestowed upon the absent
Wouldst thou inter his shade?
  HEL.   There is a custom
Among the Greeks established, that the man
Who in the ocean perishes——
  THEOC.   What is it?
For in such matters Pelops' race are wise.
  HEL. To bury in their stead an empty vest.
  THEOC. Perform funereal rites, and heap the tomb
On any ground thou wilt.
  HEL.   We in this fashion
Bury not the drowned mariner.
  THEOC.   How then?
I am a stranger to the Grecian customs.
  HEL. Each pious gift due to our breathless friends
We cast into the sea.
  THEOC.   On the deceased
What presents for thy sake can I bestow?
  HEL. I know not: for in offices like these
Am I unpractised, having erst been happy.
  THEOC. An acceptable message have you brought,
O stranger.
  MEN.   Most ungrateful to myself
And the deceased.
  THEOC.   What funereal rites on those
Ocean hath swallowed up, do ye bestow?
  MEN. Such honours as each individual's wealth
Enables us to pay him.
  THEOC.   Name the cost,
And for her sake receive whate'er you will.
  MEN. Blood is our first libation to the dead.
  THEOC. What blood? inform me, for with your
       instructions
I will comply.
  MEN.   Determine that thyself,
For whatsoe'er thou giv'st will be sufficient.
  THEOC. The customary victims 'mong barbarians
Are either horse or bull.
  MEN.   Whate'er thou giv'st,
Let it be somewhat princely.

THEOC.   My rich herds
With these are amply furnished.
    MEN.   And the bier
Without the corse is borne in solemn state.
    THEOC. It shall: but what is there beside which custom
Requires to grace the funeral.
    MEN.   Brazen arms:
For war was what he loved.
    THEOC.   We will bestow
Such presents as are worthy of the race
Of mighty Pelops.
    MEN.   And those budding flowers
Th' exuberant soil produces.
    THEOC.   But say, how
And in what manner ye these offerings plunge
Into the ocean.
    MEN.   We must have a bark
And mariners to ply the oars.
    THEOC.   How far
Will they launch forth the vessel from the strand?
    MEN. So far as from the shore thou scarce wilt see
The keel divide the waves.
    THEOC.   But why doth Greece
Observe this usage?
    MEN.   'Lest the rising billows
Cast back to land th' ablutions.
    THEOC.   Ye shall have
A swift Phœnician vessel.
    MEN.   This were kind,
And no small favour shown to Menelaus.
    THEOC. Without her presence, cannot you perform
These rites alone?
    MEN.   Such task or to a mother,
Or wife, or child, belongs.
    THEOC.   'Tis then her duty,
You say, to bury her departed lord?
    MEN. Sure, piety instructs us not to rob
The dead of their accustomed dues.
    THEOC.   Enough:
On me it is incumbent to promote
Such virtue in my consort. I will enter
The palace, and from thence for the deceased
Bring forth rich ornaments; with empty hands
You from this region will not I send forth,
That you may execute what she desires.
But having brought me acceptable tidings,
Instead of these vile weeds shall you receive
A decent garb and food, that to your country
You may return: for clearly I perceive

That you are wretched now. But torture not
Thy bosom with unprofitable cares,
O hapless woman, for thy Menelaus
Is now no more, nor can the dead revive.

MEN. Thee it behoves, O blooming dame, to love
Thy present husband, and to lay aside
The fond remembrance of thy breathless lord;
For such behaviour suits thy fortunes best.
But if to Greece with safety I return,
That infamy which erst pursued thy name
I'll cause to cease, if thou acquit thyself
Of these great duties like a virtuous consort.

HEL. I will; nor shall my husband e'er have cause
To blame me: you too, who are here, shall witness
The truth of my assertions. But within
Go lave your wearied limbs, O wretched man,
And change your habit; for without delay
To you will I become a benefactress.
Hence too with greater zeal will you perform
The rites my dearest Menelaus claims,
If all due honours you from me receive.

[*Exeunt* THEOCLYMENUS, HELEN, *and* MENELAUS.

CHORUS.

ODE.

I. 1.

O'er mountains erst with hasty tread
Did the celestial mother stray,
Nor stop where branching thickets spread,
Where rapid torrents crossed her way,
Or on the margin of the billowy deep;
  Her daughter whom we dread to name
She wept, while hailing that majestic dame,
Cymbals of Bacchus from the craggy steep
  Sent forth their clear and piercing sound,
  Her car the harnessed dragons drew;
Following the nymph torn from her virgin crew.
Amidst her maidens swift of foot were found
  Diana skilled the bow to wield,
  Minerva, who in glittering state
Brandished the spear and raised her Gorgon shield;
But Jove looked down from Heaven t' award another fate.

I. 2.

Soon as the mother's toils were o'er,
When she had finished her career,
And sought the ravished maid no more,
To caves where drifted snows appear,

By Ida's nymphs frequented, did she pass,
   And threw herself in sorrow lost,
On rocks and herbage crusted o'er with frost,
Despoiled the wasted champaign of its grass,
    Rendered the peasant's tillage vain,
    Consuming a dispeopled land
With meagre famine; Spring at her command
Denied the flocks that sickened on the plain
    The leafy tendrils of the vine;
    Whole cities died, no victims bled,
No frankincense perfumed Heaven's vacant shrine;
Nor burst the current from the Spring's obstructed head.

II. 1.

    Then ceased the banquet, wont to charm
    Both gods above and men below:
    The mother's anger to disarm,
    And mitigate the stings of woe,
Till in these words Jove uttered his behests:
    " Let each benignant grace attend
Sweet music's sympathizing aid to lend,
And drive corrosive grief from Ceres' breast
    Indignant for her ravished child:
    Now, O ye Muses, with the lyre
Join the shrill hymns of your assembled choir,
The brazen trumpet fill with accents wild,
    And beat the rattling drums amain."
    Then first of the immortal band,
Venus with lovely smile approved the strain,
And raised the deep-toned flute in her enchanting hand.

II. 2.

    The laws reproved such foul desire,
    Yet 'gainst religion didst thou wed;
    Thy uncle caught love's baleful fire,
    And rushed to thy incestuous bed.
Thee shall the mighty mother's wrath confound,
    Because, through thee, before her shrine
No victims slain appease the powers divine.
Great virtue have hinds' hides, and ivy wound
    Upon a consecrated rod;
    And youths, with virgins in a ring,
When high from earth with matchless force they spring,
  Loose streams their hair, they celebrate that god
    The Bacchanalian votaries own,
    And waste in dance the sleepless night.
But thou, confiding in thy charms alone,
Forgett'st the moon that shines with more transcendent
  light.

HELEN, CHORUS.

HEL. Within the palace, O my friends, we prosper
For Proteus' royal daughter, in our schemes
Conspiring when her brother questioned her
About my lord, no information gave
Of his arrival: to my interests true
She said, that cold in death he views no longer
The radiant sun. But now my lord hath seized
A vengeful falchion, in that mail designed
To have been plunged beneath the deep arrayed,
With nervous arm he lifts an orbed shield,
In his right hand protended gleams the spear,
As if with me he was prepared to pay
To the deceased due homage. Furnished thus
With brazen arms, he's ready for the battle,
And numberless barbarians will subdue
Unaided, soon as we the ship ascend.
Exchanging those unseemly weeds which clothe
The shipwrecked mariner, in splendid robes
Have I arrayed him, from transparent springs
The laver filled, and bathed his wearied limbs
But I must now be silent, for the man
Who fancies I am ready to become
His consort, leaves the palace. O my friends,
In your attachment too I place my trust,
Restrain your tongues, for we, when saved ourselves,
If possible will save you from this thraldom.

THEOCLYMENUS, HELEN, MENELAUS, CHORUS.

THEOC. Go forth, in such procession as the stranger
Directs you, O my servants, and convey
These gifts funereal to the briny deep.
But if thou dissapprove not what I say,
Do thou, O Helen, yield to my persuasions,
And here remain. For whether thou attend,
Or art not present at the obsequies
Of thy departed husband, thou to him
Wilt show an equal reverence. Much I dread
Lest hurried on by wild desire thou plunge
Into the foaming billows, for the sake
Of him on whom thou doat'st, thy former lord,
Since thou his doom immoderately bewail'st
Though he be lost, and never can return.

HEL. O my illustrious husband, I am bound
To pay due honours to the man whom first
I wedded, of our ancient nuptial joys
A memory still retaining, for so well
I loved my lord that I could even die

With him. But what advantage would result
To the deceased, should I lay down my life?
Yet let me go myself, and to his shade
Perform each solemn rite. But may the gods,
On you, and on the stranger who assists me
In this my pious task, with liberal hand
Confer the gifts I wish. But you in me
Shall such a consort to your palace bear
As you deserve, to recompense your kindness
To me and Menelaus. Such events
In some degree are measured by the will
Of Fortune: but give orders for a ship
To be prepared, these trappings to convey,
So shall your purposed bounty be complete.
  THEOC. [*to one of his Attendants.*]
Go thou, and furnish them a Tyrian bark
Of fifty oars, with skilful sailors manned.
  HEL. But may not he who decorates the tomb
Govern the ship?
  THEOC.   My sailors must to him
Yield an implicit deference.
  HEL.   This injunction
Repeat, that they may clearly understand it.
  THEOC. A second time, will I, and yet a third,
Issue this self-same mandate, if to thee
This can give pleasure.
  HEL.   May the gods confer
Blessings on you, and prosper my designs!
  THEOC. Waste not thy bloom with unavailing tears.
  HEL. To you this day my gratitude will prove.
  THEOC. All these attentions to the dead are nought
But unavailing toil.
  HEL.   My pious care
Not to those only whom the silent grave
Contains, but to the living too extends.
  THEOC. In me thou mayst expect to find a husband
Who yields not to the Spartan Menelaus.
  HEL. I censure not your conduct, but bewail
My own harsh destiny.
  THEOC.   Bestow thy love
On me, and prosperous fortunes shall return.
  HEL. It is a lesson I have practised long,
To love my friends.
  THEOC.   Shall I my navy launch,
To join in these funereal rites?
  HEL.   Dread lord,
Pay not unseemly homage to your vassals.
  THEOC. Well! I each sacred usage will allow
Practised by Pelops' race, for my abodes

Are undefiled with blood: thy Menelaus
In Ægypt died not. But let some one haste
And bid the nobles bear into my house
The bridal gifts : for the whole earth is bound
To celebrate in one consenting hymn
My blest espousals with the lovely Helen.
But go, embark upon the briny main,
O stranger, and as soon as ye have paid
All decent homage to her former lord
Bring back my consort hither: that with me
When you have feasted at our nuptial rite
You to your native mansion may return,
Or here continue in a happy state. [*Exit* THEOCLYMENUS.

MEN. O Jove, thou mighty father, who art called
A god supreme in wisdom, from thy heaven
Look down, and save us from our woes: delay not
To aid us : for we drag the galling yoke
Of sorrow and mischance: if with thy finger
Thou do but touch us, we shall soon attain
The fortune which we wish for, since the toils
We have endured already are sufficient.
Ye gods, I now invoke you, from my mouth
So shall ye hear full many joyful accents
Mixed with these bitter plaints : for I deserve not
To be for ever wretched ; but to tread
At length secure. O grant me this one favour,
And make my future life completely blest.
[*Exeunt* MENELAUS *and* HELEN.

CHORUS.

ODE.

I. I.

Swift bark of Sidon, by whose dashing oars
Divided oft, the frothy billows rise,
Propitious be thy voyage from these shores:
   In thy train the dolphins play,
    O'er the deep thou lead'st the way,
While motionless its placid surface lies.
   Soon as Serenity the fair,
    That azure daughter of the main,
    Shall in this animating strain
Have spoken : "To the gentle breeze of air
    Expand each undulating sail,
    Row briskly on before the gale,
Ye mariners, in Perseus' ancient seat
    Till Helen rest her wearied feet."

I. 2.

Those sacred nymphs shall welcome thy return
 Who guard the portals of Minerva's fane
 Or speed the current from its murmuring urn:
  Choral dances of delight
  That prolong the jocund night,
At Hyacinthus' banquet shalt thou join,
  Fair stripling, whom with luckless hand
  Unwitting did Apollo slay
  At games that crowned the festive day,
Hurling his quoit on the Laconian strand;
  To him Jove's son due honours paid:
  At Sparta too, that lovely maid
Shalt thou behold, whom there thou left'st behind,
  Still to celibacy consigned.

II. I.

O might we cleave the air, like Libyan cranes,
Who fly in ranks th' impending wintry storm;
When their shrill leader bids them quit the plains,
  They the veteran's voice obey,
  O'er rich harvests wing their way,
Or where parched wastes th' unfruitful scene deform.
  With lengthened neck, ye feathered race
  Who skim the clouds in social band,
  Where the seven Pleiades expand
Their radiance, and Orion heaves his mace,
  This joyous embassy convey
  As near Eurotas' banks ye stray;
That Menelaus to his subject land
  Victorious comes from Phrygia's strand.

II. 2.

Borne in your chariot down th' ethereal height,
At length, ye sons of Tyndarus, appear,
While vibrates o'er your heads the starry light:
  Habitants of heaven above,
  Now exert fraternal love,
If ever Helen to your souls was dear,
  A calm o'er th' azure ocean spread,
  Bridle the tempests of the main,
  Propitious gales from Jove obtain,
Your sister snatch from the barbarian's bed:
  Commenced on Ida's hill, that strife,
  Embittered with reproach her life,
Although she never viewed proud Ilion's tower
  Reared by Apollo's matchless power.

THEOCLYMENUS, MESSENGER, CHORUS.

MES. O king, I have discovered in the palace,
Events most inauspicious: what fresh woes
Is it my doleful office to relate!
   THEOC. Say what hath happened?
   MES.   Seek another wife,
For Helen hath departed from this realm.
   THEOC. Borne through the air on wings, or with swift foot
Treading the ground?
   MES.   Her o'er the briny main
From Ægypt's shores, hath Menelaus wafted,
Who came in person with a feigned account
Of his own death.
   THEOC.   O dreadful tale! what ship
From these domains conveys her? thou relat'st
Tidings the most incredible.
   MES.   The same
You to that stranger gave, and in one word
To tell you all, he carries off your sailors.
   THEOC. How is that possible? I wish to know:
For such an apprehension never entered
My soul, as that one man could have subdued
The numerous band of mariners, with whom
Thou wert sent forth.
   MES.   When from the royal mansion
Jove's daughter to the shore was borne, she trod
With delicate and artful step, pretending
To wail her husband's loss, though he was present,
And yet alive. But when we reached the haven,
Sidonia's largest vessel we hauled forth,
Furnished with benches, and with fifty oars;
But a fresh series of incessant toil
Followed this toil; for while one fixed the mast,
Another ranged the oars, and with his hand
The signal gave, the sails were bound together,
Then was the rudder fastened to the stern
With thongs, cast forth: while they observed us busied
In such laborious task, the Grecian comrades
Of Menelaus to the shore advanced,
Clad in their shipwrecked vestments. Though their form
Was graceful, yet their visages were squalid:
But Atreus' son, beholding their approach,
Under the semblance of a grief that masked
His treacherous purpose, in these words addressed them:
" How, O ye wretched sailors, from what bark
Of Greece that hath been wrecked upon this coast
Are ye come hither? will ye join with us
In the funereal rites of Menelaus,

Whom Tyndarus's daughter, to an empty tomb
Consigns, though absent?" Simulated tears
They shed, and went aboard the ship, conveying
The presents to be cast into the sea
For Menelaus. But to us these things
Appeared suspicious, and we made remarks
Among ourselves upon the numerous band
Of our intruding passengers; but checked
Our tongues from speaking openly, through deference
To your commands. For when you to that stranger
Trusted the guidance of the ship, you caused
This dire confusion. All beside, with ease
Had we now lodged aboard, but could not force
The sturdy bull t' advance; he bellowing rolled
His eyes around, bending his back and low'ring
Betwixt his horns, nor dared we to approach
And handle him. But Helen's husband cried:
"O ye who laid Troy waste, will ye forget
To act like Greeks? why scruple ye to seize
And on your youthful shoulders heave the beast
Up to the rising prow, a welcome victim
To the deceased?" His falchion, as he spoke,
The warrior drew. His summons they obeyed,
Seized the stout bull, and carried him aboard:
But Menelaus stroked the horse's neck
And face, and with this gentle usage led him
Into the bark. At length when all its freight
The vessel had received, with graceful foot
Helen, the steps ascending, took her seat
On the mid deck; and Menelaus near her,
E'en he who they pretended was no more.
But some on the right side, and on the left
Others in equal numbers, man to man
Opposed, their station took, their swords concealing
Beneath their garments. We distinctly heard
The clamorous sailors animate each other
To undertake the voyage. But from land
When a convenient distance we had steered,
The pilot asked this question: "Shall we sail,
O stranger, any farther from the coast,
Or is this right? for 'tis my task to guide
The vessel." He replied: "Enough for me."
Then seized with his right hand the falchion, leaped
Upon the prow, and standing o'er the bull
The victim (without mentioning the name
Of any chief deceased; but as he drove
The weapon through his neck) thus prayed: "O Neptune,
Who in the ocean dwell'st, and ye chaste daughters
Of Nereus, to the Nauplian shore convey

Me and my consort, from this hostile land,
In safety." But a crimson tide of blood,
Auspicious to the stranger, stained the waves;
And some exclaimed: "There's treachery in this voyage,
Let us sail homewards, issue thy commands,
And turn the rudder." But the son of Atreus,
Who had just slain the bull, to his companions
Called loudly: "Why delay, O ye the flower
Of Greece, to smite, to slaughter those barbarians,
And cast them from the ship into the waves?"
But to your sailors our commander spoke
A different language: "Will not some of you
Tear up a plank, or with a shattered bench,
Or ponderous oar, upon the bleeding heads
Of those audacious foreigners our foes,
Impress the ghastly wound?" But on their feet
All now stood up; our hands with nautic poles
Were armed, and theirs with swords: a tide of slaughter
Ran down the ship. But Helen from the poop
The Greeks encouraged: "Where is the renown
Ye gained at Troy? display 'gainst these barbarians
The same undaunted prowess." In their haste
Full many fell, some rose again, the rest
Might you have seen stretched motionless in death.
But Menelaus, sheathed in glittering mail,
Wherever his confederates he descried
Hard pressed, rushed thither with his lifted sword,
Driving us headlong from the lofty deck
Into the waves, and forced your mariners
To quit their oars. But the victorious king
Now seized the rudder, and to Greece declared
He would convey the ship: they hoisted up
The stately mast: propitious breezes came;
They left the land: but I from death escaping,
Let myself gently down into the waves
Borne on the cordage which sustains the anchor;
My strength began to fail, when some kind hand
Threw forth a rope, and brought me safe ashore,
That I to you these tidings might convey.
There's nought more beneficial to mankind
Than wise distrust.
    CHOR.   I never could have thought
That Menelaus who was here, O king,
Could have imposed so grossly or on you
Or upon us.
    THEOC.   Wretch that I am, ensnared
By woman's treacherous arts! the lovely bride
I hoped for, hath escaped me. If the ship
Could be o'ertaken by our swift pursuit,

My wrongs would urge me with vindictive hand
To seize the strangers. But I now will punish
That sister who betrayed me ; in my house
Who when she saw the Spartan Menelaus,
Informed me not : she never shall deceive
Another man by her prophetic voice.

   CHOR. Ho ! whither, O my sovereign, would you go,
And for what bloody purpose ?
   THEOC.   Where the voice
Of rigid justice summons me. Retire,
And stand aloof.
   CHOR.   Yet will not I let loose
Your garment ; for you hasten to commit
A deed most mischievous.
   THEOC.   Wouldst thou, a slave,
Govern thy lord ?
   CHOR.   Here reason's on my side.
   THEOC. That shall not I allow, if thou refuse
To quit thy hold.
   CHOR.   I will not then release you.
   THEOC. To slay that worst of sisters.
   CHOR.   That most pious.
   THEOC. Her who betrayed me.
   CHOR.   Glorious was the fraud
That caused so just a deed.
   THEOC.   When she bestowed
My consort on another.
   CHOR.   On the man
Who had a better claim——
   THEOC.   But who is lord
Of what belongs to me ?
   CHOR.   Who from her sire
Received her.
   THEOC.   She by Fortune was bestowed
On me.
   CHOR. But ta'en away again by Fate.
   THEOC. Thou hast no right to judge of my affairs.
   CHOR. If I but speak to give you better counsels.
   THEOC. I am thy subject then, and not thy king.
   CHOR. For having acted piously, your sister
I vindicate.
   THEOC. Thou seem'st to wish for death.
   CHOR. Kill me. Your sister you with my consent
Shall never slay ; I rather would yield up
My life on her behalf. It is most glorious
To generous servants for their lords to die,

CASTOR *and* POLLUX, THEOCLYMENUS, CHORUS.

CAS. *and* POL. Restrain that ire that hurries thee away
Beyond the bounds of reason, O thou king
Of Ægypt's realm; and listen to the voice
Of us twin sons of Jove, whom Leda bore
Together with that Helen who is fled
From thy abodes. Thou rashly hast indulged
Thine anger, for the loss of her whom Fate
Ne'er destined to thy bed. Nor hath thy sister
Theonoe, from th' immortal Nereid sprung,
To thee done any injury; she reveres
The gods, and her great father's just behests.
For till the present hour, was it ordained
That Helen in thy palace should reside:
But when Troy's walls were from their bases torn,
And she had to the rival goddesses
Furnished her name, no longer was it fit
That she should for thy nuptials be detained,
But to her ancient home return, and dwell
With her first husband. In thy sister's breast
Forbear to plunge the sword, and be convinced
That she in this affair hath acted wisely.
We long ere this our sister had preserved,
Since Jove hath made us gods, but were too weak
At once to combat the behests of Fate,
And the immortal powers, who had ordained
That these events should happen. This to thee,
O Theoclymenus, I speak. These words
Next to my lovely sister, I address;
Sail with your husband, for a prosperous breeze
Your voyage shall attend. We your protectors
And your twin brothers, on our coursers borne
Over the waves, will guide you to your country,
But after you have finished life's career,
You shall be called a goddess, shall partake
With us the rich oblations, and receive
The gifts of men: for thus hath Jove decreed.
But where the son of Maia placed you first,
When he had borne you from the Spartan realm,
And formed by stealth from the aërial mansions
An image of your person, to prevent
Paris from wedding you, there is an isle
Near the Athenian realm, which men shall call
Helen in future times, because that spot
Received you, when in secrecy conveyed
From Sparta. The Heavens also have ordained
The wanderer Menelaus shall reside
Among the happy islands. For the gods

To those of nobler minds no hatred bear;
At their command though grievous toil await
The countless multitude.
  THEOC.   Ye sons of Jove
And Leda, I the contest will decline
Which I at first so violently urged,
Hoping your lovely sister to obtain,
And my own sister's life resolve to spare:
Let Helen to her native shores return,
If 'tis the will of Heaven: but be assured,
The same high blood ye spring from with the best
And chastest sister: hail then, for the sake
Of Helen with a lofty soul endued,
Such as in female bosoms seldom dwells.
  CHOR. A thousand shapes our varying fates assume
The gods perform what least we could expect,
And oft the things for which we fondly hoped
Come not to pass; but Heaven still finds a clue
To guide our steps through life's perplexing maze,
And thus doth this important business end.

ANDROMACHE.

PERSONS OF THE DRAMA.

ANDROMACHE.
ATTENDANT.
CHORUS OF PHTHIAN
 WOMEN.
HERMIONE.
MENELAUS.

MOLOSSUS.
PELEUS.
NURSE OF HERMIONE.
ORESTES.
MESSENGER.
THETIS.

SCENE.—THE VESTIBULE OF THETIS' TEMPLE BETWEEN PHTHIA AND PHARSALIA IN THESSALY.

ANDROMACHE.

O THEBES, thou pride of Asia, from whose gate
I came resplendent with a plenteous dower,
To Priam's regal house, the fruitful wife
Of Hector: his Andromache was erst
An envied name: but now am I more wretched
Than any woman, or already born,
Or to be born hereafter; for I saw
My husband Hector by Achilles slain,
And that unhappy son whom to my lord
I bore, Astyanax, from Troy's high towers
Thrown headlong; when our foes had sacked the city,
Myself descended from a noble line
Of freeborn warriors, reached the Grecian coast,
On Neoptolemus that island prince
For the reward of his victorious arms
Bestowed: selected from the Phrygian spoils.
'Twixt Phthia and Pharsalia, in these fields,
I dwell, where Thetis from the haunts of men
Retreating, with her Peleus erst abode.
By Thessaly's inhabitants, this spot
Is from th' auspicious nuptials of that goddess
Called Thetidæum: here Achilles' son
Residing, suffers Peleus still to rule
Pharsalia's land, nor will assume the sceptre
While lives his aged grandsire. In these walls

A son, who to th' embraces of my lord
Achilles' offspring, owes his birth, I bore,
And though I had been wretched, a fond hope
Still cherished, that while yet the boy was safe
I some protection and relief might find
In my calamities; but since my lord
(Spurning my servile couch) that Spartan dame
Hermione espoused, with ruthless hate
By her am I pursued; for she pretends
That I, by drugs endued with magic power,
Administered in secret, make her barren
And odious to her lord, because I wish
To occupy this mansion in her stead,
And forcibly to drive her from his couch,
To which, at first I with reluctance came,
But now have left it: mighty Jove can witness
That I became the partner of his bed
Against my own consent. But she remains
Deaf to conviction, and attempts to slay me:
In this design her father Menelaus
Assists his daughter, he is now within,
And on such errand left the Spartan realm:
Fearing his rage, I near the palace take
My seat, in Thetis' temple, that the goddess
From death may save me; for both Peleus' self,
And the descendants of that monarch, hold
This structure reared in memory of his wedlock
With the fair Nereid, in religious awe.
But hence, in secret, trembling for his life,
My only child have I conveyed away,
Because his noble father is not present
To aid me, and avails not now to guard
His son, while absent in the Delphic land,
To expiate there the rage with which he sought
The Pythian tripod, and from Phœbus claimed
A reparation for his father's death.
If haply he can deprecate the curses
Attendant on his past misdeeds, and make
The god propitious to his future days.

FEMALE ATTENDANT, ANDROMACHE.

ATT. My queen, for still I scruple not to use
The same respectful title which I gave you
When we in Ilion dwelt; you and your lord
While he was living, shared my duteous love,
And now I with important tidings fraught
To you am come, trembling indeed lest one
Of our new rulers overhear the tale,

Yet greatly pitying your disastrous fate :
For Menelaus and his daughter form
Dire plots against you; of these foes beware.
    AND. O my dear fellow-servant (for thou shar'st
Her bondage who was erst thy queen, but now
Is wretched), ah! what mean they? what fresh schemes
Have they devised to take away my life,
Who am by woes encompassed?
    ATT.   They intend,
O miserable dame, to kill your son,
Whom privately you from this house conveyed.
    AND. Are they informed I sent the child away?
Ah me! who told them? in what utter ruin
Am I involved!
    ATT.   I know not; but thus much
Of their designs I heard; in quest of him
Is Menelaus from these doors gone forth.
    AND. Then am I lost indeed: for, O my child,
These two relentless vultures mean to seize thee,
And take away thy life, while he who bears
A father's name, at Delphi still remains.
    ATT. You had not fared so ill, I am convinced,
If he were present, but now every friend
Deserts you.
    AND.   Is there not a rumour spread
Of Peleus' coming?
    ATT.   He, though he were here,
Is grown too old to aid you.
    AND.   More than once
I sent to him.
    ATT.   Suppose you that he heeds
None of your messengers?
    AND.   What means this question?
Wilt thou accept such office?
    ATT.   What pretext
To colour my long absence from this house
Shall I allege?
    AND.   Full many are the schemes
Which thou, who art a woman, can devise.
    ATT. 'Twere dangerous; for Hermione is watchful.
    AND. Dost thou perceive the danger, and renounce
Thy friends in their distress?
    ATT.   Not thus: forbear
To brand me with so infamous a charge:
I go; for of small value is the life
(Whate'er befall me) of a female slave.
                                [*Exit* ATTENDANT.
    AND. Proceed: meanwhile I to the conscious air
Those plaints and bitter wailings will repeat,

On which I ever dwell. Unhappy women
Find comfort in perpetually talking
Of what they suffer. But my groans arise
Not from one ill, but many ills : the walls
Of my loved country razed, my Hector slain,
And that hard fortune, in whose yoke bound fast,
Thus am I fallen into th' unseemly state
Of servitude. We never ought to call
Frail mortals happy, at their latest hour
Till we behold them to the shades descend.

ELEGY.

In Helen sure, to Troy's imperial towers
  Young Paris wafted no engaging bride,
But when he led her to those nuptial bowers,
  Some fiend infernal crossed the billowy tide.

With brandished javelin and devouring flame,
  For her the Grecian warriors to thy shore,
O Ilion, in a thousand vessels came,
  And drenched thy smould'ring battlements with gore.

Around the walls, my Hector, once thy boast,
  Fixed to his car, was by Achilles borne,
And from my chamber hurried to the coast
  I veiled my head in servitude forlorn.

Much wept these streaming eyes, when in the dust
  My city, palace, husband, prostrate lay.
Subject to fierce Hermione's disgust,
  Why should I still behold the hated day?

Harassed with insults from that haughty dame,
  Round Thetis' bust my suppliant arms I fling,
And here with gushing tears bewail my shame,
  As from the rock bursts forth the living spring.

CHORUS, ANDROMACHE.

CHORUS.

ODE.

I. 1.

O thou, who seated in this holy space,
Hast Thetis' temple thy asylum made,
  Though Phthia gave me birth, to aid
Thee, hapless dame of Asiatic race,

I hither come; would I from direful harms
      Could guard, could heal the strife
      'Twixt thee and that indignant wife
Hermione, whom ruthless discord arms
To punish thee the rival of her charms,
      A captive, to the genial bed,
      Who by Achilles' son wert led.

I. 2.

Aware of fate, th' impending evil weigh,
A helpless Phrygian nymph, thou striv'st in vain
      'Gainst her of Sparta's proud domain :
Cease, to this sea-born goddess, cease to pray,
And at her blazing shrine no longer stay :
      For how can it avail
      To thee with hopeless sorrow pale
To suffer all thy beauties to decay,
Because thy rulers with oppression sway?
      Thou to superior might must bend.
      Why, feeble as thou art, contend?

II. 1.

Yet hasten from the Nereid's lofty seat,
Consider that thou tread'st a foreign plain,
      And that these hostile walls detain
In strictest bondage thy reluctant feet,
Here none of all those friends, that numerous band,
      Who shared thy greatness, is at hand,
      To cheer thee in these days of shame,
      O wretched, wretched dame.

II. 2.

A miserable matron thou art come
From Troy to our abodes, unwilling guest ;
      Though mine the sympathizing breast,
Yet I through reverence to our lords am dumb,
Lest she, who springs from Helen, child of Jove,
      Should be a witness of that love
      Which I to thee whose griefs I share,
      Impelled by pity bear.

HERMIONE, ANDROMACHE, CHORUS.

HER. The gorgeous ornaments of gold, these brows
Encircling, and the tissued robes I wear,
I from Achilles', or from Peleus' stores,
As chosen presents when I hither came,
Received not, but from Sparta's realm, these gifts
My father Menelaus hath bestowed

With a large dower, that I might freely speak
Such is the answer which to you I make,
O Phthian dames. But thou, who art a slave
And captive, wouldst in these abodes usurp
Dominion, and expel me; to my lord
Thy drugs have made me odious, hence ensues
My barrenness: the Asiatic dames,
For these abhorred devices are renowned;
But thee will I subdue, nor shall this dome
Of the immortal Nereid, nor her altar
Or temple save thee from impending death;
If either man or god should be disposed
To rescue thee, 'twere fit, that to atone
For the proud thoughts thou in thy happier days
Didst nourish, thou shouldst tremble, at my knees
Fall low, and sweep the pavement of my house,
Sprinkling the waters from a golden urn.
Know where thou art: no Hector governs here,
No Phrygian Priam doth this sceptre wield;
This is no Chrysa, but a Grecian city.
Yet thou, O wretched woman, art arrived
At such a pitch of madness, that thou dar'st
To sleep e'en with the son of him who slew
Thy husband, and a brood of children bear
To him whose hands yet reek with Phrygian gore,
Such is the whole abhorred barbarian race;
The father with his daughter, the vile son
With his own mother, with her brother too
The sister, sins, friends by their dearest friends
Are murdered; deeds like these no wholesome law
Prohibits: introduce not among us
Such crimes, for 'tis unseemly that one man
Possess two women; the fond youth who seeks
Domestic harmony, confines his love
To one fair partner of the genial bed.

CHOR. The female sex are envious, and pursue
With an incessant hatred those who share
Their nuptial joys.

AND. Alas! impetuous youth
Proves baleful to mankind, and there are none
Who act with justice in their blooming years.
But what I dread is this, lest slavery curb
My tongue, though I have many truths to utter:
In this dispute with you, if I prevail,
That very triumph may become my bane:
For those of haughty spirits ill endure
The most prevailing arguments when urged
By their inferiors. Yet my better cause
I will not thus betray. Say, youthful princess,

What reasons of irrefragable force
Enable me to drive you from the couch
Of your own lawful husband? to the Phrygians
Is Sparta grown inferior, and hath fortune
On us conferred the palm? Do you behold me
Still free? elate with youth, a vigorous frame,
The wide extent of empire I possess,
And number of my friends, am I desirous
To occupy these mansions in your stead,
That in your stead I might bring forth a race
Of slaves, th' appendages of my distress?
Will any one endure (if you produce
No children) that my sons should be the kings
Of Phthia?—the Greeks love me for the sake
Of Hector, I too was forsooth obscure,
And not a queen, in Troy. Your husband's hate,
Not from my drugs, but from your soul, unsuited
For social converse, springs: there is a philtre
To gain his love. Not beauty, but the virtues,
O woman, to the partners of our bed
Afford delight. But if it sting your pride
That Sparta's a vast city, while you treat
Scyros with scorn, amidst the poor, display
Your riches, and of Menelaus speak
As greater than Achilles; hence your lord
Abhors you. For a woman, though bestowed
On a vile mate, should learn to yield, nor strive
For the pre-eminence. In Thrace o'erspread
With snow, if you were wedded to a king,
Who to his bed takes many various dames,
Would you have slain them? you would cast disgrace
On your whole sex by such unsated lust;
Base were the deed: for though our souls are warmed
With more intense desires than those of men
We modestly conceal them. For thy sake
I, O my dearest Hector, loved the objects
Of thy affections, whene'er Venus' wiles
Caused thee to err, and at my breast full oft
Nourished thy spurious children, that in nought
Thy joys I might embitter: acting thus
I won him by my virtues. But you tremble
E'en if the drops of Heaven's transparent dew
Rest on your husband. Strive not to transcend
Your mother in a wild excess of love,
O woman. For the children, if endued
With reason, such examples should avoid
Of those who bore them, as corrupt the soul.

CHOR. As far as possible, O queen, comply
With my advice, and in mild terms accost her.

HER. What mean'st thou by this arrogance of speech,
This vain debate, as if thou still wert chaste,
And I had strayed from virtue's path?
  AND.   The words
You have been using, now at least are void
Of modesty.
  HER.   O woman, may this breast
Harbour no soul like thine.
  AND.   Though bashful youth
Glow on your cheek, indecent is your language.
  HER. Thou by thy actions more than by thy words
Hast proved the malice which to me thou bear'st.
  AND. Why will you not conceal th' inglorious pangs
Of jealous love?
  HER.   What woman but resents
Such wrongs, and deems them great?
  AND.   The use some make
Of these misfortunes adds to their renown:
But shame waits those who are devoid of wisdom.
  HER. We dwell not in a city where prevail
Barbarian laws.
  AND.   In Phrygia or in Greece
Base actions are with infamy attended.
  HER. Though most expert in every subtle art,
Yet die thou must.
  AND.   Behold you Thetis' image
Turning its eyes on you?
  HER.   She loathes thy country
Where her Achilles treacherously was slain.
  AND. Your mother Helen caused his death, not I.
  HER. Wouldst thou retrace still farther the sad tale
Of our misfortunes?
  AND.   I restrain my tongue.
  HER Speak to me now on that affair which caused
My coming hither.
  AND.   All I say is this:
You have not so much wisdom as you need.
  HER. From this pure temple of the sea-born goddess
Wilt thou depart?
  AND.   Not while I live: you first
Must slay, then drag me hence.
  HER.   I am resolved
How to proceed, and wait my lord's return
No longer.
  AND.   Nor will I before he come
Surrender up myself.
  HER.   With flaming brands
Hence will I drive thee, and no deference pay
To thy entreaties.

AND.   Kindle them; the gods
Will view the deed.
    HER.   The scourge too is prepared.
    AND. Transpierce this bosom, deluge with my gore
The altar of the goddess, you by her
Shall be at length o'ertaken.
    HER.   From thy cradle,
Trained up and hardened in barbarian pride,
Canst thou endure to die? from this asylum
Soon will I rouse thee by thy own consent,
I with such baits am furnished, but conceal
My purpose, which th' event itself ere long
Will make conspicuous. Keep a steady seat,
For though by molten lead thou wert enclosed
Hence would I rouse thee, ere Achilles' son,
Whom thou confid'st in, to this land return.
                        [*Exit* HERMIONE.
    AND. In him I place my still unshaken trust.
Yet is it strange that the celestial powers,
To heal the serpent's venom, have assigned
Expedients, but no remedy devised
Against an evil woman who surpasses
Or vipers' stings or the consuming flame:
Thus baleful is our influence on mankind.

CHORUS.

ODE.

I. 1.

The winged son of Maia and of Jove
To many sorrowful events gave birth,
And scattered discord o'er the bleeding earth,
When he through sacred Ida's piny grove
   Guided the car of three immortal dames,
   (The golden prize of beauty to obtain,
     In hateful strife engaged, who urged their claims);
To where in his mean hut abode a lonely swain.

I. 2.

No sooner had they reached the destined bower,
Than in the limpid spring her snowy frame
Each goddess laved; to Priam's son then came
With artful speeches of such winning power
   As might beguile the rash and amorous boy:
   Venus prevailed; her words, though sweet their sound,
     Proved of destructive consequence to Troy,
Whose stately bulwarks hence lie levelled with the ground.

II. 1.

When new-born Paris first beheld the light,
Would that his mother, o'er her head, this brand
Ordained by Heaven to fire his native land,
Had cast, before he dwelt on Ida's height.
Unheeded from the bay's prophetic shade
Exclaimed Cassandra : " Let the child be slain ;
Kill him, or Priam's empire is betrayed."
Frantic she raved and sued to every prince in vain.

II. 2.

Deaf was each prince, or Ilion ne'er had felt
The servile yoke, nor hadst thou, hapless fair,
Beneath these roofs, encompassed by despair,
And subject to a rigid master, dwelt.
O had he died, the fated toil of Greece,
That stubborn war through ten revolving years,
Had roused no heroes from the lap of peace,
Nor caused the widow's shrieks, the hoary father's tears.

MENELAUS, MOLOSSUS, ANDROMACHE, CHORUS.

MEN. Your son I hither bring, whom from this fane
With secrecy, you to another house,
Without my daughter's knowledge, had removed.
You boasted that this image of the goddess
To you, and those who hid him, would afford
A sure asylum : but your deep-laid craft,
O woman, cannot baffle Menelaus.
If you depart not hence, he in your stead
Shall be the victim ; therefore well revolve
Th' important question; had you rather die,
Or, with his streaming gore, let him atone
The foul offence 'gainst me and 'gainst my daughter
By you committed ?

AND. Thou, O vain opinion,
Hast with renown puffed up full many men
Who were of no account. I deem those blest
On whom with truth such honour is bestowed :
But them who by fallacious means obtain it
I hold unworthy of possessing fame,
When all their seeming wisdom but arises
From Fortune's gifts. Thou with the bravest chiefs
Of Greece, from Priam erst didst wrest his Troy ;
E'en thou who art so mean as to inspire
Thy daughter with resentment 'gainst a child,
And strive with me a miserable captive :
Unworthy of thy conquest over Troy

Thee do I hold, and Troy yet more disgraced
By such a victor. Some indeed there are
To all appearance upright, who awhile
Outwardly glitter, though they in their hearts
Are on a level with the worthless bulk
Of mortals, and superior but in wealth
Whose power is great. This conference let us end,
O Menelaus, be it now supposed
I by thy daughter am already slain:
'Twill be impossible for her to 'scape
From the pollution ruthless murder brings;
Thou too by many tongues wilt be accused
Of this vile deed, with her will they confound
Thee the abettor. But if I preserve
My life, are ye resolved to slay my son?
How will the father tamely bear the death
Of his loved offspring? he was not esteemed
At Troy so void of courage. He is gone
Whither his duty calls. Soon will the chief
Act worthy of the race from which he springs,
The hoary Peleus, and his dauntless sire
Achilles, he from these abodes will cast
Thy daughter forth, and when thou to another
In marriage giv'st her, what hast thou to say
On her behalf? "That from a worthless lord
Her wisdom drove her?" This would be a falsehood
Too gross. But who would wed her? till grown grey
In widowhood, shall she beneath thy roofs
Fix her loathed residence? O wretched man,
The rising conflux of unnumbered woes
Behold'st thou not? hadst thou not rather find
Thy daughter wronged by concubines, than suffering
Th' indignities I speak of? we from trifles
Such grievous mischiefs ought not to create;
Nor if we women are a deadly bane,
To the degenerate nature of our sex
Should men conform. If I pernicious drugs
Have to thy daughter ministered, and been,
As she pretends, the cause of her abortion,
Immediately will I without reluctance,
And without grovelling at this altar's base,
To any rigid punishment submit
Inflicted by thy son-in-law, from whom
I surely merit as severe revenge
For having made him childless. Such am I:
But in thy temper I perceive one cause
Of just alarm, since in that luckless strife
About a woman, and a vile one too,
Thou the famed Phrygian city didst destroy.

CHOR. Too freely hast thou spoken, in a tone
Which ill becomes thy sex, and that high soul
The bounds of wisdom hath o'erleaped.
  MEN.   O woman,
So small an object, as you rightly judge,
Deserves not the attention of my realm,
Nor that of Greece. But learn this obvious truth:
To any man whate'er he greatly needs,
Is of more worth by far than taking Troy.
My daughter I assist, because I deem it
A wrong of great importance should she lose
Her bridal rights: for every woman looks
On all beside as secondary ills:
But if she from her husband's arms be torn,
Seems reft of life itself. That Phthia's prince
Direct my servants, and that his obey
Me and my race, is fitting: for true friends
Have no distinct possessions, but hold all
In common. While I wait for the return
Of her long absent lord, should I neglect
My daughter's interests, I were weak, not wise.
But leave this shrine of Thetis: for the child
Shall if you bleed escape th' impending doom:
Him, if you die not, will I slay, since fate
Of you or him the forfeit life demands.

  AND. Ah me! a bitter and unwelcome choice
Of life on terms like these hast thou proposed;
Wretch that I am! for whether I decline
Or make such option, I am wretched still.
O thou, who by a trifling wrong provoked,
Committ'st great crimes, attend: for what offence
Wouldst thou bereave me of my life? what city
Have I betrayed? what child of thine destroyed?
What mansion fired? I to my master's bed
By force was dragged: yet me alone, not him
The author of that crime, thou mean'st to slay.
Thou, the first cause o'erlooking, on th' effect
Which it produces, vent'st thy rage. What woes
Encompass wretched me! alas! my country!
How dreadful are the wrongs which I endure!
But wherefore was I doomed to bear a child,
And to the burden under which I groan
Add a new burden? what delight can life
To me afford? or on what fortunes past
Or present should I turn these eyes which saw
The corse of Hector by the victor's car
Whirled round the walls, and wretched Troy a heap
Of blazing ruins? I meantime a slave
By my dishevelled hair was dragged aboard
The Argive navy; when I reached the coast

Of Phthia, and cohabited with those
Who slew my Hector; (but why lavish plaints
On past calamities, without deploring
Or taking a due estimate of those
Which now impend?) I had this only son
My life's last comfort left, and they who take
Delight in deeds of cruelty, would slay him;
Yet to preserve my miserable life
He shall not perish; for auspicious hopes,
Could he be saved, his future days attend:
But if I died not for my son, reproach
Would be my portion. Lo! I leave the altar
And now am in thy hands, stab, slay me, bind,
Strain hard the deadly noose. My son, thy mother,
To rescue thee from an untimely grave,
Descends the shades beneath; if thou escape
The ruthless grasp of fate, remember me
How miserably I suffered; and with kisses,
At his return, when thou goest forth to meet
Thy father, when a flood of tears thou shedd'st,
And cling'st around him with those pliant arms,
Inform him how I acted. All men hold
Their children dear as life; but he who scorns them
Because he ne'er experienced what it is
To be a father, though with fewer griefs
Attended, but enjoys imperfect bliss.

[*Rises, and advances from the altar.*

CHOR. I with compassion to this moving tale
Have listened; for distress, to all mankind,
Though strangers, must seem piteous: but on thee,
O Menelaus, 'tis incumbent now
To reconcile thy daughter, and this captive,
That she may from her sorrows be released.

MEN. Seize her, and bind her hands; for she shall hear
No pleasing language: I proposed to slay
Your son, that you might leave that hallowed altar
Of Thetis, and thus craftily induced you
To fall into my hands, and meet your death;
Be well assured, such is the present state
Of your affairs: as for that boy, on him
My daughter shall pass judgment, or to kill,
Or spare him: but now enter these abodes,
That you may learn, slave as you are, to treat
Those who are free no longer with disdain.

AND. Thou hast o'erreached me by thy treacherous arts;
Alas! I am betrayed.

MEN. Proclaim these tidings
To all men; for I shall not contradict them.

AND. By those who dwell beside Eurotas' stream
Are such base frauds called wisdom?

MEN.   Both at Troy
And there, 'tis just the injured should retaliate.
    AND. Believ'st thou that the gods are gods no longer,
Nor wield the bolt of vengeance?
    MEN.   We must look
To that: but you shall die.
    AND.   And wilt thou seize
This unfledged bird, to slay him?
    MEN.   No, I will not,
But give him to my daughter, who must act
As she thinks fit.
    AND.   Then how, alas, my son!
Can I sufficiently bewail thy fate?
    MEN. "Him," 'twas but now with arrogance you said,
"Auspicious hopes attend."
    AND.   Ye worst of foes
To all mankind, inhabitants of Sparta!
Expert in treacherous counsels, still devising
New falsehoods, curst artificers of mischief,
Your paths are crooked, yet though void of worth,
Through Greece by circumspection ye uphold
An undeserved pre-eminence. What crimes,
What murders, what a thirst for abject gain
Characterize your realm! with specious tongue
Uttering a language foreign to your heart,
Are ye not ever caught? Perdition seize you!
Death is less grievous than thou deem'st to me
Who date my utter ruin from that hour
When Ilion's wretched city was involved
In the same fate with my illustrious lord,
Whose spear oft drove thee trembling from the field
Into thy ships: but now against his wife
A formidable warrior art thou come
To murder me: strike, for this coward tongue
Shall never leave thine and thy daughter's shame
Unpublished. If in Sparta thou art great,
So was I erst in Ilion; but exult not
In my disasters, for on thee ere long
The same reverse of fortune may attend.

CHORUS.

ODE.

I. 1.

Two rival consorts ne'er can I approve,
  Or sons, the source of strife, their birth who owe
To different mothers; hence connubial love
  Is banished, and the mansion teems with woe.

One blooming nymph let cautious husbands wed,
And share with her alone an unpolluted bed.

I. 2.

No prudent city, no well-governed state,
More than a single potentate will own;
Their subjects droop beneath the grievous weight
When two bear rule, and discord shakes the throne;
And if two bards awake their sounding lyres
E'en the harmonious Muse a cruel strife inspires,

II. 1.

To aid the bark, when prosperous gales arise,
Two jarring pilots shall misguide the helm:
Weak is a multitude when all are wise,
One simpler monarch could have saved the realm.
Let a sole chief the house or empire sway,
And all who hope for bliss their lord's behests obey.

II. 2.

This truth hath Menelaus' daughter shown,
Furious she comes the victim to destroy;
And, that their blood may nuptial wrongs atone,
The Phrygian captive, and that hapless boy,
With impious rage unjust would cause to bleed;
May pity, awful queen, thy lifted arm impede!

But I before these doors behold the pair
On whom the fatal sentence now is passed.
Thou wretched dame, and wretched child who diest
Because thy mother to a foreign bed
By force was dragged, in her imputed guilt
Thou wert not an accomplice, thou thy lords
Hast not offended.

AND. To the realms beneath,
Lo, I am hurried, with these bloody hands
Fast bound in galling chains.

MOL. I too, O mother,
Under thy wing, to those loathed shades descend
A victim. O ye lords of Phthia's land,
And thou, my father, succour those thou lov'st.

AND. Cling to thy mother's bosom, O my child,
Together let us die.

MOL. Ah me! how grievous
My sufferings are! too clearly I perceive
That I, and thou my mother, both are wretched.

MEN. Go both together to th' infernal realm:
For ye from hostile turrets hither came.
Although the cause why you and he must bleed
Is not the same, my sentence takes away

Your life, and my Hermione's your son's.
The highest folly were it to permit
A foe to live and vex us, whom with ease
We might despatch, and from our house remove
Such danger.
  AND.   O my husband, would to Heaven
I had thy arm to aid me; and thy spear,
Thou son of Priam.
  MOL.   Wretched me! what charm
Can I devise t' avert impending fate?
  AND. My son, implore the mercy of our lord
Clasping his knees.
  MOL.   Dear monarch, spare my life,
  AND. Tears from these eyes burst forth like trickling drops
By the sun's heat forced from a solid rock,
Wretch that I am!
  MOL.   What remedy, alas!
For these dire evils can my soul devise?
  MEN. Why dost thou idly grovel at my feet
With fruitless supplications, while I stand
Firm as a rock, or as th' unpitying wave?
Such conduct serves my interests: no affection
To thee I bear, because my morn of life
Was wasted in the conflict, ere I took
Troy and thy mother, whose society
Thou in the realms of Pluto shalt enjoy.

PELEUS, MENELAUS, ANDROMACHE, MOLOSSUS, CHORUS.

  CHOR. Peleus, I see, draws near, his aged feet
With eager haste advancing.
  PEL.   You, and him
Who stands presiding o'er a murderous deed,
What means this uproar that disturbs the house,
I question, and what practices are these
Ye carry on unauthorized by law?
O Menelaus, stay thy furious hand,
And let not execution thus outstrip
All righteous judgment. O my friends, lead on;
For such a dread emergency appears
T' admit of no delay. Could I regain
That youthful vigour which I erst enjoyed
As prosperous breezes aid the floating sails,
This captive would I favour. Say, what right
Have they to bind your hands, and drag along
You and your son? for like the bleating mother,
Led forth to slaughter with her lamb, you perish,
While I and your unwitting lord are absent.
  AND. They, as thou seest, O venerable man,
Me and my son thus bear to instant death.

What shall I say to thee, whom I with speed
Not by one single messenger but thousands
Have sent for? sure thou, of the fatal strife
In these divided mansions, with his daughter,
To which I owe my ruin, must have heard:
And from the violated shrine of Thetis,
Who bore to thee a noble son, the goddess
Whom thou rever'st e'en now with brutal force
Me have they torn, nor judged my cause, nor wait
For absent Neoptolemus, but, knowing
That I and that this child who hath committed
No fault, are left alone and unprotected,
Would slay us both. But, O thou aged man,
Thus prostrate on my knees, to thee I sue,
And, though this hand must not presume to touch
Thy honoured beard, conjure thee by the gods,
Rescue us, or to thy eternal shame
Both he and I must miserably bleed.

PEL. My orders are that you those galling chains
Unbind and loose her hands, else will I make
The disobedient weep.

MEN. But I, your equal,
Who have much more authority o'er her,
Forbid them.

PEL. Com'st thou hither to direct
My household? is it not enough for thee
To rule thy Spartans?

MEN. Her I took at Troy.

PEL. She, to reward his valour, was bestowed
Upon my grandson.

MEN. Doth not all he owns,
To me, and what is mine, to him belong?

PEL. For honest purposes, but not for crimes
And murderous violence.

MEN. You ne'er shall take her
Out of my hands.

PEL. Thy head I with this sceptre
Will smite.

MEN. Draw near; if you presume to touch me,
Soon shall you rue such outrage.

PEL. O thou villain,
Sprung from a race of impious sires, what right
To be accounted an illustrious man,
And numbered with the truly brave, hast thou,
Who by a Phrygian wanderer wert deprived
Of thy fair consort, after thou hadst left
Thy house unbarred and destitute of guards,
As if thou in thy mansions hadst possessed
A virtuous dame, though she of all her sex

Was the most dissolute? nor if she would
Can any Spartan nymph be chaste? for wandering
From their own homes, distinguished by bare legs,
And zoneless vest, they with young men contend
In swiftness and in wrestling; I such customs
Hold in abhorrence. Is there any room
For wonder if the women prove unchaste
Whom thus you educate? thy Helen ought
To have proposed these questions, ere she left
Her native realm, regardless of thy love,
And by that youthful paramour seduced,
Wantonly fled into a foreign land.
Yet for her sake didst thou that numerous host
Of Greeks collect, and lead them to assail
The Phrygian ramparts. Thou that beauteous dame
Shouldst rather have despised, nor in her cause
Wielded the javelin, when thou found'st her worthless,
But suffered her in Ilion to remain,
And sent rich gifts to Paris on these terms,
That to thy house she never should return.
But thou, instead of suffering these just motives
To make their due impression on thy soul,
Full many valiant warriors hast destroyed,
Made th' aged matron childless, and deprived
Of his illustrious sons the hoary sire.
Numbered with those who owe to thee thy ruin
Am wretched I: for like some evil genius
In thee do these indignant eyes behold
The murderer of Achilles: thou alone,
Save by the missile shaft, unwounded cam'st
From Ilion's hostile shores; in burnished chests
Didst thou bear thither the same glittering arms
Which thou bear'st back again. Before he wedded,
I warned my grandson to form no connection
With thee, nor into these abodes admit
The brood of that adult'ress; for the daughters
Their mother emulate in deeds of shame.
Look well to this, ye suitors, and select
The damsel with maternal worth endued.
Then with what scorn didst thou thy brother treat,
Commanding him 'gainst reason to transgress,
And sacrifice his daughter. Thou such fears,
Lest thou that execrable wife shouldst lose,
Didst entertain. When thou hadst taken Troy,
This too I urge against thee, though thou hadst
Thy consort in thy power, thou didst not slay her,
But when her throbbing bosom thou beheld'st
Didst cast away thy sword, receive her kisses,
And soothe the fears of her who had betrayed thee.

O worthless miscreant, whom the Cyprian Queen
Hath thus debased! thou after this intrud'st
Into my grandson's palace, in his absence
Committ'st these outrages, and basely slay'st
A miserable woman, and her child,
Thee and thy daughter who shall cause to weep
Though trebly illegitimate his birth.
Oft the parched heath, when duly tilled, exceeds
The richest soil, and greater instances
Of virtue are in many a bastard found
Than in the lawfully begotten race.
But take thy daughter hence. Far better is it
To form affinity and strictest friendship
With a poor man of worth, than him who joins
Iniquity with wealth: but as for thee,
Thou art a thing of nought.

CHOR. Among mankind,
Oft from a small beginning doth the tongue
Great strife occasion: but the wise beware
Of entering on a contest with their friend.

MEN. Why do we speak in such exalted terms
Of aged men, as if they were endued
With wisdom, though in former days supposed
By the whole Grecian race to judge aright?
When you, O Peleus, who derive your birth
From an illustrious sire, and with my house
So nearly are connected, hold a language
Disgraceful to yourself, and slander me,
For a barbarian dame, whom from this land
You ought to banish far beyond the Nile,
Beyond the Phasis, and applaud my vengeance;
Because she comes from Asiatic shores,
Where many valiant Grecian chiefs lie slain.
And hath in part been guilty of the blood
Of your famed son; for Paris, by whose shaft,
Transpierced, Achilles perished, was the brother,
And she the wife of Hector: yet you enter
The same abode with her, the genial board
With her partake, allow her to bring forth
Under your roofs an execrable brood.
These mischiefs both to you and me, old man,
Foreseeing, have I snatched her from your hands
With a design to kill her. But, O say,
(For there is nought of meanness in our holding
This conference), if my daughter bear no child,
And she have sons, will you appoint them lords
Of this your Phthian land? shall they who spring
From a barbarian race, o'er Greeks bear rule?
Am I, because I hate injustice, void

Of understanding, and are you discreet?
Reflect on this; had you bestowed your daughter
On any citizen, were she thus treated,
Would you sit down and bear her wrongs in silence?
I deem you would not. Why then with such harshness
Speak you in favour of a foreign dame
Against your nearest friends? as great a right
To vengeance as her husband, hath the wife
Whom her lord injures: for while he whose doors
An unchaste consort enters, in his hands
Hath power to right himself, a woman's strength
Lies only in her parents and her friends.
My daughter, therefore, am I bound to aid:
You show the marks of age: for while you talk
Of that famed war I waged, you more befriend me
Than if you had been silent. Deep in woe
Was Helen plunged, not by her own consent
But by the gods: and this event hath proved
To Greece most advantageous, for its sons
Who knew not how till then to wield the spear,
Grew valiant. From experience, best of tutors,
Men gather all the knowledge they possess.
But when I saw my consort, in forbearing
To take away her life, I acted wisely:
And would that you had done like me, nor slain
Your brother Phocus; this to you I speak
Through mere benevolence, and not in wrath:
But if resentment o'er your soul usurp
An empire, such intemperance of the tongue
Will be in you more shameful, while my wishes
I by a prudent forethought shall attain.
  CHOR. Now both desist (for this were better far)
From such unprofitable strife of words,
O ye will both offend.
  PEL.   Ah me! through Greece
What mischievous opinions have prevailed!
When with the spoils of vanquished foes, the host
A trophy rear, they think not how 'twas gained
By those brave soldiers who endure the toil
Of battle, while their general bears away
All the renown: though he was only one
Who stood 'midst thousands brandishing his spear,
Nor any single combatant surpassed,
He gains a larger portion of applause.
The venerable rulers of a city,
Placed in exalted stations, yet devoid
Of any real merit, overlook
The populace, though many in the crowd
Of their inferiors are more wise than they,

If haply courage and an honest zeal
Unite to place them in the public view.
Thou and thy brother thus are swollen with pride,
From having led those troops to conquer Troy,
And triumph in the sufferings of your friends.
But henceforth will I teach thee not to look
On Paris, Ida's shepherd, as a foe,
More terrible than Peleus. If with speed
Thou quit not these abodes, and take away
Thy childless daughter, my indignant grandson,
By her dishevelled hair around the palace
Will drag this barren dame, who stung with envy,
Cannot endure the fruitful mother's joys.
But, if she prove so luckless as to bare
No issue, ought she therefore to deprive us
Of our posterity? Begone, ye slaves,
That I may see who dares obstruct my loosing
Her hands. Rise up: though trembling with old age,
Your chains can I unbind. O worthless man,
Hast thou thus galled her hands? didst thou suppose
Thou held'st a bull or lion in the snare?
Or didst thou shudder lest she should snatch up
A sword, and wreak just vengeance on thy head?
Come hither to these sheltering arms, my child,
Unbind thy mother's chains; in Phthia, thee
I'll educate, to them a bitter foe.
Should Sparta's sons by the protended spear
Obtain no fame, nor in th' embattled field
Their prowess signalize, be well assured
Ye have no other merit.
  Chor.   Old men talk
With freedom, and their vehemence of soul
Is hard to be restrained.
  Men.   Extremely prone
Are you to slander; much against my will
I came to Phthia, and am here resolved
That I will neither do nor suffer aught
Disgraceful: but to my own home with speed
Am I returning, and have little time
In vain debates to lavish: for a city
Not far from Sparta's gates and erst a friend
Is waging war against us: I would lead
My hardy squadrons forth t' assail the foe,
And utterly subdue them. To my wish
Soon as this great affair I shall have settled,
Hither will I return, and face to face,
When I my reasons to my son-in-law
Have in the clearest terms proposed, will hear
What he can urge; and if he punish her,

And for the future courteously to me
Demean himself, from me he in return
Shall meet with courtesy; but if he rage,
He of my rage the dire effects shall feel:
For still such treatment as his deeds deserve
Shall he experience. But I am not hurt
By these injurious words of yours; for like
Some disembodied ghost, you have a voice,
Although you are not able to do aught
But merely speak.   [*Exit* MENELAUS.

PEL.   Lead on, my boy; here take
Thy station under these protecting arms;
And thou too, O thou miserable dame,
Driven hither by the furious storm; at length
Into a quiet haven are ye come.

AND. On thee and thy descendants may the gods
Shower every blessing, venerable man,
For having saved this child, and wretched me;
Yet O beware, lest in some lonely spot
They suddenly assail us, and by force
Drag me away, perceiving thou art old,
That I am a weak woman, and my son
Is but an infant: all precautions use,
Else we, who have escaped them, may again
Be caught.

PEL.   Forbear to utter, in such language
As this, the dictates of a woman's fear.
Advance, who dares to touch you? he shall weep.
For with the blessing of th' immortal gods,
And by unnumbered troops of valiant horse,
And infantry supported, I bear rule
Over the Phthian land. I am robust,
Nor, as you deem, impaired by palsied age.
Were I, opposed in battle, but to look
On such a man as this, old as I am,
An easy conquest soon should I obtain.
Superior is the veteran, if with courage
Inspired, to many youths: for what avails
A vigorous body with a coward's heart?
      [*Exeunt* PELEUS, ANDROMACHE, *and* MOLOSSUS.

CHORUS.
ODE.
I.

My wish were this; or never to be born,
Or to descend from generous sires, and share
The blessings which attend a wealthy heir.
If heaviest woes assail, ne'er left forlorn

Without a friend are they of nobler race,
Hereditary trophies deck their head :
The records of the brave with joy we trace,
No distant age their memory can efface,
For virtue's torch unquenched pours radiance o'er the dead.

II.

Better is conquest, when we gain our right
By no reproachful means, no deeds of shame,
Than if to envy we expose our fame,
And trample on the laws with impious might.
Such laurels which at first too sweetly bloom,
Ere long are withered by the frost of time,
And scorn pursues their wearers to the tomb.
I in my household or the state presume
To seek that power alone which rules without a crime.

III.

O veteran, sprung from Æacus, thy spear
Chilled the Lapithæ with fear,
And from their hills the Centaurs drove.
When glory called, and prosperous gales
Swelled the Argo's daring sails,
Intrepid didst thou pass that strait
Where ruin oft the crashing bark attends,
And ocean's foam descends
From the Symplegades' obstructing height.
Next didst thou land on perjured Ilion's shore,
With Hercules illustrious son of Jove,
Then first its bulwarks streamed with gore :
Till crowned with fame a partner of his toil,
Europe again thou sought'st and Phthia's frozen soil.

The Nurse of Hermione, Chorus.

NUR. How doth a rapid series of events
The most disastrous, O my dearest friends,
This day invade us ! for within these doors
Hermione my mistress, by her sire
Forsaken, and grown conscious of the guilt
She hath incurred, by that attempt to murder
Andromache and her unhappy son,
Resolves to die, because she dreads, lest fired
With indignation at her guilt, her lord
Should cast her forth with scorn, or take away
Her life, because she purposed to have slain
The innocent. The servants who attend
Can hardly by their vigilance prevent her
From fixing round her neck the deadly noose,
Or snatch the dagger from her hand, so great

Is her affliction, and she now confesses
That she has done amiss. My strength's exhausted
In striving to withhold my royal mistress
From perishing by an ignoble death.
But enter ye these mansions, and attempt
To save her life, for strangers can persuade
Far better than old friends.
    CHOR.   We hear the voice
Of her attendants from within-confirm
Th' intelligence thou hither cam'st to bring:
That hapless woman seems just on the point
Of showing with what rage she by her guilt
Is hurried on : for lo, she rushes forth
From yon abodes, already hath she 'scaped
Her servants' hands, and is resolved to die.

        HERMIONE, NURSE, CHORUS.

    HER. Ah me! these ringlets how will I tear off,
How rend my cheeks!
    NUR.   What mean'st thou, O my daughter?
Wilt thou thus injure that fair frame?
    HER.   Away,
O thou slight veil, I pluck thee from my head,
And toss thy scattered fragments in the air.
    NUR. Cover thy bosom with the decent robe.
    HER. Why with a robe my bosom should I hide?
The crimes I have committed 'gainst my lord
Are clear, well known, and cannot be concealed.
    NUR. Griev'st thou because thou hast formed schemes
        to slay
Thy rival?
    HER.   I with many groans bewail
Those hostile darings, execrable wretch,
Wretch that I am, an object of just hate
To all mankind.
    NUR.   Thy husband such offence
Will pardon.
    HER.   From my hand why didst thou snatch
The sword? Restore, restore it, O my friends,
That I this bosom may transpierce. Why force me
To quit yon pendant noose?
    NUR.   In thy distraction
Shall I forsake and leave thee thus to die?
    HER. Where shall I find (inform me, O ye Fates)
The blazing pyre, ascend the craggy rock,
Plunge in the billows, or amidst the woods
On a steep mountain waste the life I loathe,
That after death the gods beneath may take me
To their protection?

CHOR. Why wouldst thou make efforts
So violent? some mischiefs sent by Heaven
Sooner or later visit all mankind.
　　HER. Me like a stranded bark, thou, O my sire,
Hast left forsaken and without an oar.
To thee I owe my ruin. I no longer
In these my bridal mansions can reside.
To the propitious statues of what God
With suppliant haste shall I repair, or fall
At a slave's knees, myself an abject slave?
I from the land of Phthia, like a bird
Upborne on azure wings, would speed my flight,
Or imitate that ship whose dashing oars
'Twixt the Cyanean straits first urged their way.
　　NUR. As little, O my daughter, can I praise
That vehemence which caused thee to transgress
Against the Trojan dame, as these thy fears
Which are immoderate. For such slight offence
Thy lord, misled by the pernicious tongue
Of a barbarian woman, from his couch
Will not expel thee: for thou art not his
By right of conquest, borne from vanquished Troy;
But thee, the daughter of a mighty king,
He with abundant dower, and from a city
Most flourishing, received: nor will thy sire,
His child forsaking, as thou dread'st, permit thee
To be cast forth: but enter these abodes,
Nor show thyself without, lest some affront
Thou shouldst receive if haply thou art seen
Before these doors. [*Exit* NURSE.
　　CHOR. Behold a man, whose dress
Is of such different fashion that it speaks
The foreigner, comes swiftly from the gate.

ORESTES, HERMIONE, CHORUS.

　　ORE. Is this th' abode of great Achilles' son,
The regal mansion, O ye foreign dames?
　　CHOR. It is as thou hast said. But who art thou
That ask'st this question?
　　ORE. Agamemnon's son,
And Clytemnestra's; but my name's Orestes:
I to Dodona, th' oracle of Jove,
Am on my road; but since I now have reached
The land of Phthia, first would I inquire
How fares Hermione, the Spartan dame,
My kinswoman; doth she yet live and prosper?
For though from me far distant be the land
In which she now resides, she still is dear.
　　HER. O son of Agamemnon, who thus make

Your seasonable appearance, like the haven
To mariners amidst a furious storm,
Take pity, I implore you by those knees,
On me a wretch whose inauspicious fortunes
You witness. Hence around your knees I fling
These arms, which ought to prove of equal force
With hallowed branches by the suppliant borne.
 ORE. What's this? am I deceived? or do my eyes
Indeed behold the queen of these abodes,
And Menelaus' daughter?
 HER.   Th' only child
Whom to the Spartan monarch Helen bore.
Mistake me not.
 ORE.   O Phœbus, healing power,
Protect us! But what dire mischance hath happened?
Or from the gods, or human foes, proceed
The evils thou endur'st?
 HER.   Some from myself,
But others from the husband whom I wedded —
The rest from one of the immortal gods.
I utterly am ruined.
 ORE.   What afflictions
Can any woman who's yet childless feel
But those which from her nuptial union spring?
 HER. Hence these distempers of the soul arise,
And well do you anticipate my words.
 ORE. Enamoured with another, is thy lord
False to thy bed?
 HER.   He loves a captive dame,
The wife of Hector.
 ORE.   This of which thou speak'st
Is a great evil, when one man possesses
Two wives.
 HER. 'Twas thus, till I avenged the wrong.
 ORE. Didst thou with arts familiar to thy sex
Plot 'gainst thy rival's life?
 HER.   I would have killed
Her and her spurious son.
 ORE.   Hast thou despatched them?
Or were they screened from their impending fate?
 HER. Old Peleus to these worthless objects showed
Too great a reverence.
 ORE.   Was there any friend
Ready to aid thee in the purposed slaughter?
 HER. My sire, who for this cause from Sparta came.
 ORE. Yet by that aged man was he subdued?
 HER. Abashed he fled, and left me here alone.
 ORE. I understand thee well: thy husband's wrath
Thou fear'st for what thou'st done.

HER.   The fact you know:
Hence justly will he take away my life.
What can be said? yet by immortal Jove,
Our grandsire, I conjure you, send me far
From these domains, or to my father's house.
Had but these walls a voice, they would proclaim
The sentence of my exile, for the land
Of Phthia hates me. If my lord return
From Phœbus' oracle, for the misdeeds
I have committed, he will strike me dead,
Or force me to become that harlot's slave
Whom erst I ruled.
 ORE.   By some will it be asked
Whence then into such errors didst thou fall?
 HER. My ruin I derive from the admission
Of these vile women, who inflamed my pride
By uttering these rash words: "Wilt thou endure
Beneath thy roof that odious slave who shares
Thy bridal couch? by Juno, awful queen,
I would not suffer such a wretch to breathe
In my polluted chamber." When I heard
The language uttered by these crafty sirens,
Artificers of mischief, who, to suit
Their purpose, in persuasive strains displayed
The power of eloquence, I was puffed up
With folly: for what need had I to hold
My lord in reverence while possessed of all
That I could wish? abundant wealth was mine,
O'er these abodes I reigned, and any children
I to my husband might hereafter bare
Would be legitimate; but hers, by mine
In strict subjection held, a spurious race.
But never, never (I this truth repeat)
Should wedded men, who have the gift of reason,
Let women have a free access, and visit
Their consort. For they teach her evil lessons:
Urged by the hopes of lucre, one corrupts
Her chastity; a second hath already
Transgressed herself, and wishes that her friend
May be as vicious: many by their lust
Are led astray; hence to their husband's house
A train of mischief rises. Guard the doors
Of your abodes with locks and massive bars;
Since from the intrusion of these female guests,
No good, but mischiefs numberless ensue.
 CHOR. Thou to thy tongue hast given too free a scope
In thus aspersing the whole female race:
Thy present woes indeed our pardon claim;

Yet every woman is in duty bound
To gloss o'er the misconduct of her sex.
　ORE. Wisdom pertained to him who taught mankind
To hear the reasons by both parties urged
In a debate.　Aware of the confusion
In these abodes, and of the strife 'twixt thee
And Hector's wife, I stayed not to observe
Whether thou in this house wouldst still remain,
Or through a fear of yonder captive dame
Abandon it : I therefore hither came,
Nor waited for intelligence from thee.
And if a satisfactory account
Of thy proceedings thou to me canst give,
I will convey thee hence.　For thou, who erst
Wert mine, with this thy present husband liv'st,
Through the perfidious conduct of thy sire,
Who ere he entered the domains of Troy
Affianced thee to me, and then to him
Who now possesses thee, again engaged,
If he the Phrygian city should subdue.
But I forgive thy father for this wrong,
When hither great Achilles' son returned,
And to the bridegroom sued that he would loose
Thy plighted hand; of all my various fortunes
Informing him, and of my present woes;
How feasible it were for me to wed
Among my friends, but that for such an exile
As I am, driven from my paternal throne,
'Twould not be easy to obtain a consort
In any foreign land : on this he grew
More arrogant, and bitterly reproached me
Both with my mother's murder, and those Furies
Whose blood-stained visages inspire dismay.
By the misfortunes of my house bowed down
To earth, I grieved indeed, but grieving bore
The weight of these calamities, and reft
Of thee my bride, reluctantly departed.
But since thy fortunes now have undergone
A change so unexpected, and involved
In woe, thou stand'st aghast ; from these abodes
Thee will I take and to thy sire convey.
For wondrous is the force of kindred ties ;
And in misfortunes nought exceeds the friend
Who from the self-same house derives his birth.
　HER. My father will take care how to dispose
Of me in marriage, nor is it my province
Such question to decide.　But, O convey me
From these loathed mansions with the utmost speed,
Lest when my husband at his first return

Enters the doors, he intercept my flight;
Or, hearing that I leave his grandson's house,
Peleus pursue me with his rapid steeds.
 ORE. Be of good cheer against that aged man,
And from thy furious lord, Achilles' son,
Who treated me with scorn, fear nought; this hand
Hath with such cautious artifice prepared
For him th' inevitable snares of death,
Of which no previous mention will I make:
But when it is accomplished, this exploit
Shall on the rock of Delphi be proclaimed.
I who my mother slew, if th' armed friends
Whom I have stationed in the Pythian realm
Observe their oaths, will teach him that he ought
To have abstained from wedding any dame
Betrothed to me. He in an evil hour
Shall claim atonement for his father's death
Of Phœbus mighty king; nor shall repentance
For these audacious blasphemies avail
To save the miscreant on whose impious head
Apollo wreaks just vengeance; by his wrath
O'ertaken, and entangled in my snares,
He wretchedly shall perish. For the gods
Subvert the prosperous fortunes of their foes
Nor suffer pride to rear her towering crest.
          [*Exeunt* ORESTES *and* HERMIONE.

CHORUS.

ODE.

I. 1.

Phœbus, thou god who with a mound
Of stately towers didst Ilion's rock surround;
And thou, O Neptune, ruler of the main,
  Borne swiftly by thy azure steeds
In a light car, who cleav'st the watery plain;
After exerting with unwearied toil
  Such skill as human works exceeds,
'Gainst wretched Troy when Mars his javelin bore,
  Why, faithless to that chosen soil,
  Left ye your city drenched in gore?

I. 2.

The steeds ye yoked on Simois' banks
Whirled many a chariot through the broken ranks;
No hero gathered in that stubborn fray
  One laurel to adorn his head:
Phrygia's illustrious rulers swept away,

Took their last voyage to a distant shore,
    And mingled with the vulgar dead,
While the polluted altars ceased to gleam
      Upwafting to the skies no more
      Their frankincense in odorous steam.

II. 1.

Slain by his wife Atrides fell;
His furious son sent to the shades of Hell
The murderess, and returned th' unnatural deed,
    That fatal stroke the god approved,
His oracles ordained that she should bleed,
When young Orestes at the inmost shrine
    Was by a heavenly impulse moved,
His hands in gore maternal to imbrue.
    O Phœbus, O thou power divine,
    How shall I think th' assertion true?

II. 2.

In Greece doth many a dame complain
Chaunting rude dirges for her children slain;
Others their native land reluctant leave,
    And to a foreign lord are brought.
Nor yet hast thou alone just cause to grieve,
Nor to thy friends hath Heaven's peculiar hate
    These signal miseries wrought:
Victorious Greece still feels as deep a wound,
      From whence the thunderbolt of fate
      Through Phrygia scattered deaths around.

PELEUS, CHORUS.

PEL. Answer my questions, O ye Phthian dames,
For doubtful is the rumour I have heard,
That Menelaus' daughter, when she left
This house departed from the realm. I come
Anxious to learn if this account be true.
For 'tis their duty who remain at home
To guard the fortunes of their absent friends.
  CHOR. What thou hast heard, O Peleus, is the truth,
And ill would it become me to conceal
The woes in which I deeply am involved:
Our royal mistress from these walls is fled.
  PEL. What feared she? say.
  CHOR.   The anger of her lord,
Lest he from these abodes should cast her forth.
  PEL. Because she plotted to have slain the boy?
  CHOR. E'en so it was. Yon captive too she dreaded,
  PEL. But from these mansions did she go, attended,
Or by her father or by whom?

CHOR.   The son
Of Agamemnon from this land conveyed her.
   PEL. What are his views ? to take her for his bride?
   CHOR. Thy grandson too he meditates to slay.
   PEL. Stationed in secret ambush, or resolved
To meet the dauntless warrior face to face ?
   CHOR. Beneath Apollo's unpolluted fane
With Delphi's citizens.
   PEL.   Atrocious crime !
Ah me ! will no one with his utmost speed
Go to the altar of the Pythian god,
And to our friends disclose what passes here,
Ere by his foes Achilles' son is slain ?

MESSENGER, PELEUS, CHORUS.

   MES. What evil tidings do I bring to you,
O aged man, and all my master's friends !
   PEL. By a sad presage which affects my soul
I of th' impending evil am forewarned.
   MES. Know then, O Peleus, that your wretched grandson
Is now no more, with such unnumbered wounds
He by the Delphic citizens transpierced,
And by that stranger from Mycene died.
   CHOR. Alas ! alas ! but what resource is left
For thee, thou hoary veteran ? do not fall;
Raise thyself up.
   PEL.   To very nothing now
Am I reduced, I utterly am ruined :
The power of speech deserts me, and these limbs
Forget their office.
   MES.   Hear me, and from earth
Arise, if, with th' assistance of your friends,
You for this murder wish to be revenged.
   PEL. How hast thou compassed wretched me, who stand
On the last verge of spiritless old age,
O cruel fate ! say how the only son
Of my deceased, my only son, was slain.
These tidings though unwelcome would I hear.
   MES. After we reached Apollo's sacred realm,
While thrice the chariot of the sun performed
Its bright career, we satiated our eyes
With viewing all around. The circumstance
Which raised suspicion first, was this : the people
Who dwell within the temple of the god
Held frequent meetings, and in crowds assembled.
Meanwhile the son of Agamemnon went
Through the whole city, and in every ear
Whispered malignant words like these ; " Behold

Him who is visiting the hallowed shrine
Of Phœbus piled with gold, the treasures given
By all mankind; the miscreant comes again
On the same purpose which first drew him hither,
To overthrow the temple of the god."
Through the whole city hence an evil rumour
Went forth, and all the magistrates, to whom
The holy treasures were consigned, assembled,
In secret councils held, and placed a guard
Behind the massive columns in the fane.
We, unapprized of this, meantime had caught
Some sheep, that fed amid Parnassus' grove,
And with our Delphic friends and Pythian seers
Approached the altar: some one said: "Young man,
What vows on thy behalf shall we address
To Phœbus? for what purpose art thou come?"
He answered: "To the god I wish to make
A due atonement for my past offence,
Because I erst from him with impious tongue
Claimed satisfaction for my father's blood."
Hence did Orestes' calumnies appear
To have great weight, suggesting that my lord
Spoke an untruth, and that he hither came
With vile designs. Beneath the holy roof,
That to Apollo he might offer up
His prayers in that oracular abode,
He now advanced, and as they blazed, observed
The victims: here a troop with falchions armed
Screened by the branching laurels stood; the son
Of Clytemnestra was the sole contriver
Of all these stratagems. Our lord stood forth,
And, in the sight of this insidious band,
Adored the god: while they with their keen swords,
Ere he discerned them, pierced Achilles' son
Unsheathed in mail. He instantly retreated;
For he as yet had by no deadly wound
Been smitten; but snatched up in his retreat
Those glittering arms which near the portals hung,
And stood a champion terrible to view,
Close to the blazing altar: with loud voice
He questioned the inhabitants of Delphi:
"Me who a pious votary hither come,
Why, or for what offences, would ye slay!"
Although the number of his foes was great,
None of them answered, but all hands hurled stones:
On every side assaulted by a storm
Thick as the falling snows, he warded off,
Extending the broad margin of his shield,
Each missile weapon: but of no avail

Was this resistance : for the spear, the shaft,
The dart, were thrown at once, and at his feet
Mixed instruments of sacrifice lay scattered.
Th' agility with which your grandson shunned
The blows they aimed, was wondrous to behold:
They in a circle gathering round, closed in,
Nor gave him space to breathe, till from the altar
Descending with a leap like that which bore
The hapless Grecian chief to Phrygia's coast,
He rushed among them : like a flock of doves
Who see the hawk appear, they turned and fled :
In heaps on heaps promiscuous, many fell,
Some in the narrow passage wounded lay,
While others o'er them trampled, and their groans
Unholy echoed through the hallowed dome.
But, tranquil as the waters in a calm,
In golden arms my lord resplendent stood,
Till from the inmost sanctuary burst forth
A deep-toned voice of horror, which impelled
The recreant warriors to renew the fight :
Achilles' son then smitten through the flank
With a keen sword, by one of Delphi fell,
Who slew him, yet ignobly, with the aid
Of multitudes.   But after he to earth
Was fallen, what sword transpierced him not, what hand
Threw not a stone to smite him? his whole frame,
So graceful erst, was with unnumbered wounds
Disfigured : till at length his mangled corse,
Which stained the altar's basis, from the fane
Drenched with the blood of victims they cast forth.
But gathering up with speed, his loved remains
To you we bear, O venerable man,
That o'er them you may shed the plenteous tear,
And grace them with sepulchral rites.   Thus Phœbus,
Who prophesies to others, mighty king,
And deals out justice to th' admiring world,
Hath on Achilles' son revenged himself,
And, like some worthless human foe, revived
An ancient grudge : how then can he be wise?
                                          [*Exit* MESSENGER.

   CHOR. But lo! our royal master, from the land
Of Delphi borne, approaches these abodes!
Wretched was he, by such untimely doom
O'ertaken : nor art thou, O aged man,
Less wretched than the slaughtered youth : for thou
Into thy doors receiv'st Achilles' son,
But not as thou couldst wish; thou too art fallen
Into affliction's snare.
   PEL.   What piteous object,

Ah me! do I behold, and with these hands
Receive into my house! we are undone,
We are undone, O thou Thessalian city;
I have no children, no descendants left,
To occupy these mansions. On what friend
Shall I a wretched sufferer turn my eyes,
And hope to find relief? O thou dear face,
Ye cheeks, ye hands! thee would to Heaven that fate
In those embattled fields of Troy had slain
Beside the waves of Simois!
  CHOR.   He in death
Hence would have found renown; thou too, old man,
Wouldst have been happier.
  PEL.   Thou, O wedlock, wedlock,
These mansions and my city hast o'erthrown.
My grandson, through the inauspicious nuptials
By thee contracted, would to heaven my gates
Had ne'er received that execrable fiend
Hermione, thy bane! O had she first
With thunderbolts been smitten! nor hadst thou,
Presumptuous mortal, charged the Delphic god
With having aimed the shaft which slew thy sire!
  CHOR. I will awake the sad funereal dirge,
And wailing pay to my departed lord
Such customary tribute as attends
The shades of mighty chiefs,
  PEL.   Ah me! at once
With misery and old age bowed down to earth,
I shed th' incessant tear.
  CHOR.   Thus hath the god
Ordained, the god's vindictive arm hath wrought
All these calamities.
  PEL.   O most beloved,
This house, ah me! a desert hast thou left,
And me a miserable old man made childless.
  CHOR. Before thy children, O thou aged man,
Thou shouldst have died.
  PEL.   Shall I not rend my hair,
And beat with desperate hands this hoary head?
O city! Phœbus hath of both my sons
Deprived me.
  CHOR. O thou miserable old man,
What evils hast thou witnessed and endured!
How wilt thou pass the remnant of thy life?
  PEL. Childless, forlorn, no period to my woes
Can I discover, but till death must drink
The bitter potion.
  CHOR.   Sure the gods in vain
Showered blessings on thy nuptials.

PEL.   Fled and withered
Is all our ancient pomp.
    CHOR.   Alone thou mov'st
Around thy lonely house.
    PEL.   I have no city.
Thee, O my sceptre, to the ground I cast,
And from yon dreary caverns of the main,
Daughter of Nereus, me wilt thou behold
Utterly ruined, grovelling in the dust.
    CHOR. Ha! who was it that moved? what form divine
Do I perceive? look there! ye nymphs, attend,
With rapid passage through the fleecy clouds
Borne onward, some divinity arrives
At Phthia's pastures, famed for generous steeds.

THETIS, PELEUS, CHORUS.

    THE. O Peleus, mindful of the ties which bound
Our plighted love, I hither from the house
Of Nereus come, and with these wholesome counsels
Begin; despair not, though thy present woes
Are grievous: for e'en I who should have borne
A race of children such as ne'er might cause
My tears to stream, have lost the son who crowned
Our hopes, Achilles, swift of foot, the first
Of Grecian heroes. But to thee, the motives
Which brought me hither, will I now relate;
O listen to my voice. Back to that altar
Devoted to the Pythian god, convey
This body of Achilles' slaughtered son,
And bury it; so shall his tomb declare
The murderous violence Orestes' band
Committed: but yon captive dame, I mean
Andromache, on Helenus bestowed
In marriage, in Molossia's land must dwell,
And her young son, the only royal branch
Which of the stem of Æacus remains;
From him in long succession shall a race
Of happy kings Molossia's sceptre wield:
Nor will our progeny, O aged man,
Be utterly extinct, when blended thus
With Ilion, still protected by the gods,
Though by Minerva's stratagems it fell.
But, as for thee, that thou mayst know the blessing
Of having wedded me, who am by birth
A goddess and the daughter of a god,
From all the ills which wait on human life
Releasing, thee immortal will I make
And incorruptible; with me a goddess
In Nereus' watery mansions thou a god

Hereafter shalt reside, and from the waves
Emerging with dry feet, behold our son
Achilles, to his parents justly dear,
Inhabiting that isle whose chalky coasts
Are laved by the surrounding Euxine deep.
But go to Delphi's city by the gods
Erected, thither bear this weltering corse,
And when thou hast interred it, to this land
Return, and in that cave which through the rock
Of Sepia time hath worn, thy station keep
Till from the waves I with my sister choir
The fifty Nereids come, to bear thee hence.
Thou must endure the woes imposed by fate,
For thus hath Jove ordained. But cease to grieve
For the deceased: for by the righteous gods
The same impartial sentence is awarded
To the whole human race, and death's a debt
Which all must pay.

  PEL.   Hail, venerable dame,
Daughter of Nereus, my illustrious wife:
For what thou dost is worthy of thyself,
And of thy progeny. I cease to grieve
At thy command, O goddess, and will go,
Soon as my grandson's corse I have interred,
To Pelion's cave, where first thy beauteous form
I in these arms received. The man whose choice
Is by discretion guided, should select
A consort nobly born, and give his daughters
To those of virtuous families, nor wish
To wed a damsel sprung from worthless sires,
Though to his house a plenteous dower she bring:
So shall he ne'er incur the wrath of Heaven.

  CHOR. A thousand shapes our varying fates assume,
The gods perform what we could least expect,
And oft the things for which we fondly hoped
Come not to pass: but Heaven still finds a clue
To guide our steps through life's perplexing maze.
And thus does this important business end.

www.ingramcontent.com/pod-product-compliance
Lightning Source LLC
Chambersburg PA
CBHW032105230426
43672CB00009B/1650